THE CANDIDATES
See How They Run

Bert Teague, Governor Rockefeller, and Hugh Gregg about to be taken for a ride.

THE CANDIDATES
See How They Run

BY HUGH GREGG

Hugh Gregg

December 17, 1990

PETER E. RANDALL PUBLISHER • 1990

© 1990 by Resources of New Hampshire, Inc.
Printed in the United States of America

Copies Available from
Resources of New Hampshire, Inc.
RFD 5–Gregg Road
Nashua, NH 03062
or
Peter E. Randall Publisher
Box 4726
Portsmouth, New Hampshire 03801

Library of Congress Cataloging-in-Publication Data

Gregg, Hugh, 1917–
    The candidates: see how they run / by Hugh Gregg.
        p.   cm.
    Includes index.
    ISBN 0-914339-29-X : $22.95
    government--1951–   I. Title
    JK2075. N42G74   1990
    324.5'4'09742--dc20   90-39553
                                                 CIP

*To my wife, Cay,
who has tolerantly withstood fifty years
of my political perambulations, and encouraged my
every endeavor, including the writing of this book.*

With a special debt of gratitude to my assistant,
Georgi Laurin Hippauf,
who first suggested and urged my writing of this book,
and whose collaboration made it possible.

Acknowledgments

I also wish to acknowledge others who have given freely of their time and advice in reviewing and critiquing this manuscript.

Steve Edwards painstakingly ferreted out missing details. Bruce Rounds embellished his own comedic recollection of events. Bert Teague, an endangered political species himself, helped to replay the Rockefeller adventure. Doctor Jim Squires and Fred Harrigan took meaningful looks at sequence and phrasing. John and Jane Pillsbury kept my courage up, though John still desires footnotes.

Dave Broder and David Black waded through an early draft and forewarned the perils of political writing. Professor Emmett Buell, Jr., educated me against misconceptions about Democrats. Joe Sakey provided leads to publishing. Rick and Helene Mann added technical support. My son, Cy, was constantly constructively critical and son Judd said I wasn't tough enough. But it was thanks to Peter Randall's meticulous custody that the pages finally came together.

Most gratifying was the attestation of my credibility to write on the subject of New Hampshire politics as willingly provided by the esteemed journalists, David Gergen and Mark Shields.

The greatest reward came from John Sears who, staking his national reputation as the longest-running and most respected political consultant in the quadrennial Republican presidential sweepstakes, contributed the foreword.

Foreword

by John P. Sears

I first met Hugh Gregg in the summer of 1967. Dr. Gaylord Parkinson, the then-chairman of the Nixon for President Committee, and I were making the rounds in New Hampshire preparatory to the 1968 Republican primary.

Already a former governor, Hugh met us at the offices of the furniture company which his family seemingly had owned for generations. There, amidst pictures and portraits of elderly gentlemen whom I assumed were ancestors, he held court, with his young son Judd at his side.

One could not escape the conclusion that in speaking with Hugh, we were not just talking to the present head of the Gregg family dynasty but were also communicating with all these bearded gentlemen on the wall. Hugh Gregg knew who he was and was proud of it. What seemed like abruptness and impatience on his part was simply a reaffirmation of his identity and a confirmation on his part that we needn't think we could persuade him to violate his strong loyalty to Nelson Rockefeller.

I came away from this meeting with great respect for Hugh Gregg, most particularly his integrity. Since then, we have been on the same side, opposite sides and somewhere in between relative to the question of who should be President of the United States, but whatever the circumstances, I never doubted his honesty or that he was fully committed to his judgment.

When I first got involved in national politics in the middle 1960s, there were still quite a number of professional politicians involved in the affairs of their parties. These men knew their states, and the people in them, far better than any poll could describe. They did not lend their support to the ambitions of presidential candidates easily but once on record, their loyalty was total. And, they kept their word. To do less was to damage the sanctity of the business they loved, and undermine the influence which they hoped to have on its evolution.

In many ways, Hugh Gregg is the last of this breed of politicians still active in the Republican Party. He abhors the so-called "professional" advertising men and pollsters who dominate politics today—their demeaning view of the people, their willingness to be hired guns to any candidate if the price is right, their propensity to claim victory for themselves if their candidate wins and talk out of school about his weaknesses should failure seem imminent. In this I totally agree with him and long for the return of the day when those who actually know the individuals who aspire to the highest office in the land have more to say about their success or failure. Politics should not be simply a matter of winning or losing; in the old days, the politicians had reason to examine what kind of *President* a person would be since their own power was affected by his performance.

On those events which we shared, Hugh and I might have different perspectives, but his opinions, drawn from a lifetime of experience, are clearly worth reading for anyone who has interest in politics at any level. New Hampshire is a unique political experience whether one is running for President or the third largest English-speaking representative body in the world, the New Hampshire Legislature.

Hugh Gregg is a unique person as well. We should listen carefully to what he has to say, not as a voice from the past but, hopefully, as an informed and experienced instructor for the future, bearing in mind that if candidates continue to use polls as a measure of what to say rather than as a tool for measuring how well their beliefs are being accepted, if candidates continue to find it acceptable to be elected as the lesser of two evils and if we continue to approach the voters having blurred the substantive issues, it is not just politics that will continue to suffer.

Freedom is a very valuable commodity if people have choices. Without clear choices, it is a false right. In whatever he has done, Hugh Gregg has always honored his tacit responsibility to give the people a choice and then accept the good judgment of the people. He believes in democracy and I wonder sometimes how many people involved in politics today could honestly say the same.

Washington, D.C.
June 1990

CONTENTS

Foreword   xi

Introduction   1

PART ONE

Chapter 1   Rocky Dis-Lodged: 1963–1964   11

Chapter 2   Ford Wagon Wrecks Reagan
             Machine: 1975–1976   37

Chapter 3   Reagan Bushwhacks George:
             1978–1980   69

Chapter 4   Vice President Bush Remobilizes:
             Postconvention 1980–1986   101

Chapter 5   Bush Races to the
             Presidency 1987   127

Chapter 6   Bush Tops the Field   151

PART TWO

Chapter 7   The Bushes Remembered   171

Chapter 8   Image: "Mirror, Mirror,
             On the Wall"   183

Chapter 9   Ode to the Organization   199

Chapter 10   The Proliferative Professionals   219

Chapter 11   Media Magic   247

Chapter 12   New Hampshire: "Always First,
             Always Right"   269

Index   293

"Since the presidency of Harry Truman, one rule of American politics has stood unchanged: Nobody can win the White House without first winning the New Hampshire presidential primary. And for close to thirty years, Republican presidential candidates—from Nelson Rockefeller to Ronald Reagan to George Bush—have courted and counted upon former New Hampshire governor Hugh Gregg for his personal help and campaign counsel. Now from the political cockpit, Hugh Gregg gives us his first-hand, behind-the-scenes account of Republican presidential candidates and campaigns from Rocky to the Gipper to Bush.

The inordinate influence of small, remote New Hampshire in determining who will (and who won't) be president has been widely questioned and roundly criticized. The case for New Hampshire—requiring presidential candidates without their media consultants or computer printouts to confront the concerns and hopes of ordinary citizens—has never been made with more commitment and first-hand experience than it is here by Hugh Gregg.

Hugh Gregg has written a political love letter to New Hampshire and that state's most important institution, its history-making presidential primary. The charge has been made repeatedly: New Hampshire voters have altogether too much presidential clout. Hugh Gregg has written a readable rebuttal in defense of his Granite State neighbors. You can't know American presidential politics unless you know New Hampshire. And when it comes to knowing New Hampshire first-hand, Hugh Gregg has few equals."

Mark Shields, Columnist, *The Washington Post*

"For forty years, the New Hampshire primary has been a crucial battleground in selecting America's next president, and Hugh Gregg knows every inch of that field by heart. Republican governor, campaign strategist, friend of presidents, staunch patriot—Hugh is all of these and more. His book on New Hampshire will prove avid reading for anyone who wants to live at 1600 Pennsylvania Avenue."

David Gergen, Editor-at-Large, *U.S. News & World Report*

(l-r) Former New Hampshire governors Hugh Gregg, John W. King, Charles M. Dale, Robert O. Blood, and New York Governor Nelson Rockefeller. (Ralph Wright photography)

Introduction

In the 1952 Republican presidential primary, General Eisenhower won every delegate-at-large to the Republican National Convention without even coming to New Hampshire. Simultaneously, Senator Estes Kefauver took every Democratic delegate-at-large against incumbent President Truman by shaking the hand of almost every Democrat in the state.

Since that time the national media has never understood the political enigma that is the Granite State. Reams have been written by the recognized pundits, newsmen, university professors, and other "outsiders," but this book is the only analysis by an "inside participant" who has been a part of the Republican process during four decades.

This commentary is based on having been elected as a native New Hampshire governor in 1952, having served in the Republican presidential primaries of 1964 as Nelson Rockefeller's state chairman, in 1976 as Ronald Reagan's state chairman, in 1980 as George Bush's state chairman, in 1984 as Reagan-Bush state coordinator, and in 1988 as George Bush's Advance chairman.

The fervor created by these campaigns underscores the pertinence and significance of New Hampshire presidential primaries. My lifelong experience is the basis for these personal observations of the procedure for electing American presidents.

As Charles Brereton observed in *First Step to the White House,* our "election's significance can be traced to two factors. First, it is the first primary. Second, it is without doubt the world's most thoroughly covered election to the number of votes cast." Former congressman Jack Kemp said, "New Hampshire is unique in the whole primary process. You are the winetasters for the whole system."

1

It's not that New Hampshire is unique; rather, our voters are bred of a wondrous environment. As early as 1612, Captain John Smith, sailing off our abbreviated seacoast, noted in the ship's log, "Here every man can be a master of his own labor and land in a short time." More than two centuries later our own Daniel Webster noted the difference: "Men put out signs representing their different trades. Jewelers hand out a monstrous watch, shoe-makers a huge boot. Up in Franconia, God Almighty has hung out a sign that in New Hampshire, He makes men."

Unfortunately there have been those incapable of sensitivity to the acclivity of a finer culture, like Massachusetts' Tip O'Neill, former speaker of the U.S. House of Representatives, who thinks of us as "an odd-ball state."

Even some who have campaigned hard here perhaps missed our true temperament, like former senator McCarthy in 1968, who viewed our image as "a suit of long underwear frozen stiff on a clothesline," or, in 1976, when Ford presidential aide Peter Kaye reflected, "A hell of a state to walk in, because if you go forty miles outside a city, there's nothing but trees and bears."

Perhaps *Fortune* magazine best put us in focus in 1978 by reporting, "It is not easy to accept the notion that the leaders of New Hampshire know what they're doing. The Granite State's politics have long had a flavor of fruitcake. It's hard to escape the aura of nuttiness—but also hard to escape the sense that they're doing something right."

Yet, aside from what others may conclude, we can easily prove we have always been different. We remain different. On January 5, 1776, New Hampshire was the first of the thirteen colonies to assert its independence from Great Britain, six months before the Declaration of Independence.

In 1820 when the presidential electoral votes were counted, President James Monroe had 231 and John Quincy Adams had only one. The dissenting vote was cast by New Hampshire elector William Plumer, who had nothing against Monroe but just wanted to demonstrate our love of political independence and opposition to unanimous elections.

Further proof of our autonomy came twelve years later, when a hardy group of our ancestors, living on northern land claimed by both the United States and Canada, formed their own nation. They called it the Indian Stream Republic. They wrote their own constitution, elected a legislature, established courts, and mobilized an army of forty fighting men. It was not until three years later, when the New Hampshire legislature finally realized the rebellious North Countrymen had seceded, that our militia dissolved their enterprise and brought them back into the fold.

Article No. 10 of our state constitution even preserves the "Right of Revolution" by decreeing:

> Government being instituted for the common benefit, protection, and security, of the whole community, and not for the private interest or emolument of any one man, family, or class of men; therefore, WHENEVER THE ENDS OF GOVERNMENT ARE PERVERTED, AND PUBLIC LIBERTY MANIFESTLY ENDANGERED, and all other means of redress are ineffectual, THE PEOPLE MAY, AND OF RIGHT OUGHT TO REFORM THE OLD, OR ESTABLISH A NEW GOVERNMENT. The doctrine of nonresistance against arbitrary power, and oppression, is absurd, slavish, and destructive of the good and happiness of mankind.

Come to think of it, probably the live potential of this clause so frightens our politicians that we haven't yet needed to take advantage of it.

We still celebrate Memorial Day on Memorial Day; motorcyclists don't have to wear helmets; our legislature is the third largest English-speaking deliberative body in the world; in many places we continue sounding the firehorns at noon, lest we miss lunch, and again in the afternoon to celebrate quitting time;

Martin Luther King's memory doesn't get us a day off, but since April 1681 we've proclaimed our own exclusive holiday (Fast Day); nor do we save a nickle by not throwing our beer cans on the highway; we don't support free kindergartens; we get one free day of fishing without a license; and we are not required to wear fluorescent orange clothing in the woods during hunting season; it remains a misdemeanor to philander with our neighbor's wife; and we're the only state (except Alaska) without a general sales tax or an earned-income tax.

Jere Daniell, a history professor at Dartmouth College in Hanover, was quoted in the *Wall Street Journal* as agreeing that we have an ethic of individualism, but went on to say, "New Hampshire is not attracted to the 19th century. It's a part of the 18th century." Of course you have to allow there are lots of liberals in Hanover.

Murray Straus, a sociology professor at the University of New Hampshire, has scientifically ranked the states by the amount of stress their residents face in fifteen stress-producing areas. It's probably significant that New Hampshire has a low stress quotient, ranking 45th in the nation, because it has relatively few illegitimate births, infant deaths, labor strikes, and natural disasters. Curiously, though, we rank ninth in per-capita sales of sex magazines—a tension omitted by the professor.

We inhabit a small, homogeneous area where our neighbors enjoy a unity of purpose and quality of life unequaled elsewhere. We honor the right of privacy and the privilege of doing our own thing. We abhor big government and resist it to whatever extent we can. That's why we'll take less in state services, because we don't want to pay the taxes. The late Jim Malley of Somersworth, long a leader of Democrats in the legislature, declared we thank God every morning "that we don't get all the government we pay for."

We're a strong home-rule state where people take part in civic affairs with enthusiasm. Political leadership comes from the grass roots, with our 400-member legislature offering everyone or their relative the opportunity to participate.

4

INTRODUCTION

It is not true, as columnist Mike Barnicle has written in the *Boston Globe,* that "some who live here take two hours to watch 'Sixty Minutes' on television." Actually, except for presidential primaries, some of us never look at TV. Just because we have more "wilderness area" than any other New England state, we are not easily lost. Quite the contrary, we appreciate the bountiful blessings of nature. It is a land 88 percent forested, replete with mountains, lakes and seashore—all within a small perimeter, thus making it possible for us to enjoy one or all of these advantages during four distinct seasons.

Yet, except with the ballot box when we speak with a voice of thunder, we tend to be a taciturn, undemonstrative people. Maybe we're just smug with pride, reflecting the well-known Granite State legend that Abraham Lincoln once said, "To amount to anything in this country, you have to come from New Hampshire."

President Nixon, a frequent New Hampshire visitor, described his visit here to dedicate the Hopkinton Dam. The occasion followed his triumphant 1959 visit to Warsaw where the Polish people by the thousands gave him the largest, most hospitable reception of his career by showering his motorcade with flowers and greetings of affection. As he drove to the Hopkinton Dam in an open car with our Senator Norris Cotton, citizens along the way were very respectful and some breathed a polite "Good morning," but there was no cheering. At the end of the trip Cotton commented on what a tremendous reception had been given the president. Nixon assumed the senator was kidding. "Not at all," replied Cotton. "A 'Good morning' in New Hampshire is the same as thousands throwing flowers in Poland."

The only one of our own who ever made it to the White House was Franklin Pierce back in 1852, but the natives turned on him when he ran for a second term four years later. Others have tried, like nine-term state representative Gene Daniell, who once teargassed the New York Stock Exchange and later founded the National Independent Party, mounting a write-in campaign for the presidency.

More recently there was our somewhat unorthodox three-term governor who treated the flag atop the State House as a yo-yo, raising and lowering it to half-mast on such events as the signing away of the Panama Canal, and on Good Friday to commemorate Christ's death. On another occasion, he brought a disorderly conduct charge against a motorist who gave him the middle finger when the governor's car wouldn't move from the passing lane. He, too, formed his own political party, the Constitution Party, and threatened to run for president.

Another Granite Stater not likely to have a historic marker on his Rochester birthplace is Lyndon LaRouche. He was constantly avoiding assassins, but it was political suicide which did him in here.

Some pontificate we don't have a proper balance of ethnic groups, commercial development, social philosophies, population enclaves, personal income, agricultural interests, or whatever, to be a reasonable thermometer of the nation's political temperature. Well, maybe we can't grow or peel bananas on the snows of Mount Washington, but long before the rest of the country has cast its vote, we have accurately picked every president since 1952.

Since the introduction of our primary process, *no candidate has ever been elected to the presidency of the United States without having first won the New Hampshire Primary.*

Meanwhile, one thing is certain: New Hampshire election results are unpredictable. Consistently, the professional pols and pollsters lose credibility in foretelling the voter's mind. They'd improve their average by reading Madame Zoysia's tea leaves. History repeats that our self-reliance does not beget humane concern for national candidates. It's more often a crap shoot who will win—sometimes somebody nobody ever heard of, or maybe somebody who wasn't even here.

Politically, our citizens are fiercely independent, with their philosophy appropriately characterized by the state's motto, "Live Free or Die." The presidential primary is the political pump primer that gets us more excited than other state elections, consistently drawing more voters to the polls. We appreciate our opportunity and obligation to play a powerful part in the selection of our president.

I have been an active Republican participant in the process for over forty years and have observed its development first-hand. What evolves in 1992 and, more importantly, how it evolves, will be a far cry from the course of 1952. New Hampshire may not continue as a bellwether state but, even if it does, the styling and derivation will be titanically different from what it represented in the past. Much more ominous are certain trends arising in the nation's body politic.

In summary, what follows are two separate books divided into Part One and Part Two.

The highlights of my association with Nelson Rockefeller, Ronald Reagan, and George Bush in their New Hampshire primary campaigns are presented in Part One of this book. The experiences from these associations contributed to my concerns regarding the drift away from grass-roots involvement to the depersonalization of the American presidential election process. The narrative in Part One is written to serve as a basis for the observations made in Part Two.

These random recollections are not meant to be a historical documentation of those campaigns. Nor are they intended as a primer on how New Hampshire presidential politics are conducted, except as may be addressed in Chapter 9 on organization. Rather, Part One is a recounting of what really happened, told from an insider's point of view, whose compelling purpose is to acclaim the enduring merit of our current system, beginning with the preservation of New Hampshire's first-in-the-nation primary.

This conviction, abetted by anxiety and apprehension, has led me to writing this book, and will be treated in Part Two. The traditional system of electing presidents is being rapidly eroded in our high-tech environment by television, pollsters, and professional political strategists, and I question the excessive manipulation from these players in the election process.

I am wary of the future, not only of its effect on the New Hampshire presidential primary but, more significantly, of what will happen to our method of choosing the president of the United States.

The final chapter of Part Two, "New Hampshire: Always First, Always Right," defines my conviction that retention of New Hampshire's first-in-the-nation Primary is essential if we are to retain broad citizen involvement in the national body politic.

Part One

Governor Rockefeller sloshes in the mud at Lorden's Lumberyard in Milford.

CHAPTER 1

Rocky Dis-Lodged
1963–1964

It is the tale of two small dogs that frames the story of my relationship with Nelson Rockefeller. You won't meet the second canine until the end of the saga.

Late in July of 1963 I received a call from Bill Treat, who was serving as Republican National Committeeman for New Hampshire, inviting my wife, Cay, and me to join Bill and his wife, Vivian, in a visit with the governor of New York and his bride, Happy, at their Pocantico Hills estate.

On August 5 we drove through an unattended gatehouse to the porte cochere of their elegant mansion, to the dismay of a somewhat confused footman who apparently did not expect us. Eventually we were led through a hall—there was no one else about—through a beautiful atrium, into their spacious living room.

Nelson and Happy soon appeared, stepping out of the elevator that fronted the atrium, and looking very surprised to see us there! In retrospect, I recognize this was his customary informality. Bill and Vivian arrived shortly thereafter. We were later joined by New York Republican National Committeeman George Hinman and his wife, Barbara. George was also a close friend, political advisor, confidant and manager of the Rockefeller interests.

Happy invited us to tour the new Japanese garden she and Rocky were in the process of designing, the focus of which was a teahouse. Nelson insisted we preserve the authenticity of the ambience by removing our shoes before entering.

During an elegant though informal dinner, we were introduced to the first of the two canines mentioned earlier. "Friendly," a playful dachshund frisking blithely between the chairs, took a special liking to me. It was a moment of considerable embarrassment when, confused by the similarity of names, I exclaimed, "Happy, you're a great pooch!" This hapless comment resulted in the dog's being banished from the dining room and I felt perhaps I should have gone with him.

After dinner Happy invited the ladies to tour the three floors of their unusual home, leaving Nelson, George, Bill, and me to discuss the governor's plans and how his presidential campaign might be handled. The importance of the New Hampshire Primary was stressed, and it was clear that Bill's recommendation of me as campaign manager was the basis of this social event.

I had never previously imagined there could develop a philosophical meeting of the minds between me and Nelson Rockefeller, even though he was a man for whom I had the greatest respect. He had been known to me and most New Hampshirites only as another illustrious member of America's wealthiest family. His name connoted images: Governor of New York, Chase-Manhattan, Rockefeller Center, philanthropist—a prominent, popular politician whose mention evoked illusions of the great society, the Waldorf-Astoria, culture, and fine arts.

Yet, on the way home from Tarrytown, I reflected on the tone of our encounter and the potential of a Rockefeller candidacy. I had genuinely liked Rocky, and could understand why he was so popular in the state of New York and considered a tactical leader by the other governors.

He sounded more conservative than I had expected. His competence, knowledge of the issues, and the depth of his familiarity with government were astonishing. Added to this was his warm, down-to-earth personality which could play well in New Hampshire.

Our state was no mecca for the jet set. In our own quiet, earnest fashion we were growing slowly but steadily, diversifying the industrial base, our largest city of Manchester inching toward a population of 90,000—meanwhile promoting the beauty of our forests and the mountains. A few fine old hotels remained amidst freshly refurbished old country inns. Still true to its reputation, New Hampshire appealed mainly to families seeking refuge from high-tax states and to many hard workers satisfied with a quiet life, including writers, craftsmen, aspiring artists.

How would a Rockefeller play here? Could we promote him into a viable candidate? How would he stand up against Goldwater and his ardent conservatives? How would we handle the marital issue? Could we transpose our previous statewide experience of running gubernatorial, senatorial, and congressional campaigns into the makings of a successful presidential primary organization—our first?

Predominant in my thinking has always been the conviction that in electing a president, the substance and character of the man are considerably more important than his position on specific issues. Another consideration was that his would be a challenging campaign because, clearly, he would be the underdog in our conservative state.

Ten days later, George Hinman visited me in New Hampshire. It was a particularly awkward situation for him as he arrived on Cay's birthday and had to sit through a family party in Rye's Saunders Restaurant.

Later that evening we discussed the upcoming campaign in great detail. George was persuasive and tenacious in soliciting my active involvement. It was this visit that led me to agree that I would serve as chairman for the Rockefeller Primary campaign. In his quiet, competent manner, George had as much to do with this decision as did the governor himself.

Bert Teague, who had been my administrative assistant when I served as governor and who had previously served Senator Styles Bridges, agreed to work with me. Bert held fond memories of Nelson Rockefeller, who had delivered the commencement address at his graduation from the University of New Hampshire in 1939. (Nelson remembered the event very well, as it was the first commencement address he had ever delivered.)

Soon after Bert joined the campaign, we went to meet Rockefeller at his New York offices. Extending his hand in hearty welcome, Rocky greeted us warmly: "Gentlemen, this is really a privilege and a pleasure!"

Bert's vast political experience was invaluable as we established the Rockefeller organization. "Having been raised under Bridges and tutored by Gregg, I was a trained ultra-conservative, as I can prove by my public record," relates Teague.

Our initial personal encounters with the candidate, getting to know nim, had assured Bert and myself very quickly of his viability. First of all, we both liked him and thought the voters would, too. His commanding persona elicited affection, not just excitement.

Observing Rockefeller throughout the campaign, Bert recognized that on domestic issues the candidate did sound like a conservative. When he spoke on any platform in New Hampshire, he always recommended financing the state by bonds in advance of receiving any federal funds in order to get the project finished before the funds arrived. This taking care of the necessities of life, "paying as you go," was the very foundation of his claim to fiscal integrity.

Rockefeller, at that time, had a clear record of following this practice, yet he was perceived as a liberal. He pursued what Bert believed was true conservatism, but we were never able to get that point across during the campaign. "The other thing about Rockefeller that always impressed me was that people used to say, 'If he doesn't like South America he'll buy it,'" Bert jested. "I often thought, wouldn't that have been wonderful!"

With Rocky we dealt with a glamorous reality. Though an instinctively shrewd politician, his charm was inbred. His vibrant personality and professional accomplishments were real. All we had to do was come up with a brilliant plan to package and market what should have been "a natural," a perfect presidential specimen, to a somewhat skeptical, though persuadable public.

We looked forward to the challenge of introducing this new leader, new promise, new ideas to the body politic of the Granite State. It had exciting potential; it looked as though even the issues would play into our hand.

Bert and I began weaving a network of Rocky's personal and professional friends, many of whom lived in the upper Connecticut River valley, where a natural constituency formed readily.

An advantage was that over the years Rockefeller had seen a lot of New Hampshire as an unusually devoted Dartmouth alumnus (class of 1930), having missed few opportunities to revisit the hallowed halls of the Hanover college.

Elsewhere, we set up interviews, meetings, speeches—there was never the problem of "Nelson who?" as with George Bush fifteen years later. Almost everyone knew who he was and wanted to meet him, and were glad they did.

Another factor that impressed everyone about Rocky, though it was not a saleable product at the time, was that no one had ever heard of an official serving in an administrative office of government, such as governor of New York, who could get up on a platform and answer any question on his state's financing. Rocky had an unbelievable memory for facts and figures. He had the answers. He would talk about the budget of New York as if it were the budget of the towns of Hollis or Merrimack.

There was little need for special staging, because Nelson had charisma: he could carry the show.

Incredibly, he knew all the people he was working with on a first-name basis. He was very human. In Bert's opinion, "Rocky would have been by far the best president the country ever had."

John Stylianos later wrote in Nashua's *Telegraph* that he sensed Governor Rockefeller as a regular fellow for two reasons. One of them was his general attitude and humor, and the other was his humility despite the reputed Rockefeller wealth. At a dinner rally in Hudson's Alvirne High School, this same reporter had observed Nelson smiling to indicate he wanted more ice cream.

John remarked, "Now anyone who likes ice cream must have a soft spot, and a concern for others." I wonder what he would have written had he known Rocky's favorite dessert was brownies.

Liaison with the national Rockefeller campaign was Alex ("Sandy") Lankler, a friendly guy who related well to everyone. We all agreed that the campaign would be structured low-key, to bring the governor one-on-one with New Hampshire residents, and without the usual hoopla one would expect to see in a Rockefeller entourage. We felt this would surprise a lot of Granite Staters, though it was an easy approach for the governor to assume, this being his customary style.

Our plan was to put him in a bus, with press and supporters, and tour the state, town by town. The days were strategically scheduled to cover the pre-primary period. In about three weeks we were to travel over four thousand miles crisscrossing the state, appearing in over eighty communities.

Nelson Rockefeller was the first to announce formally for his party's presidential nomination in the New Hampshire Primary. Early on the morning of November 7, 1963, he stated his intentions at the State House in Albany, New York, then was flown immediately to New Hampshire in a small plane, all alone, unpretentiously, and without fanfare—part of a carefully wrought strategy.

We were supposed to have been notified by telephone of his departure from Albany and estimated time of arrival in Nashua, but the information was never conveyed until after his arrival. As a result, it was almost by chance that he was met at the Nashua Airport where he had disembarked, by Cay, who had impulsively decided to head for the airport by herself. Meanwhile, the reception committee was still waiting in my business office in downtown Nashua.

Our intentions worked too well. We had overdone it. He arrived so inconspicuously that nobody knew he had landed. This was our first proof to the candidate that the great state of New York and the name of Rockefeller could easily be deflated in New Hampshire.

Directly from the airport we followed a full campaign schedule, to demonstrate his energy and the sincerity of his intentions, starting with a public gathering at the Olde Coach Inn on old Route 3. The best luck we had all day was that it rained very hard and everything got soaked. The state had just suffered through a long drought so, as wet as everybody was, we were all thanking Rockefeller for having brought the abundant weather.

Rocky himself was not so grateful. Later that day a brief visit to Lorden's Lumberyard in Milford found him over his ankles in mud, gallantly shaking hands with five or six people. "If this is your idea of campaigning I'm not so sure I want any more of it," he chuckled.

When we returned to my house for the night, we were both dripping wet. I brought him in through the woodshed door lest there be complaints if we tracked mud through the front door. The contrast between the introduction to my home and our arrival at his Pocantico Hills estate was graciously glossed over, probably because we quickly had him drinking beer in a Dartmouth mug.

His shoes were soaked through from the day's torrential rains. "I did not expect to need an extra pair of shoes," he said. And Cay offered to stuff them with newspaper, then put them on top of the furnace to dry. Characteristically, Nelson wanted to oversee the process.

We soon found out he was skilled at taking care of himself, apparently a reflection of his stoic upbringing, picking up his own room and tending to his clothes. He could easily take command of any situation. This man, a stout individualist, was usually followed by a retinue which he certainly didn't need.

His only request was whether there was a phone in his room, because he wanted to call Happy. He made a few other calls as well, then quickly rejoined us in the living room. At first we talked about Dartmouth. "Tell me about the rest of the state," he asked, wasting no time in learning all he could about life in New Hampshire, immersing himself to its unique, though heterogeneous, ethos.

17

Thereafter, when he traveled in the state, he was accompanied only by Eddie Galvin, his genial personal bodyguard, a plain-clothes officer of the New York State Police. Ed was thoroughly efficient, deftly easing his charge through a crowd with more dexterity than an entire cordon of security personnel which would normally surround important personages. All of this was in direct contrast to the large retinue that normally traveled with him, particularly when he was making public appearances as governor of New York—an entourage which was frequently preceded by sophisticated advance teams.

We designed our own New Hampshire schedules which never had to be sent out-of-state for approval. Nor did we have any relationship with the staffers who constituted his routine advance teams in New York. We were given full authority to set our own agendas, and Rocky never questioned our direction when he was in the state.

Eventually we opened Rockefeller's headquarters at the New Hampshire Highway Hotel in Concord, creating the precedent of using that facility for untold numbers of subsequent political campaigns. Richard Morton, who had built it as an eleven-room motel in 1951, was known to have enjoyed Nelson Rockefeller as one of his favorite candidates. "He spent a tremendous amount of money in the state and a great deal with us," said Richard's son Matthew, who added that Rockefeller, unlike some other political hopefuls, paid his bills.

Matt had better luck than Pete Wing, the Nashua chairman, and myself who, prior to the establishment of a legal campaign account, had jaunted over to the Manchester post office and naively subsidized an $8,000 mailing. We've often wondered whether our early exuberance had not marked us as rank amateurs, because we were never able to collect reimbursement!

The headquarters were humble at first, only a small room to which, eventually, several others were added. Though Bert Teague's New Hampshire staff was small, there were plenty of volunteers. Rocky would mingle with the office personnel, a practice unique to this candidate. He was always upbeat, smiling pleasantly, cheering up the volunteers. He was extremely well-liked and effective at keeping the workers happy. "The most down-to-earth guy you'd ever want to know," said Bert.

Our only simulated Advance team was made up of young volunteers like Bernie Streeter, now the governor's senior executive councilor. His job was to insure a prepared setting and convenient access to typewriters and telephones for the traveling press corps. Early on we learned the hard way that events should be scheduled in small halls, to make the crowd look big—in case we got one!

Rocky was a collector of facts, a collector of art, a brilliant man who looked into things avidly, an ardent student who would learn the vernacular and use it skillfully, at the appropriate level, to ease his way in with the players. He spoke five languages fluently. He was practical, too. In preparation for his South American business trips, he would take a brushup course in Spanish.

On a campaign visit to Berlin, a typical pulp and paper town near the Canadian border with a largely a Franco-American population, the local arena was jammed with hockey fans. Rocky stole the show between periods when he went down on the ice and addressed the crowd in French. The fans loved it.

Although he was relatively small in size, Rocky's presence was commanding, his face handsome and relaxed. He was tireless, never halting to rest, working from the campaign bus from town to town for full twelve-hour days, often late into the evening. Rocky was charismatic, captivating, and enthusiastic. He projected warmth and sincerity, adapting easily to grass-roots politics. Always pervasive was the added aura of the Rockefeller mystique.

A devoted parent, he talked frequently about his children, about his son, Michael, tragically lost in the seas off Dutch New Guinea. He spoke especially about Happy, about his life, his family, the way he was brought up, strictly and frugally, even while at Dartmouth.

19

Lunchtime: Cay Gregg Serves Governor Rockefeller his animal crackers. (Robert Swenson photography)

He talked about the marriage of his son to the Swedish girl who had been employed in their Pocantico Hills home and of his hope for their happiness. He enjoyed telling the story of how the whole family flew over to Sweden for the wedding. Upon arriving they had been brought into a starkly cold airport waiting room. Spotting an enormous black stove in the middle of the room, Rocky dispatched an aide to find some wood, while he proceeded to explore the appliance himself. When he opened the stovelid, he found a newspaper reporter hidden inside.

Rockefeller was no ordinary politician, unmatched as a grass roots campaigner. He needed no coaching. I suppose the average citizen was surprised at his warmth, his direct gaze, and his expression of genuine interest. Hardly anyone would have so imagined a Rockefeller. An extrovert, he related to the man on the street, hand outstretched and always with a smile, sometimes introducing himself as "I'm Nelson Rockefeller" or beaming his irrepressible greeting of "Hi, fella!"

Occasionally, on an early morning visit to a small town, we would be lucky to field a crowd large enough to fill its phone booth. Yet Rocky, attuned to the fervency of campaigning in New York City, was always good-humored. He would have loved Bob Hope's comment, made many years later, when the comedian overnighted at the home of the Vic Manginis in Greenfield. In midevening Bob, accompanied by his hosts, took a leisurely stroll on its Main Street when one car passed by. "Wow," hooted Hope. "There goes the action for tonight."

Along the campaign trail, my wife, Cay, would often meet the bus, toting a picnic lunch with Rocky's favorite brownies, or bringing some fresh laundry. Rocky might ask her to sew on a button which he, himself, had firmly retrieved from an overly ardent fan. Apparently his buttons were a collector's item. As much as he enjoyed people and seemed to revel mid the fray, he always caught the button snatchers to reclaim his dignity.

The days always started early, following some tough itineraries, covering lots of territory. While Rocky was an excellent speaker, he was no orator. He could be forceful, deep, and eloquent in probing the issues, sometimes too profound or too complex. He risked losing his audience.

Rockefeller was a brilliant manager, enjoying some of the strongest labor support of any Republican governor in the early 1960s. Labor had come of age in the 1930s under the impetus of the Wagner Act, and many industries had fought long and bitter battles against unionization. At the outset of his career, as a young executive of Rockefeller Center in the 1930s, Nelson had helped formulate a labor relations policy that kept the huge real-estate enterprise free of labor trouble for many years.

It was a farsighted formulation for the times. The acceptance by the Rockefellers of labor's right to organize was an important psychological factor in shaping the thinking of many employers. "I felt," Rockefeller had said," and I still feel that employers and employees have to recognize they are mutually dependent on each other."

He loved children and frequently, in the middle of a crowd, would bypass adults in favor of the kids—though he had not inherited his grandfather's tradition of handing out dimes! Kelly's drugstore in Newport almost ran out of ice cream when he bought cones for all the youngsters.

At the same time he had a practical approach to the disposition of the Rockefeller fortunes and his dedication to the arts. He wanted to visit historic Strawberry Banke in Portsmouth but Captain Carl Johnson, its director, said the facility was closed for the season. They wouldn't shovel the snow even for a Rockefeller. Rocky smiled, "Maybe they won't come to the Rockefeller Foundation for a contribution."

There were minor gaffes, like the time Rockefeller went into a small Whitefield gift shop to buy a present for Happy. In this tiny little store he pulled out a $100 bill, big in Whitefield at that early morning hour, then had to borrow $20 from me when the astounded clerk was unable to make change. Rocky had simply forgotten where he was, momentarily, but the incident received nationwide publicity.

The national press was always with us, usually in the second of two buses, covering every move. Rocky rode in the first bus, again a contrast to campaigning for governor of New York, where one bus was for staff, the second for press, while the candidate and his wife were comfortably ensconced in a limousine.

The two of us had a major difference in opinion on how to handle the press. Rocky had always played to the press, astute at grabbing great photo ops. He had his national image in mind, quite predominantly, whereas I wanted to concentrate on winning New Hampshire. We knew we had to get him close to the people here first, and there was so much work to do, so much adverse publicity to counter.

New Hampshire's weekly newspapers did not have the personnel to cover the campaign, except when the candidates were in their immediate area of circulation. To stir their interest we would invite a representative of their publication, usually the owner or editor, to ride the bus in their neighborhood.

Clint White, editor of the *Coos County Democrat*, was accorded such treatment. (Lest the reader be confused by "Democrat," the paper's editor then and even now would deny any Democratic allegiance; rather, their political philosophy has been in the best tradition of New Hampshire's motto, "Live Free or Die.") White related how he was "invited to sit" with Rockefeller in the bus during the round trip from Lancaster to Groveton. NBC News filmed them on the trip North and on their return they "discussed several matters in depth."

Even the dailies, except the Manchester *Union Leader*, relied heavily on the State News Service (a joint venture of several New Hampshire dailies), wire service stories, or our press releases. The only way most of them could do an in-depth article was for the candidate to visit the newspaper office—a practice which led to a tradition that became increasingly complex in subsequent presidential primaries.

Barry Goldwater, originally predicted to be Rockefeller's major opponent, announced his candidacy on January 3, 1964, from his home in Phoenix, Arizona: "I have not heard from any announced Republican candidate a declaration of conscience or of political position which would offer the American people a clear choice in the next presidential election." Nelson Rockefeller was the only other announced candidate at that time.

Goldwater's late formal entry in the race was delayed in part by the assassination of President Kennedy on November 22. The president's death cast a pall on all politics at every level.

Our candidate was scheduled to arrive on the twenty-fourth for a three-day campaign swing, which was promptly canceled. All promotional trappings were taken down outside the hotel, including a huge billboard photograph. The schedule was scrapped. The whole country was in mourning for a period of thirty days.

When Senator Goldwater finally arrived in the Granite State in early January, he was limping badly from an operation on his right heel, causing him later to remark that he "remembered every footstep" of his three-week tour here.

Goldwater had been described by the Rockefeller camp as "extreme" in his views. He was plagued by some of his positions: NATO commanders in Europe should be allowed to use tactical nuclear weapons at their discretion (later he said he meant to limit such authority to the supreme NATO commander); TVA should be sold; "Let's lob one into the men's room of the Kremlin"; "Sometimes I think this country would be better off if we just saw off the eastern seaboard and let it float out to sea."

But the most critical damage to Goldwater in New Hampshire came at a news conference on January 6, when he urged that Social Security be made voluntary. At that time, only three states had a higher percentage of senior citizens than ours. This statement continued to haunt him for the balance of the campaign, and for the Rockefeller forces, it provided the focal issue.

Goldwater's style, while hard-hitting in his criticism of liberals, was sometimes inconsistent, particularly in his handling of the press. He was a most effective speaker but no match for Rockefeller in the hand-shaking, back-slapping department. As Theodore White observed, Nelson was the most energetic hand shaker we had seen in the state since Estes Kefauver in 1956 who had campaigned by dogsled. Senator Goldwater (everybody loves him now) was a bit too peptic for even our Graniteers to digest. Rocky's suavity was just the right antacid, smooth and easy to swallow.

Even before these two had announced, on October 12, 1963, Rockefeller had challenged Goldwater to a debate on Republican policy, repeating the offer on many occasions. Goldwater adamantly refused on the theory that Republicans should debate with Democrats, never with each other. He countered that Rockefeller had always rejected invitations to debate with his own rivals when seeking the governorship of New York. The ritual of televised candidate debates had not yet been mandated. In subsequent New Hampshire primaries, debates among the major candidates became a factor in determining winners. This was not the case in 1964.

Initially the direction of the New Hampshire campaign had been given to us carte blanche, but as momentum gained, outside influences became pervasive. Consultants from New York began appearing on the scene who insisted on setting strategy, especially on policy matters. The better things went in New Hampshire, the more pressure we received from New York.

Previously, with the exception of Sandy Lankler, there had been very little outside input. Sandy never got into policy matters. But later Hugh Morrow emerged as Rockefeller's speechwriter; Tom Stevenson, who stayed at the New York level, had considerable influence; and Karl Spad became the key liaison who handled all his public relations. Ann Whitman was Rocky's secretary and a close friend of Rose Mary Woods, who later became Richard Nixon's personal assistant.

New Hampshire television was still relatively unimportant. WMUR-TV was the only New Hampshire station and its equipment was limited. Most media placement was done with Boston stations which covered New Hampshire.

One serious mistake was that the Rockefeller TV ads did not feature our state's background nor its environment. They originated from some remote cottage in Long Island or Cape Cod. Rocky's coterie of media consultants presumed New Hampshire's dumb hayshakers would not know the difference.

This became a typically negative influence sponsored by "foreign" advisors. All TV publicity was produced and directed from Madison Avenue, some of which the New Hampshire leadership never had the opportunity to preview.

While there were other candidates in the race, they did not figure prominently in the Primary. Neighboring Maine Senator Margaret Chase Smith made a couple of appearances. The public was not about to entertain the concept of a woman in the Oval Office.

Former vice president Richard Nixon—always well regarded in the state—received a sizable write-in vote resulting from an effective program directed by former governor Wesley Powell, who rallied Nixon's long-time, ardent loyalists.

It proves the appeal and popularity of our Primary that Harold Stassen also participated in this contest. He was a quadrennial player in New Hampshire over several decades. In 1989, back home in Minneapolis, he won $99.50 on his eighty-second birthday by calling in on a celebrity radio talk show—a better prize than he ever won here!

Eventually it became apparent that we weren't really fighting Goldwater, but rather Bill Loeb and his Manchester *Union Leader*, New Hampshire's most powerful news medium. For every inch we gained in a day, the *Union Leader* would whack us back a foot with the next day's headlines.

According to Professor Eric Veblen in his book *The Manchester Union Leader in New Hampshire Elections*, from January 1 through Primary Day, March 10, "the *Union Leader* carried 109 'positive' or 'neutral' stories about Goldwater and 50 about Rockefeller; 26 photographs of Goldwater and 19 of Rockefeller, the latter including five clearly uncomplimentary photos; and 80 editorials favoring Goldwater, attacking Rockefeller, or both. An all-out effort."

The *Union* editor characterized Rocky in various ways: "spoiled, rich kid"; "this snob from New York just wants to kid us peasants along until he gets New Hampshire's votes, and then the royal train will move on and we'll get the back of his hand."

A New Hampshire newsman, Rod Paul, aptly described Loeb in the *New Hampshire Times* as a "curmudgeon who had an uncanny ability to pick out an issue and make it outrageous."

As late as 1974, when Ford chose Rockefeller as his running mate, Loeb remained bitter. In an editorial on August 21, 1974, he vituperated, ". . . never in the history of the republic have we had two such 'lemons' in the White House—and they are there, not because the people elected them, but because of a sinister conspiracy by certain powerful groups in this country which violated the U.S. electoral process and placed the nation in the most serious danger it has ever faced in its history."

Loeb's most caustic attacks were directed against Happy, whom he consistently referred to as "the woman for whom Governor Rockefeller swapped his wife." Nelson's divorce from his first wife had occurred in 1961. On May 4, 1963, Rocky had married Margaretta Fitler "Happy" Murphy. She was 36; he was 54. (A Gallup poll taken just before his remarriage had given Rockefeller a 20% lead over Goldwater among Republican voters. One taken shortly after the remarriage gave Goldwater a 5% lead.)

Happy, who had given up custody of her own four children to marry Rocky, frequently campaigned with her husband. A lovely and charming woman, though somewhat shy, nothing came easily for her. We felt it was necessary that she appear as frequently as possible in New Hampshire to offset the messy publicity of the marital situation.

At a fall Dartmouth versus Holy Cross football game in Hanover, Dean Thad Seymour of Dartmouth, a rabid Rockefeller supporter whose sense of humor was legendary, had suggested

Governor and Happy Rockefeller leave the New Hampshire Highway Hotel for the daily trek. (Ralph Wright photography)

Governor and Happy Rockefeller on the campaign trail. (Ralph Wright photography)

that the college band, as a promotional stunt, should march down the gridiron playing "Happy Days Are Here Again."

Later that night we drove Nelson and Happy from Hanover to his brother Larry's hotel in North Woodstock, Vermont. On our way back to New Hampshire, Bert Teague's wife, Joanne, remarked, "Fellas, you have more problems than you thought you had. Happy Rockefeller is pregnant!" Subsequently, Dorothy Kilgallen announced in her column that the new Mrs. Rockefeller had indeed visited her obstetrician and the pregnancy had been confirmed.

She was constantly embarrassed by the press, many of whom were cruel in their questioning. On many occasions it became necessary to shield her from reporters, for which she was extremely grateful. It was increasingly difficult to schedule events in which she could feel comfortable. The public remained skeptical.

Some women were particularly petty and insulting. During a visit to the Dublin town hall, Happy was just coming up to the top of the steps while three dowagers stood watching. Obviously well-rehearsed, as they were approached by Happy who stepped forward to shake hands, one of them said, "Oh, Mrs. Murphy (Happy's name by her first marriage) how nice to see you . . . and, where are your children?"

The minister of a Baptist church in Manchester publicly questioned Rocky's moral fitness to be president, in light of the divorce and remarriage. The governor had planned to attend a Sunday worship service at his church, so I talked with the reverend about his condemnation. The minister felt that such a visit might be "embarrassing" and suggested he would like to speak personally with Rockefeller.

A meeting was arranged at which the churchman said he asked pointed questions for forty-five minutes, eventually admitting he had been "too hasty" in his conclusions. "I think neither party got his divorce simply to satisfy a love affair," he added.

Thereafter, Rocky went to the Brookside Congregational Church and the Baptist minister declared he was going to cast his vote for Harold Stassen.

Rocky was solicitous of his wife, whether or not she was with him. Happy was so enamored of her husband, it seemed she had lost her own sense of place. She didn't like politics but persisted, for his sake, rarely verbalizing her feelings about the campaign or the day's events. She was not a stimulated participant but, rather, a gracious, loyal, and loving companion to Rocky.

Cay traveled with her quite often at first, until she needed a secretary. As she became uncomfortably pregnant and Cay tried to keep her interested in campaigning, doing things we thought would help the cause, she began to balk and, eventually, became a stumbling block. Perhaps she should have persisted longer, perhaps not. She had already made tremendous sacrifices.

In 1964 Rocky's domestic difficulties were so fresh in everyone's mind that, in my view, this was the single, most destructive influence on his campaign. Yet, ten years later, when he was chosen by President Ford as his vice president, it was hardly an issue—except from the pen of William Loeb.

As the campaign progressed it became obvious that both Goldwater and Rockefeller were being outflanked by an invisible candidate, Henry Cabot Lodge, who was serving as American ambassador to South Vietnam. Four out-of-staters, encouraged by his son, George, had the brilliant idea of initiating a "Draft Lodge" campaign. The Lodge name, respected in adjacent Massachusetts, was favorably known here. Thus, the timing was excellent, as most New Hampshire Republicans were seeking an alternative to the two leading candidates. Nonetheless, it was a response against Rockefeller and Goldwater, not necessarily pro-Lodge.

Some GOP regulars were uneasy. The Goldwater-Rockefeller fray might splinter the party and weaken it for the fall election; there was danger of a fratricidal brawl. Congressman James Cleveland was only one of those who, fearing divisiveness after the Primary, remained neutral.

In retrospect, it seems that the real coup for New Hampshire, which could have changed American history, would have been to slate Rockefeller and Goldwater on the same ticket. The match could have been consummated, as the two were good friends who had great respect for each other. Goldwater in his memoirs concurred that it would have been a definite possibility. Settling which of the two would top the ticket might have strained their mutual admiration.

Unknown to us at the time, Bill Treat, who had lured me into the Rockefeller campaign, had been approached by George Lodge, who entreated Bill to make the long journey to Saigon and speak to his father. Treat was a trustworthy neutral, totally familiar with the New Hampshire political process and its current status. Rockefeller had not been advised of Treat's voyage, which occurred only a couple of months before the election.

Meanwhile, the four public-relations Lodge promoters assembled a group of New Hampshire citizens, under the leadership of J. Richard Jackman, the well-respected head of Rumford Press in Concord. As Jackman told David Broder, "I figured that any man who has been as strong in international affairs as Lodge would be strong in domestic affairs, too—a strong President." They organized a slate of delegates, as required for the ballot. Most of them were political neophytes, virtually unknown.

We were not immediately disturbed by this development, since Rocky had assured Bert and me that Lodge, before going to Vietnam, had pledged his support. Nelson felt comfortable with that guarantee, believing that Lodge didn't know what was happening and would certainly disclaim any interest if it reached a meaningful level.

The Lodge write-in campaign was expertly designed, with effective literature mailings and a TV film presentation. The coup de grace was a unique sample ballot, mailed to Republican voters, by which even a Democrat could learn to write in Lodge's name without any fear of its invalidation.

As we recognized that Lodge fever was rising, we began to worry. Rockefeller's initial reaction was to write a friendly letter of reconfirmation to Lodge. As the situation became more troublesome, we decided that Rocky should phone Lodge in Saigon to determine the seriousness of his interest in the project. Several unsuccessful attempts were made from the Highway Hotel to complete the long-distance call.

While I don't remember the specific day, I vividly recall an operator's advisement that a call would reach the ambassador at a precise midmorning hour. Our schedule required our being in transit at that time. How could we remove Rockefeller from the bus, for an unscheduled stop, without alerting the accompanying press?

It was accomplished by momentarily stopping the bus in front of a private home along Route 3 in Boscawen, to allow Rockefeller "a pit stop." We told the press the halt was a matter of personal privilege and the tight schedule did not allow time for anyone else to disembark. To this day, and to the best of my knowledge, the fact that the call was completed at that time, under those circumstances, was known only to the insiders, never disclosed elsewhere.

Lodge had replied he would not discourage the write-in. Rockefeller felt double-crossed. He was visibly disturbed. Back inside the bus and sitting next to Cay, he asked whether Bert and I were concerned about the escalating sentiment for Lodge.

The more he thought about it, the more he recognized the potential catastrophe ahead. Thus, he decided to call Lodge again to express total disappointment with his refusal to halt the movement. Up until this time Rockefeller had presumed the ambassador was playfully enjoying the publicity, as most politicians would. Rocky understood that posture and was willing to accept it. He remained confident of Lodge's eventual support.

We still considered it vital to conceal from the press any indication that Rocky and Lodge were in direct contact. But at Franconia College the same afternoon, prior to a major event, the final call to Saigon was completed—most dramatically.

Over the auditorium's loudspeaker came the announcement, "Governor Rockefeller, your call to Saigon is ready." At that very moment the press knew that the call had been made and a critical discussion was about to take place. It made the front page for the next few days.

ROCKY DIS-LODGED: 1963–1964

As the nation knows, the New Hampshire Primary election begins at midnight in Dixville Notch. It leads the parade in casting its ballots, corraling its handful of residents to vote at 12:01 A.M. of Primary Day. The anointed voters of this bellwether precinct are blessed with twenty- four hours of international media recognition.

For Dixville to retain this distinction, state law requires that the ballots of all registered voters be recorded before a count is taken. This famous quadrennial event is held at The Balsams, a world-renowned resort in the North Country. Most of these voters are involved, directly or indirectly, with the hotel and its subsidiary operations.

On the fateful night of March 10, a nefarious schemer from the Rockefeller campaign sent Bertie Parker of neighboring Colebrook a case of booze, hoping to lure a few more of those extremely valuable Dixville votes.

Even while all the national TV networks were set up in the hotel awaiting the witching hour, one recalcitrant townsman (who had been sued by the Balsams) refused to join the festivities.

We dispatched Judge Fred Harrigan, the area's most influential civic leader, who, fortunately, was a Rockefeller chairman. In the missing voter's kitchen, he found the family poring over Henry Cabot Lodge's delegate mailer. He managed to cajole an absentee ballot, probably for Lodge, and so saved the Dixville tradition, but not the race.

A total of nine Republican votes were cast and at least the liquor paid off as Rocky beat Barry two to one—that is, we got two votes and Goldwater got one. It probably should be mentioned that Lodge and Nixon got three each!

We were all aware that every vote for Lodge was a vote away from Rockefeller, not from Goldwater. Still we were concentrating on defeating Goldwater. Even then it never occurred to us that Lodge would win the election and take all of New Hampshire's seats at the Republican National Convention. Both leading camps completely underestimated the surging power of the Lodge crescendo and prepared no counterattack.

Rocky listened to the returns in New York on that fateful evening of March 10. At 12:40 A.M. of March 11, he wired me a personal telegram of thanks including the message: "Be of good cheer. We will continue to fight." He had taken the bitter disappointment in stride and was off to the west coast the next day.

My days with Rocky had been filled with unusual moments, rare insights, a type of bonding inevitably growing out of an intense, though temporary experience. It was easy being his friend and sharing a love of politics, he showed confidence in what I said and thought. We shared a mutual respect and he had always been accessible to me.

As it turned out, fourteen Lodge delegates and their alternates were elected. The defeat was complete. Neither Rockefeller nor Goldwater received even one delegate, not even Norris Cotton, who observed, "When I failed to be elected delegate to my own party's national convention, that was the only defeat I had from the time I went to Congress until the time I retired as senior senator."

It's interesting to remember that in those days, the use of write-in votes was popular and easy to accomplish. All the votes were hand counted, except for six machine precincts in Portsmouth. On Election Day, the combined Lodge and Nixon write-ins totaled 48,594, whereas Rockefeller and Goldwater combined, whose names were printed on the ballot, garnered only 40,196.

This result was somewhat reminiscent of the 1952 election when Senator Robert Taft, who had campaigned vigorously, was defeated by General Eisenhower who (though on the ballot), like Lodge, had not even visited the state. .

The year 1964 was the last that demonstrated the power of the write-in vote. The outcome was later described by Guy MacMillin, editor of the *Keene Sentinel* as "the perfectly pointless Republican write-in victory of non-candidate Henry Cabot Lodge."

Today, there are occasional successful write-in efforts in New Hampshire, but always at the local level and normally in those communities where paper ballots are still used. Increasingly

If this gang could have voted, Rocky might have won the Primary. (Robert Swenson photography)

more precincts have installed automatic voting machines, making the process more difficult and almost impossible in a major statewide race.

In 1960, before I had met him, friends of Rockefeller had previously launched a leaderless write-in campaign in an attempt to block Nixon from gaining the Republican nomination. It failed badly. Again, in 1968, a write-in effort was sponsored by friends of Rocky to stop Nixon. It was an unorganized, spontaneous movement which netted only a few votes.

Had Henry Cabot Lodge not been a player in the 1964 campaign, had he kept his promise to his old friend Nelson, in my view, Nelson would have won, perceived as the lesser of two evils.

Further, had it not been for the untimeliness of his second marriage and the public's strong negative reaction to it, the campaign would have probably succeeded in focusing only on the issues, and thus he would have earned the confidence of the electorate, able to withstand the upsurgent write-in effort for Henry Cabot Lodge. Even Bill Loeb would have been short of ammunition.

In my view, the couple did an amazingly good job. Submerging his worldliness and erudite sophistication, and having made so many friends in the chilly hills of New Hampshire—which to the Rockefellers was but a dot on the map—proves the mettle of the man.

Even the old pro, Theodore H. White, wrote in *The Making of the President 1964*, "It is this reporter's opinion that Nelson Rockefeller would have won by a flat majority, gone on to a larger majority in Oregon and then probably carried California to defeat Goldwater conclusively."

Now enters the second pup! On the day of the election, a black and white mixed-breed canine walked into the Concord headquarters. She was especially friendly and frisky, like Happy's Friendly, an endearing creature which immediately captured the affection of us all. The next day, after we had lost the election, we discovered she had been abandoned at the hotel. She was promptly and appropriately named Happy "Loser" Rockefeller. She turned out to be an exceptionally bright dog and spent the next twelve years as the most respected member of the Cay and Hugh Gregg household.

She never seemed to mind the nickname "Loser."

CHAPTER 2

Ford Wagon
Wrecks Reagan Machine
1975–1976

On Sunday, August 24, 1975, John Sears, Ronald Reagan's campaign director, and his assistant, Jim Lake, made a social call at my home on behalf of "Citizens for Reagan." This was the first time I had met either of them, and both impressed me with their low-key, good-natured approach to the selling of their candidate.

Later I came to respect Sears as a cool, calculating scoundrel who had a penchant for sequestering himself, then coming up with real hardball decisions. Whenever we had subsequent contacts, I always sensed I was being psychoanalyzed; thus, it was with some relief I later learned John had previously wanted to become a psychiatrist.

Traveling around with Jim Lake, by contrast, was like romping with one of the big, friendly Newfoundlands that were part of our household (along with Loser) and with whom I always felt both comfortable and befriended.

John and Jim were in the process of making courtesy acquaintance calls to scout the political landscape. Reagan's potential candidacy in New Hampshire was discussed, but no offers were suggested nor were commitments requested. While I had never met Ronald Reagan informally, he had visited the state in 1971 and 1974 to address Republican state dinners.

September 11 was a fascinating day. Reagan had unobtrusively arrived in New Hampshire the night before, accompanied by Sears and Lake. They were staying at the Holiday Inn West in Manchester, where I had an apppointment to meet them at 8:30 A.M.

This was my first one-on-one with the governor. He had just awakened, and I don't think he was focused on me. Yet on this occasion they were very up-front in asking for my help in the forthcoming effort, but only for a commitment of support. No offer of chairmanship was made.

The very same morning President Ford was to land in Keene for a motorcade swing through the southern tier, ending with a major address at the University of New Hampshire in Durham. While it was billed as an official presidential visit, the real purpose was to boost Congressman Louis Wyman's ailing senatorial campaign.

As previously with Reagan, I had never met President Ford informally, though I had attended a State House reception for him hosted by Governor Thomson in April of 1975. However, I was invited to meet him that day during his noon luncheon stop at the home of Phyllis Brown in Amherst. The invitation had come from Senator Cotton, who had suggested to the President (as he confirmed to me by letter afterwards) that I would be "an excellent choice" for Ford's New Hampshire campaign chairman, even though some overtures had been made previously to Congressman James Cleveland for that position.

Cotton had no problem with Cleveland, a close friend, but advised the president that "Cleveland's contacts had previously been largely confined to the Second Congressional District while yours, as a former Governor of the State and one active in Republican campaigns, had been state-wide." I was flattered by the senator's totally unsolicited recommendation and anxiously looked forward to the opportunity of conversing with the president.

My respect for Gerald Ford, a former football player and graduate of the University of Michigan, had begun while we were both at Yale. Ford was a law student and dated Phyllis Brown, a glamorous blonde from Connecticut College for Women in New London. Phyllis skipped school on occasion to moonlight in New York City as a Petty calendar model. Ford became macho man on campus when he took off with Phyllis on a well-publicized, long-weekend ski trip in Vermont.

Now, the prospect for me of being greeted by both Gerry and Phyllis was tantalizing, but the fantasy turned out to be only nostalgic. She was a different Phyllis Brown!

Until I told them later, Governor Reagan and his representatives were unaware of the plan for me to meet with Ford. I genuinely liked both candidates and had not yet made the choice in my own mind. Thus I explained my indecision to Sears and Lake. Perhaps the afternoon meeting would help decide what I should do. We agreed to keep in touch.

Presidents don't come to Amherst every day, and Ford was probably the first to come since Amherst-born Horace Greeley popularized the phrase, "Go West, young man, Go West." Nobody was heeding Greeley that day because people came from all directions.

When I arrived at the Browns' house, the crowd was so large it was obvious there would be little chance for privacy either in the house or on the grounds. With tremendous agility Cotton managed to maneuver the president and me into the "woodshed" by ourselves.

Cotton soon excused himself to seek a photographer, allowing the president and me to speak freely. Ford asked me to head up his New Hampshire campaign. I showed qualified interest, subject to talking with his campaign aides. Thereupon he called Don Rumsfeld, his presidential assistant, into the shed, with instructions that I should be put in touch with Bo Calloway (his campaign chairman who was not on the trip) for discussion of such an arrangement.

A few days later, Cotton learned from Calloway that the latter had settled on Cleveland even before my meeting with Ford and it would have been beyond change. Ford had not known this.

Fortunately I heard nothing from Calloway for a week, which allowed me the time to reason things out. During that interim, I pledged my support to Jim Lake. Calloway eventually did call, but by then it was too late for both of us.

When I later became chairman of the Reagan campaign, Stuart Spencer (Ford's political director), the Ford press, and other Ford disciples gave me a "bad rap" by alleging that my action in signing with Reagan resulted from having been declined the Ford chairmanship.

Fortunately, a letter in my file from Senator Cotton states, "I can negate any suggestion that you either sought or were refused the position of campaign chairman for President Ford in New Hampshire." At that time I never disclosed the true facts of what happened in the woodshed because I did not want, in any way, to embarrass Norris' relationship with Jim Cleveland.

The climax of that unforgettable Thursday occurred the same afternoon on my way north, back to the Waumbek in Jefferson, a resort complex under my management. As I passed Profile Lake I was intercepted by Cay, who was driving through Franconia Notch on her way south to our Nashua home. We stopped, appropriately, under the shadow of the Old Man of the Mountain who blesses all our citizens, and I advised her we'd likely be in another campaign. She added her blessings to those of the Old Man—later proving to be of no avail.

After calling Lake with my commitment, I invited him to join me for the weekend at the Waumbek. We related well to each other and spent most of the time completing an extensive phone canvass of my friends and Republican activists. The pulse for Reagan was surprisingly good.

On the following Wednesday Sears returned to New Hampshire and officially anointed me as chairman. I wonder on how many occasions thereafter Lake questioned his announcement statement: "In getting Hugh Gregg, we were trying to establish we were not the candidate of the kooks."

Some of the press were predicting the New Hampshire situation would be a classic confrontation between the moderates supporting Ford and the conservatives backing Reagan, similar to the Rockefeller- Goldwater fiasco of 1964. But I tended to agree with Nick Thimmesch, the *Los Angeles Times* columnist, who wrote, "Ford's message would be applauded by Reagan if Reagan weren't running."

Nonetheless, it was obvious that the state's traditional Republican hierarchy would line up behind Ford, thereby ranking Reagan as the underdog in the Primary. Not only have I always presumed an identity with homeless dogs, but there's always more freedom for gamesmanship in running against an incumbent.

From my vantage point, while Ford and Reagan perhaps shared a similar political philosophy, I came to believe the latter was more electable. He had exceptional charisma and the advantage of not being in any way tarnished by the Watergate scandal or marked with the Washington beltway tattoo. More importantly, he had demonstrated administrative excellence as governor of California, and had twice successfully satisfied millions of voters, whereas the appointed president had been a legislator elected only by the people of a congressional district.

The record here has often demonstrated that the winner is not necessarily the person who receives the most votes. It was on that postulate that I plausibly predicted Ford, a sitting president, would be regarded as the loser if Reagan garnered 40% and Ford only 60%. Dave Broder agreed this analysis had a certain reasonableness, inasmuch as President Nixon had received slightly more than 70% of the primary votes in 1972 against two vigorous opponents. Even the *Portsmouth Herald* suggested Ford needed 75% to be a viable candidate.

The inbred party members were rallying around the theory that it would be suicidal to repudiate an incumbent president at a time, as Cotton said, "when there aren't enough members of the Republican party to man a small fleet of lifeboats." Thus, initially my 40% figure was not substantively or seriously questioned; however, in the final days of the contest the percentage strategem became the most important part of it.

From the beginning it was apparent that our balance sheet had an unusual equiponderance with both its major assets and major liabilities simultaneously being the same two personages, namely, Governor Meldrim Thomson and publisher William Loeb of the Manchester *Union Leader.* It would be a gross understatement to admit they were exceptionally influential and equally, exceptionally, controversial. We had to contend with the latter aspect.

In January of 1974, when Reagan appeared at the Republican banquet, Thomson was the first significant public official to announce his support, recognizing the California governor as a great American statesman.

Shortly thereafter, at a National Conservative Political Conference in Washington, Thomson openly endorsed Reagan over Ford. He was later quoted as saying, "With the great issues of prayer, decency and morality, Ronald Reagan is fortunate to be on the side of God." Loeb had always been a fervent follower who thought of Reagan as "a man uncontaminated by the Washington cesspool."

In early November I received a friendly letter from Loeb suggesting I invite Governor Thomson to be honorary chairman: " . . . I think his nose has been out of joint because of the fact that he wasn't consulted enough on the general situation regarding the Reagan campaign." It also contained a vague reference that Thomson might possibly be considering Connally.

My polite negative response to Bill's request was based on our feeling that such an appointment would dissuade many of our workers who were uncomfortable with the governor's lack of party loyalty. He had occasionally displayed a predilection to drift.

Loeb's reply to me was not quite as cordial when he wrote that the governor was really "teed off" and that neither he nor the governor would continue his support on the basis of the current campaign hierarchy. "If you want to lick yourself over a silly little matter, you go right ahead and do it." He affirmed that Thomson wanted to have a major hand in selecting the delegates to the Republican convention.

Sears recognized that a planned strategy should keep Mel at a distance, yet carefully, so as not to antagonize the more radical rightists in his camp. We wanted him quiet, allowing us to woo moderates to our cause, while Ford people wanted him quiet to allow their proselytizing of conservatives. Since he was going to run for re-election anyway, I gave him some peer advice that he should spend his time in the State House as good former governors had done. We all had doubts that my suggestion would take.

Immediately we began building a town-by-town organization, opening a headquarters at the New Hampshire Highway Hotel in Concord on October 16, 1975. It was permanently staffed by only seven people, four of whom were volunteers, under the direction of Colonel "Hap" Watson. They nurtured a close, cordial relationship with our town chairmen.

Governor Reagan himself entered the Concord headquarters only once or twice for formal functions, accompanied by his serge-stripe suited John Sears and dapper Charles Black, a most imposing trio. They didn't stop to chat.

By contrast, the opposition appeared to work like a Xerox machine, more concerned with handbiting than handholding. Our proudest pat on the back came from Mary McGrory who wrote, "They greet the press with a cordiality that surpasses understanding in a conservative camp." Eventually we had eight offices around the state, all staffed by volunteers.

Though it was an expensive innovation, proprietor Matt Morton agreed to a temporary replacement of the wording on the huge sign atop the building, from "Highway Hotel" to "Reagan for President." This action created an ostentatious precedent, as all subsequent candidates who used the facility worked the same deal, for which Matt should pay me a royalty on the revenues he received. Now that this historical monument of political history has been razed, I guess my collateral went with the sign.

On the morning of November 20, Reagan formally announced his candidacy with a press conference at the National Press Club in Washington, leaving shortly thereafter with Nancy and a large

Hugh and Cay Gregg, Nancy and Governor Reagan at the Manchester Airport upon arrival for First Citizens' Press Conference.

entourage in a chartered plane for a second declaration in Miami, then ending up the same night at the Sheraton-Wayfarer in Bedford for an hour-long third one. The Reagans were greeted here by a well-organized crowd of a thousand enthusiastic supporters. Governor Thomson had attended the Washington event, then had gone from there directly to the Governors' Conference in Kansas.

Standing before a red, white, and blue campaign banner, it was the first of what became accepted as a "Citizens' Press Conference," unique in its ground rules that questioning was exclusively limited to nonmembers of the press. The concept was not welcomed by the media but they soon found it interesting because novel, unrehearsed questions sometimes introduced new issues.

In his opening remarks Governor Reagan ruled out, in the event of his losing the nomination, any thought of a third-party bid, by commenting that Republicans should stand together, then go after the balance of the electorate which he felt was disillusioned with both major parties. After his opening statement, he impressively fielded seventeen friendly audience questions. Ron and Nancy left the next morning for North Carolina.

Personal invitations had been extended and not accepted by the local Ford leadership to participate in this first open discussion meeting. Instead they badgered Reagan via letters to the editor and news releases on a number of issues. It gave us the chance to fire the initial volley that Reagan would not need surrogates to speak for him.

During the Christmas holidays, schedules were prepared which would bring Reagan back to the state for six multiday tours between the first of the year and primary day on February 24. Meanwhile, active days were not to begin before 9:00 A.M. and provision was to be made for the candidate to have an hour's rest, preferably early every afternoon.

Columnists Jack Germond and Jules Witcover noted that during Reagan's first campaign in California a rest period was integrated into his daily schedules, whereas in New Hampshire his stamina lasted for longer hours. It led them to conclude that the candidate had "1) learned to pace himself better; 2) found ways to conceal his nap time more skillfully; or 3) both." We take credit for having devised alternative 2. Nonetheless he did wage an occasional exhausting thirteen-hour day.

Arrangements were made with Stewart Lamprey, a former speaker of the New Hampshire House, and his newly formed Direct Mail Systems to telephone every Republican household, some 90,000 of them. With his partner, Ray Burton, who later became an executive councilor, they had presumably picked up checklists from every precinct and added phone numbers to the addresses of the Republican names.

The statewide twelve-hour-per-day phone bank was to be operated out of a storefront location in Laconia, with professional phone callers. Later, when we attempted direct mailings from the lists they had prepared, we received wholesale "wrong address" or "addressee unknown" returns from the post office. In many instances, the phone operators were so politically naive, it would have been better if they had been working for Ford.

On December 16 Bo Calloway stumped the state, promising that other Ford advocates would be following him after the first of the year. Meanwhile his aides were saying they'd been searching futilely for some sign of a Reagan organization beyond its state chairman.

On January 5, when Reagan arrived on his first campaign swing, they found out the hard way that we were still very much around. We ran a full-page ad which listed the names and phone numbers of 236 local chairmen, ready to lead every community in the state. The whomp of this impact was so revolutionary that it shocked the enemy. The revelation so jolted the opposition and the press that the chairmen identified in the ad began receiving phone calls to verify they were real!

Reagan's introduction to electioneering in New Hampshire began on that bitterly cold and snowy January day. He had solidified the frigidity with a speech entitled "Let the People Rule," given at the Chicago Executive Club the previous September, when he had proposed removing $90 billion of social programs from the federal budget to make them a state responsibility. The challenging concept was intended to save money and increase control at the local level.

The Ford people contrived an ambush, attacking the transfer of the taxing authority as a subterfuge for foisting a sales tax on the state. Shooting your mother would get you less criticism in New Hampshire than suggesting a sales tax.

The crux of his plan was to negate the notion that a dollar which comes from Washington comes free, and it was an attempt "to do away with the freight charge" by not sending our money there in the first place. The trouble was that the scenario had not been scripted carefully enough for even a former actor to put on a good performance before the continually repetitious questioning on the subject.

The *Portsmouth Herald* editorialized, "Reagan's proposition, no matter how the fanatics explain it, means horrendous new taxes in New Hampshire." Meanwhile, Bo Calloway had a hit with his version of the "ninety-billion-dollar boondoggle."

The governor's scheduled arrival in Laconia on the first day was suddenly vetoed at the last minute by the Secret Service. Weather conditions probably would have obscured the relatively unsophisticated instrument landing system at Laconia Airport, resulting in the United Airlines chartered 727 putting down at Manchester. Nancy was to join the trip later.

It meant quick cancellation of preplanned events in Meredith and Center Harbor; but, more importantly, we immediately became aware and alarmed that new personnel had been added to our scheduling department. The Service was constantly with us thereafter, sometimes fouling up logistics even more than I did.

It was twelve degrees below zero when we arrived at the packed Lions Hall in Moultonboro where the excitement was electric—many, of course, just coming to see a live movie star. A sled dog team met us at the door with a sign, "We can't vote but you can. Vote Ronald Reagan." Bruce Rounds, a legislator in charge of Advance, had also set up a horse-drawn sled for a photo op with a horse's blanket emblazoned, "I'm pulling for Reagan."

Subsequently we came to suspect all kinds of artifices from Bruce's cunning hand. With the cookies and jelly beans consumed, a few words of greeting, and with handshakes for everyone, in a half-hour the candidate was on his way, to West Ossipee, ten minutes up the road.

There the program was repeated, at the Flanders Motel, except Bruce got Ann Flanders to haul out a giant pink elephant as a welcoming gift. Because the room was smaller, the press outnumbered the natives and pushy TV camera crews made no friends. There were complaints that it was ridiculous to crowd out the townsfolk when the media had been with him all day.

Nonetheless, many were elated to see themselves the next morning on ABC national news.

At 6:30 P.M. we arrived at the Red Jacket Inn at North Conway, the overnight stop for the whole entourage. NBC had a charter flight standing by in nearby Fryeburg, Maine, to fly out film to be shown on its "Today Show" the next morning, of both the day's activities and the Citizens' Press Conference planned for eight o'clock that evening.

The bulk of the camera equipment and heavy-duty suitcases hauled and manhandled by the networks was awesome. In addition there was a filming unit directed by the advertising agency to capture ambience for future commercials.

Reagan had left Los Angeles at 6:30 that morning, barnstorming all that day, dressed like one of us in two sweaters topped by a ski parka. With only an hour's rest he reappeared from his private room in a well-cut blue suit, white shirt, and red tie, ready for the quick drive to Kennett High School where we had gathered an audience of over one thousand to await him.

Upon reaching the podium and noting a sign hoisted by a protester in the back of the hall which proclaimed "Death Valley, USA," the Governor warmed the crowd with, "It may have been Death Valley to some—for me it was bread and butter."

While the overwhelming majority of the questioners were warm and receptive, it was our first exposure to the antagonistic group identifying themselves variously as "People's Bicentennial Commission" (PBC) or "Bicentennial Common Sense." This well-oiled and organized tribe became our constant companions wherever the candidate appeared, always endeavoring to embarrass him. Well-equipped with a truck, loudspeaker, van, cars, well-written promotional literature, and placards, their objective as economic revolutionaries was to blame big business and giant corporations for all of America's ills.

In one of PBC's initial pamphlets appeared the shocking query, "The Russians have the Communist Manifesto, the Chinese have the Quotations of Chairman Mao. Do Americans have a political document to lean on for guidance?" Obviously they didn't know New Hampshire had adopted the nation's first constitution nearly 192 years earlier, but it was rather surprising they hadn't heard of the Declaration of Independence or the United States Constitution. Jeremy Rifkin was one of their leaders. Near the end of the Conway meeting one attendant rose to ask, "Who the hell invited all those Reagan haters from Taxachusetts here tonight?"

As though it wasn't sufficient to have them as our constant uninvited guests, the Ford committee provided its "Truth Squad," which followed us around with open recorders. They didn't bother us much because they didn't ask questions. They only stole our better ideas, making the match more competitive.

At one session it was obvious the kibitzers couldn't correctly interpret their own recorders. We accused them of deliberately attempting to misrepresent Reagan's stand on Social Security. This free-for-all ended up with Reagan propounding the Eleventh Commandment, "Thou shalt not speak ill of a fellow Republican." Ford retorted he'd give the Republicans a choice between his record and Reagan's rhetoric, and the campaign stayed on a relatively high level thereafter.

Another group which occasionally made its presence known was Common Cause. It had requested thirteen of the Republican and Democratic presidential candidates to comment upon a set of campaign standards it had dreamed up. Common Cause was particularly upset with our Citizens' Press Conferences as there was no opportunity for follow-up questions on specific issues. Governor Reagan just ignored their queries. He was in full accord with Senator Eugene McCarthy's chairman who replied, "You can take your enclosed standards and stuff them in your ear."

This first major campaign appearance before a large gathering in North Conway was singular in that Reagan began his remarks from a prepared text, a format scrapped afterwards at similar events. It addressed what was to be his perennial theme—that government is not the solution, it is the problem.

In subsequent freewheeling, off-the-cuff remarks, he began introducing characteristic one-liners which became the real people pleasers at quick stops on the campaign trail. On deficit spending he compared balancing the budget to protecting a woman's virtue: she has to learn to say no. For prevention of higher taxes we need to get the government off our backs and out of our pockets. Berating national health insurance. he'd comment that one cannot socialize the doctor without socializing the patient.

At the end of the meeting he was chauffeured among the well-wishers by the Secret Service, but their security apprehensions restricted the autograph seekers. Nonetheless we seldom found the Service to be unduly difficult in coordinating their concerns with ours. ("Horseshit," exclaims Rounds. "You weren't out in the field with them.")

Commiserating with Bruce, I admit it was upsetting on the following day at the Balsams, when they only permitted the governor to sit in a snowmobile and wouldn't let him drive it. To the disdain of its proud owner we told the camera crews that it wouldn't work.

At nine o'clock the next morning we were off to the North Country—another piercingly cold day. Reagan was in high spirits. When we stopped at Bob Morrell's frigid, unheated workshop at Storyland, Reagan asked Bob if he could do anything about adjusting the air conditioning.

What became a permanent accoutrement of travel was a table fitted at the rear of the first bus which would accommodate a working area for four people, two riding backward. The governor took what became his customary position next to the window, facing forward. State and national media representatives would be invited to take fifteen-to thirty-minute turns sitting across the table for one-on-one interviews. Usually either Lyn Nofziger, Reagan's press secretary, or I would sit next to the candidate. We always kept a recorder on the table to tape everything. A Secret Service agent sat across the aisle.

Nancy, when on the trips, was seated in the right front seat of the bus. Revolving with each stop, influential women were her invited guests and seat companions. Meanwhile, she kept a watchful eye on her husband, frequently shepherding him when they were off the bus.

Reagan was close to no one except his closest confidants, with Nancy his constant companion. She called the shots on her husband's schedule and she, like no one else, had constant access to him. The two were almost inseparable, spending considerable private time together in their hotel suite; it seemed she generally would not allow anyone to hover too closely without her scrutinous approval.

After the first trip, Reagan's availability to us for campaigning was limited, with the days usually beginning about 9:00 A.M., a rest period allotted for almost every afternoon, then terminating in the early evening except for specific events.

The long bus rides were filled with activity. Any private conversations we had between us related to the campaign—people he had met, events—political talk. He never criticized his opposition publicly but his extraordinary sense of humor was irrepressible. Inside jokes abounded, sometimes even about Gerry Ford.

In the briefcase Reagan carried himself were stacks of four-by-six-inch white cards on which were inventoried boundless facts and statistics on a limited number of subjects. While I was never privy to its contents I'm sure the *World Almanac* would be only a primer in comparison. How he was ever able to recall anything specific from this bottomless encyclopedia remains a mystery to me. It also contained a selection of jokes and one-liners which he constantly upgraded. My favorite was the one he used in elderly nursing homes about the man whose Social Security check stopped because the government thought him dead, but he managed because it also sent him a $700 check for his funeral.

On his own, strolling in and out of the bus, Reagan was jovial, cavorting with the press, traveling staff, or supporters, always ready with a sharp retort. He was a natural, talented politician who identified well with the average guy—he had been very union-minded in those days when he was a Democrat—comfortable in any situation, though more reserved than the backslapping Rocky.

The ease with which he campaigned was perhaps best illustrated by the following exchange with a *New Hampshire Times* reporter:

"If Shakespeare had to write this scene of running for the presidency, what play do you think he would put it in?"

"Well," Reagan drawled, "I guess he would probably put it in *Much Ado About Nothing.*"

He never complained about his accommodations. Lunch was bought along the road and eaten en route. He did not show fatigue, though his staff remained watchful and protective of his physical comfort.

Wherever he went, he always had a large entourage and, when not with Nancy, would confer with us, Jim Lake and myself, or with his staff. Mike Deaver, Lyn Nofziger, Marty Anderson, and the Secret Service were usually hovering about, and the press rarely left us.

Lake and I worked well together. We ran a good road show featuring a Hollywood star, a witty performer. Wizened from the sixties, when Goldwater overspilled with rhetoric and underestimated the impact of the press, there'd be no free-for-all with candidate Reagan. The times, they sure had changed.

On each leg of the trek newsmen, selected on a rotating basis, also rode the first bus along with the campaign staff. The balance of the press contingent boarded the second one. This arrangement seemed to work reasonably well with the media. It offered local radio and newspapers opportunity for exclusivity, and also somewhat assuaged the national press which was barred from asking questions at the Citizens' Press Conferences. Still, some of the New Hampshire dailies were childish and naturally embittered because we could not visit their homerooms.

The procession, which always included a fleet of private vehicles behind the buses, stopped at the Skimobile where skiers were

Governor Reagan makes an unscheduled flag stop in the north country.

congregating. Reagan allowed that Ford was a skier, but that he preferred horseback riding.

At the Fireside Hotel in Gorham he showed courage in accepting a glass of orange juice because he wasn't sure whether it came from Florida or California.

In the jammed Salvation Army hall in Berlin he was presented a framed sketch showing him in a rocking chair. We guessed the artist must have been a Democrat who thought Reagan had reached that age, or maybe he was just a leftover Kefauver supporter.

The highlight of this trip occurred as we started toward Dixville Notch and were passing through the remote environs of Errol. There in the middle of the desolate, steeply snowbanked highway (and only Rounds could have known when the column would reach that point) were several lonely ladies waving an early American flag and unfurling a homemade Reagan banner. It was just too good for anyone to miss, especially Reagan. Everybody was instantly out of the buses for fantastic photos of "the whole Damm family"—that is, the family of William Damm. Better yet, they all turned out to be Republicans, except the growling Damm dog, obviously a Democrat.

Once back in the bus, still in a state of exhilaration, the parade had passed through adjacent Millsfield before I realized it. A two-family town with only seven voters, it had nearly shattered our coup of getting a chairman for every precinct of the state. It was so important that we backtracked the long string of vehicles and the candidate met Genevieve Annis, his chairman, to receive from her a balsam pillow "for sweeter dreams."

The next stop was the nationally famous midnight place of Dixville. True to its traditional flair, the Balsams Hotel welcomed the governor with premises-produced "Reagan for President" balloons, sumptuous refreshments worthy of the Cordon Bleu, and the pianist at the grand fingering "I Left My Heart in San Francisco." After trudging through the heavy snow all day, feeling frostbitten to the bone, the city-clad, ravenous press plunged toward the plentiful buffet in total disbelief.

Then on to Colebrook where fellow newsman Judge Fred Harrigan, publisher of the local *News & Sentinel* and sage of the North Country, confided to his peers that the only picturesque New Hampshire types are confined to the North Country, and that southern New Hampshirites were becoming practically indistinguishable from commuters in greater Boston. In theory Fred was probably correct, but the press seemed to have little difficulty in scavenging "characters" wherever we went.

It should not be overlooked either that there were colorful Democrats in this race, other than Jimmy Carter, such as Billy Joe Clegg who campaigned under the motto, "Free Spirit for freedom with Jesus Christ and the Holy Spirit as my foundation and guide." Lee Packwood, his vice presidential running mate, observed the need for stockpiling food to survive the famine of 1982 which would be caused by the alignment of the planets. "Keep Roll-in-son with Rollinson" and his wife, the "Magic Princess," were running on the platform of his being an honest man. Then there was Robert Kelleher who didn't want to be president, rather probably prime minister, because he wanted to replace Congress with a Parliament.

Nightfall brought us to a packed house at the White Mountains Regional High School for another Citizens' Press Conference. By now the absolution that had been allowed to the PBC fanatics (whose American Revolutionary "Don't Tread On Me" flag flew to the constant accompaniment of an amplified recording of "Yankee Doodle Dandy") had begun to wilt. When one of the young lady protestors asked why Reagan was so supportive of big business, he cracked, "Tell me, from whom did you buy that loud sound truck you're foisting on everyone?"

The answer to a question of whether Reagan would be willing to debate the president was strongly affirmative, with an offer to do so even in the White House; but no confrontation between the two men ever took place.

Fulminating against his favorite whipping boy, the federal government, Reagan pledged he would get it out of the business of running the schools and return that responsibility to the local level. Overheard was a bystander's comment, "He talks my kind of game, but so did Nixon before he was elected."

We spent the night in Littleton, where somehow a room for Bruce was omitted from the manifest and he had to sleep on the floor of someone's living room. Next morning when I told Reagan of our star advance man's plight, he willingly autographed a photo: "To Bruce, Next time we'll share the red carpet suite together." I had asked him to substitute the words "presidential suite" but Reagan wouldn't do it as he thought it would have been "presumptive." In retrospect, I guess he meant by "presumptive" that he would never share a room with Rounds!

The following day (January 7) we wound up the first three-day tour, having drawn eager crowds in sixteen communities. On the way through Franconia Notch where the photographers wanted a background shot of the Old Man (not Reagan), the candidate obligingly threw a snowball at a highway sign, followed by a Lyn Nofziger zinger: "George Gipp would have knocked the sign down."

Another exhausted aide who had not stepped out of the bus remarked, "Some guys will do anything for the cameras," to which the candidate grinned, "Some guys will."

The visit had been a total success in achieving our objective of bringing this relatively unknown Californian (other than as a movie idol) to the grass roots of New England. He remained easygoing, outgoing and authentic. When he did well, as he usually did, there was often some realist, or a Democrat, calling to one's attention, "Well, he is an actor after all."

The five ensuing journeys through the state were equally triumphant and conducted similarly. Of course, there were always the amusing incidents, such as when in Dublin, State Senator Rob Trowbridge, chairman of the senate finance committee and a dedicated Ford zealot, presented Reagan with a basic economics textbook.

Credit for the smooth operation of these junkets went to our two advance teams. The first consisted of representatives of the Secret Service with both New Hampshire and national staffs. They would carefully case every detail of the proposed schedule and route. The major problem was that we had a candidate who insisted on talking with everybody about everything. On the day of his arrival the governor was immediately preceded by a second advance team which frequently tried to make last-minute adjustments to the previously planned program.

One of the missions of the Advance team was to prep the welcoming host at each stop with appropriate words of greeting to the candidate upon his arrival. Nancy did not like the way her husband was introduced at the Bow firehouse, so she wrote out her own suggestion for future salutations. Her version was then carried ahead for use at each location. It worked for a while, until the press started questioning the rote remarks repeated whenever the bus halted.

February 6, 1980, was the date of the big secret, that is, Reagan's sixty-fifth birthday and his eligibility for Social Security. The timing did not tie in well with our resolution to overlook the age issue. We were paranoid that the press would note the milestone. A good job was done all day. No one had said a word during the tedious, cold day's tour.

After the very last event of the day, a dinner in Sunapee, in marched the chefs ceremoniously shouldering a giant birthday cake ablaze with at least sixty-five candles. Our secret was blown wide open and made headlines everywhere the next morning.

Another secret now being disclosed for the first time could have mooted the entire 1976 Primary. The press had been advised that Reagan's filing papers, officially entering him in the race, would be presented to the secretary of state on the final day of the mandatory filing period.

The secretary's office closed at five o'clock and by midafternoon we had not received the candidate's filing papers. We had been calling the California campaign office for a couple of days. There had been a major foul up and the filings never arrived. I was the only one who knew.

Locking myself in a private room at the Highway Hotel, I began practicing the governor's signature. The forgeries were detectable.

Fortunately Georgi Hippauf, who was in charge of the headquarters and later became my personal assistant, came to my rescue. Now that the Statute of Limitations has run out, she says it's okay to disclose that she committed the peccadillo and that's how Reagan's name got on the ballot.

One of the more memorable episodes occurred later when a Catholic priest traveled with us in the press contingent. He represented a diocesan newspaper and was properly credentialed as a reporter.

During one afternoon Citizens' Press Conference he removed his media ID, stepped away from the press section, and, masquerading as a local, boldly asked Reagan a question.

At dinner that evening, Bruce Rounds chastised him for unprofessional conduct. As the confrontation heated up, Bruce became more incensed and ended up calling the pseudo-newsman an "asshole."

The next morning the priest cornered Reagan to complain that a member of the governor's staff had spoken an obscenity. Reagan, after listening to the true recitation of what had happened, looked the priest right in the eye and said, "I agree with Bruce."

On February 7 President Ford made the first of only two campaign trips to the state. The major event was his address to the Annual Chamber of Commerce dinner in Nashua, which was rather ironic as it was in honor of the "Man of the Year," Sam Tamposi, who happened to be our finance chairman. We felt comforted and maybe even somewhat sympathetic when a PBC kook showed up in a gorilla suit to ask the president loaded questions.

Ford was accompanied by his wife, who Mary McGrory called the "open Ford," adding that the Ford managers wanted Betty as the president's only advocate, yet feared her proabortion views would trigger needless nasty Loeb editorials. Loeb was already waging a pretty good battle without additional ammunition by dubbing the president as "Devious Gerald," whose supporters were "piling every lie, every dirty trick, every underhanded attack they can against this newspaper and anyone who supports Reagan."

In the light of the campaign that developed four years later, it may have been prophetic that the editor of the *1590 Broadcaster* wrote, "If Ford's pardon of Nixon weren't enough to turn most voters off—his appointment of George Bush to head the critical CIA should do the trick."

Nonetheless, the Ford people did recruit and dispatch a series of bureaucratic surrogates, including Elliott Richardson, secretary of commerce, who Ford's honorary state chairman, Senator Cotton, called a "cream puff"; and Rogers Morton, councilor to the president on energy matters. Even Henry Cabot Lodge showed up in New Hampshire to have lunch with Ford on the final weekend of the campaign as the final step of their endearment program.

Our payoff came from Mitchell Koblinski, within a week after he had been appointed as head of the Small Business Administration and before he could have found his desk in Washington. Koblinski checked in here to visit special ethnic groups encouraging votes for Ford. He didn't bother to contact Bert Teague, who was then the District SBA chief; rather he called Polish and Lithuanian clubs, and Faustyn Jaskiel, a Reagan supporter and prominent member of the Polish community in Manchester.

Jaskiel noted the call was possibly a political coincidence and the next coincidence he'd expect would be "a call tonight suggesting that, for a fella with my limited academic background, which is zero, that I've been appointed to be an overseer of Harvard."

While Reagan made no use of proxy speakers, on the last weekend he was accompanied by actor Lloyd Nolan. Nolan, aged 73, was introduced at each stop and was appreciatively recognized by at least some of the adults in the audiences.

Ford's staff took astute advantage of Air Force I by advertising its arrival as though the passenger was an afterthought. They were probably right, because lots of Reagan people showed up at the airport to be awed by the splendor of the plane, and that's how they mustered a crowd.

Except for his presence at our Manchester headquarters, Governor Thomson was invisible until we stopped at the Pittsfield firehouse on February 11. There the New Hampshire governor rode shotgun with Reagan in a small buggy wagon drawn by a Shetland pony, appropriately named "Tippy Toes." Over the pony was draped a sign reading, "Reagan Makes Horse Sense." Obviously Rounds didn't know the difference. Mel gave a warm introduction to Ron, saying, "Any of you who farm know the prevailing winds come out of the West. A great wind has come out of the West to honor us today." It got the hot air flowing—quite befitting two politicians.

Perhaps it was in this euphoria that Thomson first dislodged our underdog status, to our consternation, by predicting Reagan would win well over 50% of the vote. Reagan, too, became somewhat overzealous on that occasion in acceding that he had not ruled out anyone as a possible vice presidential running mate, including Thomson.

A few days before the Pittsfield love-fest, Lake had received a carping letter from Loeb, critical because we were spending too much time looking for votes from the Ivy League and in the woodland, rather than on the seacoast and in southern New Hampshire. In his typical editorial style he wrote, "You'd better get off your ass and do something or you are going to get a hell of a licking."

Probably Loeb's wrath had been agitated by Reagan's visit to Lebanon, a town Loeb felt was contaminated by osmosis from the liberals at nearby Dartmouth, where he had been introduced to a Reagan gathering by Senator Cotton. The senator, who was Ford's honorary state chairman and a Yankee gentleman, expressed his great respect and admiration for the candidate, stating that the governor was a tower of strength in the Republican party and "my kind of fellow." The accolade even included a testimony that Cotton would support Reagan with enthusiasm, were he the nominee.

When we selected our twenty-one (out of 2,259) nominees for delegates to the Republican National Convention, we had a serious problem of few well-known names, with all the heavy hitters playing on the Ford team. Thomson had told a Washington Post reporter in December that he had a "commitment" to head the Reagan delegate slate and would have a say in naming its other members, but we knew of no such promise. He was not chosen, primarily because of his own contested reelection for governor.

It was a wise, farsighted decision, as later he stalked off the reservation when Reagan picked Senator Richard Schweiker as his runningmate. Even Loeb scolded him for not supporting Reagan's choice.

After Thomson, piqued, said he wouldn't even attend the convention, he went anyway as a free spirit. He wanted to make a seconding speech for Reagan's nomination and was treated with cautious courtesy, given a limousine and a box seat with Nancy. Nonetheless, the Reagan high command, fearing he would become a loose cannon, assigned a staffer to accompany him at all times under the code name "The Muzzle."

All our lists, correspondence, and records were prepared manually, within the limitations of photocopiers and typewriters. The traveling staff carried a telecopier to use when Reagan was in the state, so that overnight articles from first editions of the Washington and New York papers could be retrieved. From these, news summaries were prepared. Though Reagan used a teleprompter in other primary states, it was not done here.

Innovating incidents to whet the appetites of the wire services was a constant challenge. We were really reaching at Mount Sunapee ski area when we lured the governor to kneel in deep snow next to a sleepy Saint Bernard with a barrel under its collar. It was a question of which one was lost. Meanwhile Ford was taking advantage of his office by inviting editorial writers and reporters from local radio, TV, and newspapers to the Oval Office of the White House.

Traveling reporters were expected to file a steady stream of stories relating the campaign's progress, which meant news had to be generated every day. If they didn't get a good scoop during the day, prankster Lyn Nofziger could always make headlines at the bar in the evening, like the time he mischievously suggested to the British press that Jimmy Carter had "the clap."

From the repetitious routine of our daily schedules, the media ceaselessly probed for fresh images or photo ops, and we tried to oblige. Sometimes they became very colorful in their descriptions. Andy Merton described Dover City Councilor Geraldine Sylvester at a Reagan meeting as being dressed in a white business

61

suit with bright red high-heeled shoes and a Miss America-type red, white, and blue sash across her chest, emblazoned "REAGAN." He commented, "She rarely dresses that way for City Council meetings."

Others, like NBC newsman Tom Pettit, exposed a finagling. The candidate had just told employees of the State Liquor Commission, "I have a feeling this is the first time I'm among a group who won't challenge a state being able to run certain programs that have been loused up by the federal government." As he was about to exit the building I passed a bottle of liquor to a woman spectator on the outside, which she was to present "spontaneously" as he came out. The *Wall Street Journal* used this as an example of politicians contriving media events, proving that network reporters aren't always patsies.

On the Friday before the Primary, at a general news conference, a reporter noted that President Ford had portrayed Reagan as too far to the right to be electable, whereupon Reagan disclosed the startling secret that Ford had previously offered him the cabinet positions of secretary of commerce and secretary of transportation. The follow-up query was to learn if the offers were made to keep the governor from running, to which Reagan wryly replied, "No, I just thought he recognized my administrative ability."

When the primary process began, no one believed the challenger could receive more votes than the president, although he could be the accredited victor by coming close, perhaps with only 40% of the vote—which had been my prediction.

As the windup approached, speculation was growing that it might be a standoff. A few pollsters were going both ways.

Still, based on the traditional New Hampshire experience that quantified (not veritable) numbers count, I safely upped my estimate to 45%. Though somewhat suspect in some quarters, it was widely accepted as a defensible figure until Governor Thomson declared on "Meet the Press" that Reagan "would win easily with 55% of the vote."

Governor Reagan and Nancy as he addresses the crowd. (Donald P. Jones, Contoocook)

As soon as Mel made that prediction, I knew we were in deep difficulty. It not only raised media standards of expectation but, much more seriously, it meant that some Reagan supporters would lose the stimulus to turn out at the polls.

On election night security was the tightest we had ever witnessed, with a half-dozen Secret Service agents behind a roped-off area at the entrance of the Highway Hotel, checking cameras and going through handbags, all without the speed of mag machines. They issued nearly one thousand press credentials. There were reporters covering reporters, with many of them only gathering material to write books, some about themselves.

A couple of days before Primary eve, former president Richard Nixon had landed in Peking for a nine-day tour of China. Early on Primary night, when results were running ahead for Reagan, Stuart Spencer and Bo Calloway, looking worried, commented that Nixon's trip had slowed down the momentum of the Ford drive in the closing hours, by triggering shadows of Watergate and the pardon. At 11:30 P.M. Ron Nessen, Ford's press secretary, said it would be a cliff-hanger.

With a razor-thin lead at midnight, Reagan appeared before our cheering, jubilant troops recalling that he had embarked on the New Hampshire Primary race seeking only 40% of the vote, "but we've far exceeded our expectations. I feel that what's happened tonight is a victory."

When the tallies were finalized the next morning, we had lost by a statistical margin of 1,587 votes, or 49% (53,569) to 51% (55,156). Of course, I claimed we had won. Jim Cleveland, Ford's chairman, put the picture in a more practical posture for the press by reacting, "Hogwash, a victory is a victory and we won." And that's the way the story played.

Fred Harris, who was simultaneously being wiped out by Jimmy Carter on the Democratic ticket, explained his loss much better than we did, saying, "Our problem is that the little people were not able to reach the vote levers."

Reagan dauntlessly wisecracked, "One Primary does not a summer make." More seriously, he contended he was happy to have ended in a virtual tie with the incumbent president. But Senator Cotton prophesied that both candidates had bloodied each other's noses so that both of them were at the bottom of their popularity, while Carter was at the height of his.

The *Portsmouth Herald* said Ford did well to come out alive and that Thomson was a greater burden than Reagan could carry.

Mary McGrory summed it up in her syndicated column by writing, "New Hampshire had spoken, and said nothing."

The morning after the Primary, Nancy Reagan dispatched an aide to headquarters to visit the senior members of the staff who had labored hard and well for her husband. Each was given a very nice pin from Governor Reagan of California, but there had been no personal exhange, no personal note, not even a handshake, yet the two had been staying only a few doors down the hall.

The Reagans were never guests in the Gregg house. They were certainly more private than the Rockefellers and, as it turned out, the Bushes. We did not develop a close personal relationship with them, although our working rapport was excellent. Cay had only a few occasions to visit with Nancy. It was difficult for the two women to converse, as they shared few common interests.

Nancy was always the actress, always on stage, mentally and physically. She never let the curtain fall. She enjoyed campaigning, being front center, occasionally speaking on selected subjects. She was an asset and, as always, his closest ally.

How did they feel about New Hampshire? For Nancy's part, one day she asked Cay to find her an outhouse—a present for her husband, as a joke reminder of the state.

She also wanted to buy something from every state that was indigenous to it. Someone suggested a blanket made in Harrisville, from our own sheep wool. "Good, how much?" she asked. "Seventy-five to a hundred dollars," was the reply. No sale, as it turned out. She didn't want to spend any more than ten dollars.

As for Ron, I think he genuinely liked the state and found it fun campaigning here. The close, personal nature of our politics was probably new to him but the constant presence of his cohorts and the Secret Service lessened some of the commingling with the populace which Rocky had encountered.

Until Nancy Reagan published her book, *My Turn*, I did not know that the Reagans had been prepared for a Granite State win, which was one reason for their return here on election night.

They apparently had anticipated basking in the klieg lights of victory. It is inconceivable that their national handlers would have assumed her husband would receive more than 50% of the vote. Certainly no one on the New Hampshire staff did.

———————

For ourselves, the volunteers and staff of the campaign organization, the fifteen-hour days and hundred-hour weeks were over. For five solid months we had labored with unrelenting intensity and purpose, building a statewide organization from only a handful of supporters. But now, the hunt was ended. In any other business, we might have reveled in our technical success. It was probably gratifying enough that we had brought a relatively obscure political candidate to the threshold of the presidency.

But the dismantling of a political campaign is worse than the legendary postpartum blues, and it has to be done in a day. The clock ticks against us, as every hour spent is a dollar spent, while the money is needed elsewhere, for the next foray, in Florida, Illinois, or North Carolina.

Because I had already taken so much time away from the responsibilities of my business during the campaign, I did not want my name on the ticket as a delegate to the Republican National Convention scheduled for the fall. Sears and Lake insisted it was necessary, so I reluctantly agreed, expecting not to be elected anyway. As it turned out, I was the only Reagan delegate-at-large who did win; thus, I went to the convention in the company of district delegate Tom Hynes, and thereafter was happy the opportunity had been offered to me.

Campaign workers are probably the most expendable commodities on earth. Some will seek to continue, following their hero to the end. If, after long months of personal contribution at little or no pay, the candidate should win the general election, a fortunate, eager few may find positions in the new administration.

The primary campaign of 1976 was certainly memorable and, until the fall of 1979, my communication with Ronald Reagan was infrequent but pleasant. Once I had committed to George

Bush, as will be discussed in the next chapter, obviously the personal relationship was terminated and never rekindled.

For myself, I sought no compensation for time, services, or monies expended, though I had asked for one simple personal favor: John Sears promised me that Ronald Reagan would make a campaign stop at my new restaurant in Sarasota, Florida.

I left New Hampshire immediately, eager to prepare an elaborate welcome for his visit and, a few days later, Reagan did come to Sarasota—and lunched at a competitor's establishment!

But such is the vicissitude of politics, and there has never been any question of my friendship and admiration of John. That we share mutual respect was demonstrated several years later when he told a public policy conference at the College of William and Mary in Virginia that I was a man who had devoted himself "in the proper way to this business of politics and who should be president."

Dave Bates, candidate George Bush with son, Neil, seeking votes house-to-house.

CHAPTER 3

Reagan Bushwhacks George 1978–1980

If Hollywood had scripted this chapter it would be entitled "Snow White and the Seven Dwarfs," with its popular actor Ronald Reagan playing the role of Snow White. I wouldn't dare associate the familiar names of the dwarfs with specific candidates, but their real names were John Anderson, Howard Baker, George Bush, John Connally, Philip Crane, Robert Dole, and Harold Stassen (he's thrown in out of respect to his perseverance and to make it seven).

The Primary was set for February 26, 1980. Yet all these major Republican aspirants, plus a few minor ones, had begun their energetic scouting in early 1978, thus setting a new endurance record for campaign longevity.

My first exposure to this campaign came when Paul Russo phoned me in early February of 1978. Paul had helped us as a most effective Reagan staffer four years earlier, but in the interim his allegiance had switched to Senator Dole. Paul arranged for the two of them, Paul and the senator, to join Cay and me for dinner at our Sarasota restaurant, Greggs Greenhouse, and spend the night at our beach cottage there on February 16.

I had long admired Senator Dole for his exemplary war record. This was the first time I had met him in a relaxed ambience—a most pleasant social experience, the highlight of which was his facile political wit. He would have been a great match for Will

Rogers. Later in the fray, for example, he joked that neither Reagan nor Connally would dare make speeches outdoors on a windy day, lest they should drop their notes!

Dole had served as Ford's running mate in 1974 and carried Ford's endorsement in 1980, but did not emerge as a serious contender in this race. While he fantasized himself as an alternative, a younger Ronald Reagan, realistically he was concerned about giving up a safe Senate seat. He suffered the added problems of a revolving-door staff and insufficient financial backing.

On September 9, 1978, Phil Crane came to my home in Nashua for a social visit. During mid-summer he had stayed overnight at Bill Loeb's mansion at Prides Crossing, Massachusetts. Bill, within a month thereafter, dubbed Crane's intent to run as egoism and a "stab in the back" to Reagan for wanting to divide the sensible conservative element of the Republican party.

It's unlikely that Crane, a former college history professor, could have foreseen the biography of himself that Loeb would subsequently publish on the front pages of the Manchester *Union Leader*. Loeb labeled him as a heavy drinker, a playboy, and a womanizer. Crane wrathfully accused Loeb of vile innuendoes while good-naturedly admitting he was a passionate Protestant who had eight children because he wanted eight children. Still, the charges were so acerbic that even the New Hampshire legislature passed a resolution of apology—but permanent damage had already been done.

Crane had started much earlier, making more trips to New Hampshire in 1978 than anyone else. He was the first participant to show organizational activity. At a time when Gordon Humphrey was an unknown airline pilot, Phil was the first prominent public officeholder to endorse Humphrey's initial Senate run and assist him in raising money. Thus, Gordon was a close friend upon whom Phil was counting for a base of support. What a surprise for him when the coup de grace befell his candidacy: Humphrey endorsed Reagan!

70

Governor Reagan phoned me on September 10, 1978, to advise he would again be a candidate for president in 1980. His call was followed up by one from Lyn Nofziger, still a Reagan deputy, two days later. Lyn and I agreed to get together to discuss the part I might play in the forthcoming effort. On October 20 he flew to Boston and we met in the American Airlines Admiral's Club at Logan Airport.

It was from a mixed mind-set that I advised Lyn I might not get involved in the next presidential primary and not, in any event, in the Reagan campaign. In the earlier Reagan venture I had dedicated substantial energy and resources, to the detriment of my own business obligations, and felt perhaps it would be personally unwise to do it again.

Though I blanch to admit it now, it was my sincere opinion that Reagan's name, after ten years pursuing the presidency, had become "shopworn" (a term which did not endear me with Nancy) and perhaps the country was ready for a fresh face on the Republican ballot. Also, fearing the restrictions of his age (with myself not yet over seventy at that time), I was convinced the rigors of a campaign and certainly a couple of terms in the Oval Office would be more of a physical strain than Reagan could handle. How wrong I was!

Meanwhile, prior to my meeting with Nofziger, George Bush had been making intermittent forays into the state, meeting Republican leaders under the sponsorship of Congressman Jim Cleveland and former national committeewoman Victoria Zachos, our perennial Young Republican.

Bush had written to me on August 30 suggesting we get together on one of his subsequent visits. His letter read, "I note that some there are labeling me a 'liberal'—not true!! Why do we Republicans always try to label each other and divide?" In a later note he said again, "I've always deplored 'labeling.' I have a sound voting record in Congress—fiscally conservative."

It was not until October 26, 1978, that I first met Bush, a fellow Eli (six days after the meeting with Nofziger in Boston). Jim

71

Cleveland had arranged our initial introduction at the home of Gerrie Porter in Amherst.

I was never privileged to have similar private encounters with the other major contenders in the 1980 race, nor with their representatives. Nor did any of them become significant players in the contest.

John Connally blew into the state in his garish purple, pink, and white corporate jet. While his appearance was that of a powerful silver-maned statesman, Granite Staters saw him as a cross between a buccaneer and the Marlboro Man. Then, too, there was his status as a turncoat Democrat, the milk fund bribery trial, and the White House wheeler-dealer image.

Loeb summed up Connally's slick demeanor by calling him a real patent-medicine salesman. As a tactician, the Texan also underrated our unique political folkway when he declared if he couldn't organize us in twelve months, "I'll turn in my gun and start selling shoes."

John Anderson joined the chase as the only avowed liberal against a cluster of conservatives, describing himself as the "thinking man's candidate" for president. As David Olinger pictured the course, Anderson was "the only candidate trying to run in the left lane," a dangerous place because New Hampshire frequently has no center line. Though a ten-term congressman, he was so unknown that even his own advertising promoted "John Who?" He was an effective speaker but his campaign schedules were generally limited to the southern counties. Neither did he make friends by advocating a federal fifty-cent per gallon gas tax in this sales-tax-free environment.

Senator Howard Baker joined the fray far better known and more respected than the other also-rans. His best card was a toehold of local support from then-senatorial candidate Warren Rudman and former governor Walter Peterson. Although thoroughly informed on all aspects of government, as the *Boston Globe* reported, his delivery was passionless, even when speaking of passion for the American political process.

In Baker's own promotional piece George Will was quoted, "Baker, like chamber music and other subtle things, is an acquired taste." A camera zealot, he was sometimes taking as many photos of others on the campaign trail as the media took of him. He had a delightful sense of humor, allowing, for example, that his major competitor, George Bush, had always been such a good friend that "I may give him a job in my administration."

The day before my meeting with George Bush at Gerrie Porter's, Reagan had lunch with Bill at Loeb's Massachusetts home. Thereafter he flew to Concord to be the main speaker, for the second time, at a Governor Thomson fundraiser, telling reporters he had not determined whether he would again be a presidential candidate. Thomson was running for a fourth term and to the surprise of no one, there were mutual endorsements.

Later Thomson refused to support Reagan as long as John Sears was Reagan's manager. Colorful as always, he was quoted by Jonathan Kirsch in *New West* magazine: "They'd like to have me on the campaign if I sat in the back pew and read my hymnal at the proper times and otherwise kept my mouth shut."

On November 7, 1980, Thomson was defeated by Democrat Hugh Gallen.

Unknown to me, Bruce Rounds, coworker with Bush in the CIA. and formerly resolute Reagan worker, had sent a telegram to Bush on the day after Thomson's defeat, noting that the latter's rejection at the polls was also a defeat of the Reagan-Loeb axis, thus leaving leaderless the responsible New Hampshire conservatives. He added, "The time is most propitious for you to make an overt move here before the national Reagan organization can recover from what must be a most disheartening setback."

My conversation with Bush at Gerrie Porter's was strictly social. Jim Cleveland and George had served together in Congress and were close friends. George and I also seemed to relate well to each other, resulting in my inviting him to visit me in Sarasota the week before Christmas, when he planned to be in Florida.

He came as my overnight guest and, after jogging three miles on the beach at Siesta Key, had dinner at our Greenhouse restaurant. We discussed the New Hampshire situation and my reluctance to undertake another presidential campaign.

It didn't take much of a discourse to recognize that Bush, like Rockefeller, was not a liberal, as he'd been so often stereotyped. Rather, he had steadfastly opposed the Panama Canal and Salt treaties, cancellation of the B-1 bomber, the Democrat attacks on the defense budget, and called for sound fiscal policies as an antidote to inflation.

His experience in foreign policy far exceeded that of his competitors, and he was the only one with a business background. Furthermore, his impeccable reputation of personal integrity and decency had never been questioned.

More important to me, he outlined his intention of aggressively soliciting votes in every hamlet of the state, while engendering assuredness he would actually do it. He said he was going to win because he'd work harder than anyone else.

At age fifty-four, Bush obviously had the vigor and stamina to withstand the rigorous physical demands of an active presidency. His affability and sincere interest in people qualified him as a natural handshaker for the hustings. Best of all was his gifted, incisive intelligence, complemented by an unpretentious personality. Needless to say, he sold me.

Some days later Jim Baker, Bush's national campaign manager, called from Houston and offered me the New Hampshire chairmanship. I accepted.

In assuming this responsibility, at least one familiar characteristic was common to earlier campaigns with which I had been involved. Our candidate was starting so low in the polls that he had only dogs to worry about. On January 8, 1979, the *Los Angeles Times*, in the first major survey of New Hampshire voter attitudes, released opinions asked of 353 registered Republicans, with the following results:

REAGAN BUSHWHACKS GEORGE: 1978–1980

Reagan	37%	Crane	4%
Ford	36% *	Dole	3%
Baker	11%	Bush	2%
Not sure	7%		

*Ford did not run; endorsed Dole.

The poll concluded, "The potential candidate with the dimmest current prospects . . . is George Bush."

On a return trip from Puerto Rico, George and his aide, Dave Bates, flew into Boston at noon on Sunday, January 7, 1979. Jim Baker also came up from Washington. My son Judd, an executive councilor at that time, Bruce Rounds, and I joined them for an hour at Logan Airport. It was a get-acquainted meeting for Judd and Bruce, both of whom had also been solicited by the other candidates.

Some preliminary ground rules were established. At our request, we were to be given the authority to call the shots in New Hampshire, we could select the delegates to the national convention, and Secret Service protection would not be solicited until after the Primary.

The meeting was held in a corner of Eastern's big Ionosphere Room. There was no privacy. We had a tough time holding George's attention as he kept gravitating toward a nearby TV set—the Houston Oilers were in the play-offs. They lost.

Fortunately the easiest first step was the assembling of experienced, competent, and loyal associates. The four top-doers from the 1976 Reagan venture were enthusiastic about trying again. Because we had worked harmoniously through stressful situations, we were tolerant of each other's idiosyncracies, mostly mine.

Georgi Hippauf served as my efficient administrative assistant. Bruce Rounds acted as campaign director, Jim Chamberlin as coordinator, and Lucy Muller took charge of the Concord headquarters. Additionally, we were joined by Congressman Jim Cleveland, who had headed up the 1976 Ford opposition, and his popular, talented wife, Hilary, agreed to be finance chairman.

Except for Georgi's professional expertise, all of us were one hundred percent volunteers.

George and Dave Bates spent the first two nights of what eventually became an intermittent long-term residency at our home in Nashua on January 28 and 29, 1979. Unlike most presidential candidates, Bush never had a traveling retinue until after Iowa. He didn't need one—he had Dave Bates. A fledgling Houston lawyer, Dave was a friend of George's son Neil, and initially became acquainted with Bush through tennis matches arranged by Neil.

Neil had suggested his dad needed a young, versatile aide as a permanent travel companion. The choice was perfect. Constantly cheerful and easygoing, Dave was always at George's side. He carried the burdens of everything from being Houston headquarters liaison to reminding the candidate to write a note thanking Mrs. Postlethwaite for her party, noting special appreciation for the brownie baked by her five-year-old daughter, Penelope . . . "Also you'd better enclose a pin for Penelope," Dave would recommend.

Our house was the habitual overnight accommodation for the two men and occasionally George's gracious wife, Barbara. It served as a convenient base from which we launched our daytime excursions, though Bar found the house cold and suggested we spend more money on Texas oil.

Beginning from that first visit and for the forty-odd overnights thereafter, George was never able to communicate with our cat, Morris. Morris enjoyed sleeping with the next president but the feeling was not mutual.

At first, when George politely advised us he was a dog man, it was embarrassing to us and offensive to Morris, who considered himself more intelligent than any dog. When Bush became more proprietary, after several visits, he pronounced, "Morris can sleep on my bed if he wants, on the understanding he leave when I return." The hostility was finally diffused three years later when Morris received a Christmas card from the vice president's house in Washington with the note, "I miss you, you furry devil."

On Sunday evening, January 28, we held our first organizational session at the Vesper Country Club. In attendance were Bush, Chamberlin, Tom Hynes (who had been a Reagan district delegate), my son Judd (then governor's councilor and currently governor), Rounds, Charlie Sullivan (a judge, he could not participate in the campaign), and myself.

This get-together was followed by regularly scheduled meetings of a much-expanded advisory committee which set the policy and direction of the campaign. Long-range schedules were established which would plow the grass roots of every community in the state during the next year. The committee also served as a sounding board for tracking the adversaries.

Bruce's recollection of the first meeting with Bush was his advising the former ambassador it would be necessary that he abandon his $500 suits and start sporting flannel shirts. Bush, taken aback, blurted out, "This isn't a $500 suit, it's an $800 suit and my mother gave it to me." When next they met, Bush brought up the subject again, explaining he had checked with his mother who said she had not paid $800, rather, they were on sale and she had bought two for $1,500. After that one, Bruce was sure he liked George.

When George and Dave Bates left Nashua in a rented car on the morning of January 30, they headed for Vermont to meet Senator Norris Cotton at a prearranged stop in Lebanon, New Hampshire. Ben Thompson, a Cotton confidant, was to greet them and arrange for Bush's autograph of the popular senator's biographical book, while seeking an endorsement. Cotton held Bush in the greatest respect but his assistance turned out to be ambivalent.

The standard routine when George stayed with us was a knock on his bedroom door at 6:30 A.M., followed by Cay's quick breakfast, then our departure in my 1977 Pontiac station wagon for a physically exhausting day of "one-on-ones" with voters all over the state. The day rarely ended before 11:00 P.M., at which time Cay would have a bowl of hot buttered popcorn or Locke's vanilla ice cream, a specialty from Hollis, waiting for him to enjoy before he retired for the night.

George seldom asked about the daily schedule until we were in the car and under way. He rolled with the punches and took them as they came. Service clubs or other groups were worked into the itinerary whenever possible, along with breaks for jogging.

The only time he ever complained was when we allowed less than twenty minutes for lunch, getting downright unruly on really busy days with his six-minute sandwich. Once he commented, "If I'm such an elitist, how come you don't at least serve me watercress sandwiches?"

I always drove and George sat in the front seat, with Dave in the rear, frequently with local chairmen who would accompany us in their districts. Occasionally there would be a newsman aboard, but the press had little interest in what we were doing until after the Iowa caucus a year later.

George's perpetual good nature and delightful sense of humor made these rides fun, as there was always an inexhaustible series of situations bordering on the bizarre—such as the recurrent confusing of our candidate with Busch beer, or when he barely avoided shaking hands with a mannequin in a department store.

My most prized memento of the association with Bush is an ornate, sealed scroll (see page 170) which he appropriately executed on Air Force I after his election "in a flight over New Hampshire." Duly acknowledged and certified by Jennifer Fitzgerald and Chase Untermeyer of the Bush staff, it reads, "I spent more time in Hugh Gregg's station wagon than I spent in any other four-wheel conveyance anywhere in the world during 1979 and 1980."

In the early stages, when name recognition was zero, we gained a superb assist from a "Dear Fellow American" letter composed by Lowell Thomas, proffering his first lifetime endorsement of any presidential candidate by writing, "Based on my fifty-odd years of covering the global political scene I feel the leader we need for the 1980s is George Bush."

The identity crisis was so bad that sometimes, other than our arrangers, only a half-dozen people would show up for a well-publicized meeting. I recall that early in 1980 a Derry manufacturer requested we bring George through his plant. I told him we had done it last June. "Oh, was that George Bush? I didn't remember him."

Routine staff-staged teas were held in towns to acquaint their voters with the candidate. Frequently guests would politely introduce themselves: "We wanted to meet you, Mr. Bush, but we're for Ronald Reagan." In Jaffrey, even the servers of petit fours were wearing Reagan buttons. George chuckled, "I expect him to eat the cake, but why should I get the icing!"

Regrettably, small children cannot vote, because Bush, like Rockefeller, bewitched them like the Pied Piper. One day at Goodnow's store in Keene, mocking his own serious side, he waved his finger at an infant and jokingly proclaimed, "We've got to hold the growth of federal spending and regulation" and, as reported in the *Keene Sentinel* the tot broke into a broad grin.

Same thing with the elderly. At a senior citizens' center in Derry he entered just as they were singing "This land is your land . . . This land was made for you and me." George, as related in the *New York Times,* clutched an old woman, kissed her heartily on the cheek, then joined in singing "God Bless America." It was deeply sincere and a spontaneous display of patriotism. After he left, we learned he had taken every vote in the house.

By fall we had opened the main headquarters at the New Hampshire Highway Hotel in Concord. It was déjà vu from four years earlier, in the same office space, with only the name changed on the big sign atop the building.

Lucy Muller took over as though she had never been away, with three paid professionals and a flock of volunteers. She kept the files, handled correspondence, manned the telephones, greeted visitors, controlled expenses, and accomplished the myriad of miscellaneous tasks generic to a campaign. Georgi commuted between Concord and my Nashua office where she created the newsletters, kept the books, and generated the schedules. Parkie Fisher from Meredith, staunch Bush fan, joined us as a full-time volunteer.

Monthly upbeat newsletters entitled "The Bush Beat" served as the lifeline to our 236 chairmen and 664 key workers. A four-page, in-house publication, it was attractively designed and contained valuable data on the candidate's positions on major issues, "how-to" tips, schedules, and confidential information "not for media or public distribution."

Who were the Zekes? Everyone wanted to know. They were unpaid (except for expenses), energetic, dedicated, and productive young people, mostly from other states, who wanted a grounding in the political process. Their primary assignment was to work with the local chairmen in recruiting workers, setting up meetings, advancing for Bush, and serving as liaison to me.

We had tough weekly indoctrination sessions which earned me the unflattering title of "The Ayatollah." This innovative use of amateurs contrasted dramatically with our competitors, who were largely dependent upon professional field representatives. Many of our survivors have since established political prominence of their own, both here and in the nation's capital.

Pat Durkin from Connecticut, for example, ended up at Dartmouth's Amos Tuck School of Business Administration, then went on to speechwriting for the secretary of the treasury and eventually to a big- shot Wall Street job (so he says) with The First Boston Corporation. He still returns to New Hampshire to mock me for having advised, "You'll never get theah from heah." His brother, Dan, joined us in the 1988 campaign and thereafter moved on to the Commerce Department in Washington.

Thanks to the good fortune of his name, probably the best known of the Zekes was Neil Bush, the number-three son. A humble guy, he'd be the first to say he didn't do anything. On second thought, it was a jovial group, so maybe the others would be the first to say he didn't do anything!

Neil worked out of our Nashua office, always cheerful and eager to put in endless hours. His personal, handwritten thank-you notes to everyone he met on his daily rounds were too numerous to count—a trait inherited from his father and mother. It got to a point where he said, "Sometimes I feel like I'm the one running for office." Neil acknowledged the romance of campaigning in the Granite State by marrying one of its own, Sharon Smith, whose vivacious personality and beauty graced the entire campaign.

Joel Maiola, one of our enterprising Zekes, devised an innovative connivance to catch press attention with his announcement of the "First Great Presidential Worm Race" to be held at Claremont. Each of the candidates agreed to field a contestant. Joel figured if our entry won, it would generate lots of conspicuous publicity.

I must admit that "Bushwhacker," resting on his purple velvet chaise in his gold box, looked pretty impressive before the race. Though Joel said he had been dug up in the garden only two hours earlier, Bushwhacker even looked rested and ready.

And a great mudder he was. It was unbelievable how easily he crawled away with the race. The judges never found out he'd been given a quick shot of ammonia. The publicity wasn't quite like selecting Miss America but anything was better than nothing on an otherwise dull media day.

After George Bush announced his intention to run in the New Hampshire Primary, we confounded the media by taking "run" literally. Jogging became a part of the grand strategy of contrasts, as we knew Reagan wasn't about to compete in a road race. Our best photo op of the campaign occurred at 6:30 one morning in Jefferson, where John Harrigan, publisher of the *Coos County Democrat*, accompanied George for a three-mile run.

The photo identifying George and John appeared in the paper's next edition with the caption, "George Bush (left) who is really more to the right . . ." The editor also noted that a couple of farm dogs checked Bush's calfs to see if they were as inviting to bite as those of local legs.

Bob Novak, who witnessed this otherwise unheralded Olympic event, also took photos and unkindly quoted me in his nationally syndicated column: "I'd like to see Reagan doing this. We couldn't even get him out of bed this early." A few months later Bush stopped at Harrigan's home and found him cutting wood. George instinctively shouldered the axe for a different photographic exercise.

There was a pleasant sequel to this relationship when seven years later Harrigan, planning a trip to Florida via Washington, wrote George partly in jest saying, in effect, "Hello, former Running Partner, here are the dates I may be traveling on." In reply he got a prompt phone call from the White House advising that the vice president was in Tunisia, but would return so they could go running again.

Sure enough, when John landed at National Airport there was "a huge Lincoln with all kinds of antennae sticking out of it. The Secret Service gave me a badge and waved us right through the gates, tank traps and all."

While John waited in an inner sanctum, people like Ed Meese and Vance Packard wandered around "exchanging low but yet powerful murmurs." When he was admitted to George's office the vice president was stuffing his briefcases and advised, "We've got to go to my house to change before we run." At the vice presidential mansion they had to sneak up the back stairs to avoid a ladies' fundraiser hosted by Barbara.

From there it was another limo and motorcade ride to a boys' school where the vice president asked permission of the track coach to run with the school team. He gave it. George, an aide, John, and four Secret Service agents formed a moving cluster. The kids ran faster, so every time the veep's corps heard "a shrill post-pubescent voice ring out 'track' we'd all leap off the track and run on the grass while skinny kids flashed by, all legs in a blur of sneakers."

John Harrigan, the Vice President, and Ron Kaufman, on the track. (Dave Valdez)

Afterwards they went back to the mansion for a shower, a beer, and catching up on the "cultural differences between northern New Hampshire and Washington." George later dropped me a note: "John Harrigan came by and we went running."

A postscript to John's adventures with George is a vintage story which his father, Fred, relates. The elder Harrigan recounts that whenever George was in Colebrook he utilized the comfort facilities of Fred's *News & Sentinel* office. After Bush succeeded to the presidency Fred felt he should memorialize the john with a brass plaque: "The President __ __ __ here." But, thinking better of the idea, he settled for a photo of the chief executive above the bowl.

Then there was the day we nearly lost the candidate. He was scheduled into an exercise class at the Concord YMCA. After a grueling thirty minutes of aerobics consisting of sprints, sit-ups, jumping jacks, and push-ups, he lay on the floor gasping for breath. Unable to find his pulse, Bush conceded, "I must be dead. I knew campaigning in New Hampshire was rough, but this is absurd."

In retrospect maybe we overdid our loading his schedules with physical feats, as George admitted to the *Fort Worth Star,* "If I'm alive after New Hampshire I'll be soaring up above the rest of the crowd, and if I'm not, I'll be deader than the depleted . . . whatever the hell it might be, so forget it."

John Anderson took a shot at Bush when the latter told the *Los Angeles Times* a nuclear war was "winnable." Anderson dubbed the statement "appalling." What Bush had meant was that if there were to be a nuclear holocaust, it would be better to be a "survivor" than a loser. But just the mention of nuclear war was enough to frighten a lot of people.

At about the same time, Congressman Anderson was also cracking that Bush was a Ronald Reagan in a Brooks Brothers suit, describing them as Tweedledum and Tweedledee.

It was customary for George to ignore such attacks from any of the opposition, or to attest he would abide by Reagan's Eleventh Commandment of not speaking ill of other Republicans. At the same time he launched a sneaky counterattack against what some of them were saying by proposing his own Twelfth Commandment: "Don't make any phony promises."

I still get a chuckle from George Will's advice that for Bush to relate to blue-collar America, it would be necessary for him to do something ungenteel, such as drinking water from a fingerbowl. Columnist Will should have been with us at the Hopkinton Fair.

After stepping over natural obstacles in a stall, the candidate stooped under the Jersey cow being milked from the opposite side by its owner: "Hi, I'm George Bush, running for president." Somewhat irked, the farmer snapped back, "President of what?" "President of the United States," George proudly answered. "A'yud, that's nice," and the milking continued. A good example of what we meant by running a low-key campaign.

George has a fantastic memory for faces and names. As president he has been known to identify individuals in a White House reception line whom he met, maybe only once, twelve years earlier while campaigning here. Incredibly, more often than not he'll even recall the circumstances—and sometimes those circumstances were fleeting.

One afternoon we were walking down the street in Manchester, in consort with a coterie of curious onlookers. I forewarned him we were about to enter a store where he'd meet one of his ward chairmen. With a grin Bush said, "Have you told her I'm the guy in the green coat?"

Because the media picks up on them, private polls are bad enough, but mock elections sponsored by commercial interests are worse. For example, the Mall of New Hampshire set up a computer terminal in its atrium for easy access to its swarming crowds of shoppers. Blown-up photos of each candidate were on display and the public was invited to press the key of their choice, providing they first entered the voter's name and social security number.

The arrangement offered us the opportunity for mischief and an early victory, without Bush's knowledge. The names were easy—we took them from the phone book—but matching names with numbers was trickier, working up more imaginative ID numerical combinations than were ever played in the New Hampshire Sweepstakes lottery. When the polling results were published, a genuinely pleased and surprised George Bush declared, "Gee, I'm overwhelming the others."

Trilateralists may have been associates of Jimmy Carter and George Bush, but they became mythical bogeymen to the good citizens of the Granite State, thanks to early warnings from Bill Loeb. In case the reader doesn't know, and we didn't, the Trilateral Commission was founded by David Rockefeller in 1973 to discuss the virtues of international competition, particularly between Japan, Europe, and North America. To some this group of tycoons and politicians represented a shadow world government, to others a nefarious conspiracy to elect George Bush. George had been a "dangerous" one of them, but had resigned in September of 1978.

Wendell Woodman, a Manchester *Union Leader* columnist, wrote, "The Trilateral Commission means the abolition of democracy." Loeb called them a closed, nonpublic group of important people who elected Jimmy Carter to the White House. "Now, apparently," he further editorialized, "the Trilateral Commission feels Carter has outlived his usefulness so they will put a Republican counterpart in his place, a man who will be equally incompetent because that is exactly what George Bush would be."

While most people had no real knowledge of the commission's purpose or objectives, antagonism formed quickly. Bush's detractors were eminently successful in moving the issue negatively. On one occasion, responding to a planted question, Bush tried to explain that he had never advocated world government, and he was drowned out by boos. On the Sunday before Election Day, the Committee of Concerned Voters from Houston and the Florida Conservative Union of Miami ran half-page ads in the *New Hampshire Sunday News* warning voters of impending catastrophe if they supported David Rockefeller!

The ironic sequel to their hoopla occurred in March of 1981 when Lou Cannon reported that President Reagan had invited David Rockefeller and a delegation of Trilateralists to the Oval Office.

In November, to promote the traditional slogan, "As Maine Goes, So Goes the Nation," Republicans there conducted a nationally focused straw poll. It was "wired," according to Jack Germond, in favor of Senator Baker. Bush was the winner, to the surprise of everyone, except perhaps some of our Zekes who assisted in staging the ambush. The resulting extensive publicity substantially improved our position because, as the *New York Times* reported, Bush's "rousing oratory" came out ahead of Baker's first serious organizational effort.

Before the straw poll in Maine, contributions to George's campaign were averaging $20,000 per day. Afterwards, they doubled.

According to the *San Francisco Examiner*, a story making the rounds following the Maine episode recounted how Senator Howard Baker's motorcade had pulled ahead of my station wagon. Baker supposedly commented, "That's the first time we've led George Bush in a while." Whereupon, according to the reporter, "The Bush car took off in a cloud of dust and burning rubber, leaving Baker far behind." Obviously it never happened, because we always drove slowly so that George could wave at the bystanders.

Bob Goodman had been employed to produce Bush's national TV commercials. He perceived the candidate as an authentic American hero, an American eagle, and coined the slogan, "A President we won't have to train." During the fall of 1979 nearly $100,000 was allocated for Boston television to boost name recognition. Because the primary vendor was out of state, the full amount of the expenditure was not charged against our New Hampshire budget.

The ads were unique. To stirring music George personalized the identity of Granite State citizens, about forty of our chairmen, in this fashion: "Mike D'Agostino grows some beautiful roses. More important to Exeter, Mike's been responsible for a lot of good will between the military and the people of the seacoast area. The success of our campaign comes from people like Mike."

Viewers paid attention, hoping to hear mention of their neighbor's name. The ads were a switch. Instead of the natives talking about Bush, he was talking about them. As a bonus we soon learned that those mentioned in the spots were receiving inquiries from friends wanting to know why Bush was their candidate.

As in all professions, certain duperies are acceptable. Bush was supposed to land by private plane in Lebanon where Goodman's film team and well-rehearsed supporters were gathered to make a commercial of an airport rally. Heavy rains made flight impossible so we brought him to Lebanon by car, put him in a small plane, taxied around the airport and ended up in a hangar for the filming. The debarkation, the crowd, the fanfare—it all looked like the real thing.

Unfortunately, a CBS-TV crew was on hand doing a segment for "60 Minutes." Those who later saw the commercial on their television sets would not have known the difference unless they had watched "60 Minutes" or had read in the *Union Leader* about the airport charade under the heading of "Bush League Tactics."

We made out much better while filming a commercial on the porch of the general store in Judd's hometown of Greenfield. It was a typical cracker-barrel, old New England setting. He had assembled an odd assortment of local characters (at least made to look like them) on the steps and in the rockers, carrying on in their "native tongue"—all to the amusement of a large press contingent.

But we relished the last laugh when one of the inquiring big-city reporters, determined to expose the ruse, asked one of the flannel-shirted hayseed types, "Have you lived here all your life?" Fortunately he had picked an irascible genuine Yankee and got the traditional answer, "Not yet."

Simultaneously, radio advertising was having a favorable effect. It expanded a thought expressed by George when he spoke at the Vocational-Technical College in Berlin. He told the students there that he saw the race as one with several hares, and he was the tortoise—thereby accentuating his persistent plodding by his frequent visits to the state.

The radio theme was simple: "In New Hampshire, we see a lot of presidential candidates come into our state, put on their big show, and then they go. But with George Bush, there's a difference. With George Bush, it's like he never left."

On June 7, 1979, Reagan, accompanied by his political advisor, Jim Lake, returned to Concord for a "strictly nonpolitical" visit to address the Brotherhood Council awards banquet in Concord. En route to the dinner, by an extraordinary coincidence, he stumbled into a meeting of the members of his own recently announced campaign advisory committee. Bob Monier, state senate president and one of the members, conceded it was only a social call. At least we had the satisfaction of knowing that he was eating directly underneath the sign on the roof of the hotel which proclaimed "Bush for President."

The California governor and Lake returned on September 28 for yet another nonpolitical foray to address the Merrimack Rotary Club. This time, en route to the luncheon, he stopped in Bedford for an hour's meeting with supporters. By then Gerry Carmen, his state chairman, Steve Thayer, Jim Barry, Elaine Lyons, and Joe Zellner had a full-time political operation in play.

Bill Loeb offered his front-page welcome to "The Happy Warrior." With his usual one-liner, Reagan disposed of the age issue by quipping, "The doctor told me I was sound as a dollar and I fainted away."

The Bushes' grand family and their countless out-of-state friends were also active campaigners. On weekends some would come in groups by bus, others individually by private car. They served as "Bushwhackers," canvassing voters and handing out literature. One busload came all the way from Pennsylvania and a chartered plane brought loyalists from Texas.

The premier family event was a bicycling call-to-arms with sixty riders fanning out for a day of political proselyting on the roads leading into Manchester. Among the cyclists were Barbara Bush; her brother, Scott Pierce, and his wife; George's brother,

John; Dorothy, Marvin, and Neil Bush; cousins Jamie Bush and Kent Pierce; along with many Bush-family children. The sport was capped with a rally and prizes at Victory Park. Who received the award for the longest ride? Mrs. Barbara Bush.

Secret Service protection was offered to the major candidates and most accepted. On our advice George did not avail himself of it until after he left New Hampshire. Based on the experience of the last presidential campaign we felt their guidelines would be too restrictive for Bush's "press the flesh" style; also, working out of our home would have made the logistical requirements quite uncomfortable.

Besides, as Morton Kondracke pointed out, where Reagan was traveling with the trappings of an incumbent president, Bush's soldiers resembled a guerrilla force trying to defeat a plodding army—and sometimes the guerrillas do overcome the odds.

Because Bush had been director of the CIA, not using Secret Service was a calculated risk. Thus, we were fortunate when Bob Gambino, who had been director of the Office of Security at the CIA, volunteered his time to join us during the final weeks. George seemed very happy with the arrangement, telling the *New York Times* he didn't need "the aura of big-shot-ism."

In the beginning when Bush was a mere asterisk in the polls, Loeb concentrated on sanctifying Reagan by defaming the Democrats with such choice portrayals as having seen "a democratic president turn the White House into some sort of whorehouse." Criticism of our candidate was mild at that time. When corresponding with George's cousin, Loeb said that Bush would be the "last lad" in the world for whom he'd ever vote because George was "the candidate of the liberal Republicans."

Occasionally we'd get a front-page editorial reminding other voters that George was the candidate of the sales taxers, "clean fingernail, silk stocking" Republicans, and the darling of the Republican "crown princes."

We were not too unhappy with this kind of critical treatment, as it meant publicity that cost us nothing. Often when he'd say something vexing about Bush, Loeb would also run George's picture which, for people who couldn't stomach the editorials, might have succeeded in getting us votes.

Soon the pace and nastiness intensified. Like a pack of hungry hyenas Loeb's entire editorial staff and insider columnists joined the attack, except for the State House political reporter, Donn Tibbetts, who did not participate. Wes Powell, Warren Pease, Jim Finnegan, J. W. McQuaid, and Paul Tracy all took mouthfuls. As noted by one of his former reporters, there was no longer any doubt as to who was becoming the strong threat to Reagan and for whom the *Union Leader* was getting out the hatchet.

Hodding Carter III reflected in *The Wall Street Journal* that William Loeb never gave us a tasteless bowl of boiled mush. And reading the *Union Leader's* morning edition while riding in my station wagon, George would often say he "detected" an editorial bias.

Loeb was magnificent at crafting sources from which to create issues. He reprinted a piece by an unfamiliar writer named Robert Mauro who claimed that at a reception in Florida Bush had told an annoying questioner, "Aw, go vote for someone else." Then, according to the article, Bush leaned over with one hand to the side of his mouth and said, "Go _ _ _ yourself." Maybe it staggered Bill Loeb to conceive that a product of the Greenwich Country Day School, Phillips Andover Academy and Yale could make such an unpresidential remark, but it sounded just like George to me.

Congressman Paul McCloskey prepared a study which disclosed that during twenty-six days in February, 1980, the *Union Leader* ran ten editorials, one cartoon, and seventy-one columns favorable to Reagan; whereas there were twenty-six editorials, five cartoons, and fifty-four articles critical of Bush. McCloskey commented that when a newspaper is used in such a manner it becomes a major campaign document worth tens of thousands of dollars.

Because advertising space had to be committed in advance, and not knowing what last-minute scurrilous charge might need refuting near the campaign's end, we reserved the masthead of Loeb's papers for the weekend preceding election Tuesday.

When it came time to compose the copy, there had been so much offensive material published that, in very bold type, we ran a statement from George: "Sure, I have a sense of humor. Bill Loeb's editorials always give me a kick."

Bill got the last word by running a box directly under the masthead in which he graciously thanked Bush for paying $1,300, "kindly donating to us today by this ad at the top of our front page." His gratitude was flanked on one side by an editorial entitled "Only a Bush Leaguer," and on the other by a column headed "George Bush Is a Liberal." George responded by asking what more one could expect from a guy who was so tough that he only gave Bo Derek a "3."

Reagan and the political prognosticators were dumbfounded on January 21 when Bush carried the Iowa caucus. "Big Mo" (George's shorthand for "big momentum") had spun for Bush. Reagan had spent only three days there, had not participated in an all-candidates debate, and Sears had previously been quoted as saying the governor would not campaign here because he had the state sewn up. Mortification set in on the local Reagan establishment. Loeb was furious, his paper claiming that in Iowa Reagan had been 'searscomsized'."

At Loeb's urging the Reagan strategy was promptly revamped to return his "personal touch" here on a sustained basis, to ride the bus every day, and to work people-to-people stops as he had done for us four years earlier. He arrived with an entourage safariing from Massachusetts that was sometimes larger than the communities he was visiting. Yet, as Jim Perry reported in the *Wall Street Journal* "the old movie star hasn't lost his magic." Except for Harold Stassen, Reagan's effort was even then the longest running show in presidential primary history.

In mid-July of 1979 Paul Laxalt, Reagan's national chairman, had written to each of the inherited 236 New Hampshire chairmen, whom we had recruited in 1976, to ask for their recommitment. We already knew from contacting them that a large number were reluctant to be involved a second time for Reagan unless the candidate himself rekindled their enthusiasm. They still liked Reagan but were passively sitting on their hands. If Reagan had stayed out of New Hampshire, many of them would have supported Bush, and quite a few made the switch anyway.

Four years earlier I had been very proud that we had created such loyal, dedicated disciples for a person who was then relatively unknown here as a politician. Now I was grieved by our folly, because we were aware that the state's most effective conservatives were lukewarm on Bush.

Nonetheless the great communicator appeared and the only negatives were minor flaps he provoked himself, such as the ethnic joke: How do you tell the Polack at a cock fight? "He's the one with the duck." How do you tell the Italian? "He's the one who bets on the duck." How do you know the mafia was there? "The duck wins."

On another occasion, by a slip of the tongue (guess he'd forgotten his sound 1976 training), he allegedly suggested to a factory worker in Pittsfield that the state should consider a broad-based tax!

Bush, in sharp contrast to Reagan, had an erratic way of signaling with his two hands when describing things during a speech. Unwittingly, sometimes it looked like an obscene gesture. Rhetorician Rounds had cautioned him about the impression, so George dutifully began using only one hand.

Things were much improved until a photo came out in the Colebrook News & Sentinel of Bush emphasizing a point with an extended middle finger. Bruce sent the picture to Bush, humorously suggesting he should go back to using two hands. Bruce promptly received a reply: "I was thinking of you when I did that."

93

Hugh Gregg, Bruce Rounds, and Charles Clough arriving at a Bush reception in 1979. (Walter Hippauf)

As an Election Day incentive for our chairmen we offered them a double victory by winning for themselves while winning for Bush. A contest was designed whereby the winners would be the three who turned out the highest percentage of votes for Bush against the total number of Republican ballots cast in their respective communities. The prize was dinner with the Bushes at their Kennebunkport summer home.

One of the achievers was Etta Sweatt, who took on the job of chairman in her town when the vote was two to one in favor of Reagan. In these big cities of the North Country, everybody knows everybody. How you play your cards on Election Day can make or break your social circle.

Etta fearlessly accepted the challenge, garnering six out of eight possible votes, leaving Reagan with only the vote of his own chairman and her son.

Etta described the reward dinner: "Mrs. Bush helped serve the meal. Everyone cleared the table just like at home. It was just like we'd known them all our lives and dropped in for supper."

It was along about this time when Cay read that in Iowa, as a fund-raising gimmick, followers of presidential hopeful Phil Crane were auctioning off souvenirs of his visit to that state, including his bedsheets. Cay figured we had amassed a small fortune, except that George insisted our cat Morris should be part of her laundry auction package.

———

After the Iowa victory most of the professional pollsters were ranking the two front-runners neck-and-neck. We were ecstatic to have progressed from an asterisk to upper case. But in any campaign, you can count on that point in time when a candidate does something or says something; does not do anything when he might have; or should not have said something which he did say . . . when his action, or lack of it, becomes either the springboard to his victory or the trapdoor to his defeat. The door opened for George at the Nashua High School gym on February 23, 1980.

Copious copy has been written about the abortive Nashua debate, most of which has been totally inaccurate in important details. There is sufficient material in my files and memory to compose an entire book on the subject, but the review here will be a very short, though correct, abridgement.

One circumstance omitted by all other writers was detail of the lively briefing sessions preparing Bush for the debate, along with preparation for another held a few nights earlier in Manchester in which all the candidates participated.

Bush was coached by Barber Conable, David Gergen, Pete Teeley, Jim Baker, and other confidants. When and where they were held has never been disclosed. As things turned out, it remains a nugacious secret better forgotten.

Gerry Carmen, Reagan's New Hampshire chairman, had repeatedly requested publisher Bob Foster of *Foster's Daily Democrat* in Dover (without our knowledge) to use his paper for underwriting a debate between his candidate and Bush. Foster was unwilling to become guarantor unless all the presidential candidates were invited. The Reagan forces were adamant. It was their absolute prerequisite that it be a two-man event.

After being refused seven times by Foster's paper, arrangements were made with the Nashua *Telegraph*, which agreed to sponsor the one-on-one format.

We accepted Reagan's challenge on the basis of a written agreement with the *Telegraph* for a "one-on-one encounter." The other candidates promptly filed complaints with the Federal Election Commission about being excluded. This action caused the agency to rule it would be an illegal corporate contribution for the newspaper to absorb the expenses for such a limited forum.

In light of this decree we advised the *Telegraph* and the national press that we had no objection to a panel including all the others.

Unfortunately, most recorders of the event did Bush immeasurable injustice by not having their facts straight on this particularly significant detail. For example, political science professor David W. Moore at our own state university wrote, "Bush's petulant insistence that the other Republican candidates not be allowed to participate . . . contrasted sharply with the apparently more generous Reagan."

Even Nancy Reagan repeated this misunderstanding when she wrote in her book that, after her husband had explained why the other candidates should have had a chance to speak, "the Bush people would not allow it."

It was the host paper's exclusive decision to retain the restricted two-man structure.

Because we had not sought the debate and were already concerned about exceeding our federal spending limit, Reagan offered to absorb the $3,500 expense, but not the sponsorship nor the supervisory right to change the format.

Until we arrived at the gym that fateful night, we did not know that Reagan had unilaterally invited the other candidates to participate anyway, as his guests. Although invitations had been extended before noon, it was not until three o'clock that afternoon that editor Jon Breen, the *Telegraph* representative and evening's moderator, first learned from the press that the others had been invited.

Breen advised the Reagan deputies that Reagan had no such authority and the event would proceed as already planned. We still had not been extended the courtesy of being informed of what was taking place, by either Reagan or any of the other participants.

When George took his place on stage he was followed by Reagan and, to the total surprise of both Breen and Bush, by the other candidates (we knew they were in the building, as Jim Baker had visited with them on his arrival). At that point George still felt obligated to his host, the *Telegraph,* and remained pledged to the agreement that had been made between Reagan and the newspaper.

As indicated earlier, if Jon Breen had decided to change the rules and admit the others, Bush would have been pleased to assent. George, unlike Reagan, had never ducked any all-candidate debates. But Jon was steadfast. Even though the Reagan campaign had picked up the tab for the event it remained the exclusive prerogative of the sponsoring host, not Reagan, to set the rules.

Reagan's calamitous "I paid for this microphone . . . ," triggered the trapdoor, with George Bush the victim of adherence to the standards of protocol and etiquette.

The other candidates left the stage in a fit of rage, unaware that they had been used to embarrass Bush and dupe the press. *Foster's Daily Democrat* summed it up editorially by saying they were like bit players on "Twenty-Mule Team Borax's Death Valley Days," and Bush had "been bushwhacked by an aging cowboy whose hat isn't as white as it once was."

In retrospect, why is it that no one has recognized that Bush's propriety during these odd theatrics by our Republican leaders was perhaps not only in keeping with his own sense of fairness, but rather the only correct behavior which was sorely required at that historic moment?

Had Bush, too, added public vitriole, the thoughtful members of the audience and perhaps even his angry competitors would have suffered considerably more embarrassment from what was really a childish public display.

Walter Cronkite came to my house at about eleven o'clock that night to review the details of the event. He said there is a very thin line between a clever political maneuver and a dirty trick. Loeb capitalized, writing, "Bush showed himself for what he really is, a spoiled little rich kid who has been wet-nursed to success and now, packaged by David Rockefeller's Trilateral Commission, thinks he is entitled to the White House as his latest toy."

On Election Day we got clobbered by a Reagan landslide, 50% to 23%, with the others far behind. After a recount demanded by Congressman Anderson, the final tally was Reagan 72,886 and Bush 33,527.

Admittedly it was not a two-man race like in 1976, but it's interesting to note that four years later Reagan's total percentage of the vote remained about the same.

As *Newsweek* reported, once again New Hampshire had accomplished what it had set out to do by establishing the nation's first primary—to make or break the presidential candidates.

But the magazine underestimated George Bush's intrinsic competitiveness. As he outlined in his autobiography, *Looking*

Forward, "No matter how bad a situation may look, something good can come of it." He had demonstrated that it was now a two-man race and he was eager to tackle Reagan in other states. For George it was not over; rather, it was a new beginning.

Peter Hannaford wrote in his excellent book, *The Reagans*, that a primary reason Reagan later chose Bush as his running mate in July at the Republican National Convention, was because George "had virtually earned it by running the gauntlet of all the primaries gallantly."

It is both ironic and an incredible tribute to our elective process that from the display of great political theater at Nashua, the remarkable Hollywood thespian and the talented diplomat from Washington ended up as one of the most complementing, perfectly cast presidential/vice presidential teams in history.

Vice President George Bush and Hugh Gregg share a good laugh.
(Dave Valdez)

CHAPTER 4

Vice President Bush Remobilizes Postconvention 1980–1986

(Author's comment: The reader should be aware that my tracking of political activity in the state from the 1980 Republican convention, when Bush became vice presidential nominee, until 1987 is sketchy, and limited only to those circumstances which I consider pertinent to Bush's forthcoming 1987-88 campaign. My view of the events that happened during this period is written exclusively from this perspective.)

While acknowledging to Governor Reagan unlimited esteem for his sound judgment in choosing George Bush as his running mate in July of 1980, it was George's own indomitable never-give-up spirit that earned him his selection as the vice presidential nominee. Even when it was rumored that former president Ford was going to receive Reagan's nod at the Republican convention, Bush was a team player, exhorting the convention to support a united Republican ticket.

His integrity, gentle manner, deep concern for principle, great love of country, and dedication to achieving his goal had gained a tremendous loyalty among those of us who had worked for him in New Hampshire. We also knew that the rare kinship we felt for him was exchanged in kind for his special Granite State supporters. The next eight years confirmed this mutual sentiment.

Initially my role during this six-year interval was liaison between George and those who had served here as his insiders.

But, as the association grew, my part became a somewhat unofficial source of information on a wide variety of matters dealing with people and events in New Hampshire.

I would forward job applications, requests for his appearance, news clips of special interest, and, when asked, make suggestions concerning local political matters. There was a close and sometimes confidential understanding between us. We had considerable personal correspondence and met occasionally, both in Washington and Kennebunkport.

George often communicated with me by self-typed letters which sometimes contained spelling or grammatical errors. It was quite an admission for a Phi Beta Kappa graduate who breezed through Yale in only two and a half years to write, "Pardon any typing glitches that might have occurred above (spelling too)." My faith as a fellow Eli was restored when I read in the *New York Times* that if he made it to the Oval Office, a staffer would be assigned to retype all his original drafts and correct misspellings as a "standard operating procedure." In retrospect, now that he's there George still zings off personal notes. Apparently that staffer hasn't found him yet.

Shortly after the 1980 convention, our stock improved immediately when the Manchester *Union Leader* repented mildly: "We may have to live with George Bush as the number two man on the GOP team, but Ford would have been the worst choice of all ...and we will continue to support Reagan though we feel the Bush move was a mistake."

Its view was totally opposite to mine: after two vigorous campaigns as New Hampshire chairman for both, the pairing of the two men was like winning the daily double at Rockingham Race Track!

Under the chairmanship of former governor Lane Dwinell, who had been serving as Reagan's honorary chairman in 1980, a Reagan-Bush committee was formed. On paper it represented the merger of their two primary campaign organizations.

Bush made one further visit to the state prior to the November general election, when he addressed a luncheon meeting of the

Southern New Hampshire Association of Commerce and Industry on September 26. Although Governor Dwinell and I greeted him, the Bush group had not been invited to participate in planning for the visit. Even after the fall election, in December Loeb was warning, "Reagan has yet to learn that when you take one foul ball in the administration, as he did with Bush, you are in trouble."

For the fall campaign the national media advisors had designed a radically new concept. It featured a taped presentation, simultaneously shown to Reagan-Bush groups nationwide. In New Hampshire, key workers from both camps were brought together at the Holiday Inn West in Manchester. The space was arranged like a classroom. The meeting proceeded pursuant to an orderly agenda, reinforced by a slick, thick promotion packet. No time for repartee.

At the appointed bewitching hour a smiling Reagan and happy Bush appeared on a giant TV screen which dominated the room. It was strictly Madison Avenue all the way. We were being processed.

———

During 1981, George, as vice president, twice attended homecomings in appreciation for his New Hampshire friends. On Easter Sunday he came to honor retired congressman Jim Cleveland when the latter was presented the Robert Frost Contemporary American Award by Plymouth State College. Then on August 22 he drove his cigarette power boat "Fidelity" from Kennebunkport to Newcastle in support of a fund-raiser for my son, then congressman Judd Gregg.

His kindheartedness was further evidenced in April when he solicited funds to retire the political debt of his former opponent, John Connally. In September of the following year, he did the same thing for his brother, Prescott Bush, who had aborted a Senate race in Connecticut. Both men had also worked hard to help elect the Reagan-Bush ticket.

Meanwhile, we had encouraged Bush to strive for a softening of Bill Loeb, which was working very well. They had exchanged letters, with Bill noting that he was a member of Zeta Psi at Williams while George was at Yale. In reply, George disclosed that his brother, Pres, was therefore a fraternity brother (also a member of Zeta Psi) of Loeb, and "I now know where my brother Pres got his charm and courtesy—Zeta Psi, of course." Bill was so moved by this synthesis that he ran a photocopy of George's hand-written note, dated July 17, on his front page with a caption, "Some Common Ground Found."

The irony of this coincidence which could possibly have ignited a tolerable relationship between the two men was abruptly ended when Loeb died on September 14, 1981. Four years later Bush honored him at a controversial memorial dinner in Washington. It is unfortunate that the George Bush-Bill Loeb cycle was completed posthumously.

It reminded me of the political postulate that successive successful seekers of public office know so well: your enemies of yesterday can be your friends of tomorrow.

———————

In the 1980 Primary campaign Senator Gordon Humphrey had characterized George as a liberal, based substantially on Bush's social background. They had had a confrontation on the night of the disastrous debate in Nashua when Bush angrily advised Gordon, "I don't need a lecture from you on party unity." Nevertheless, George came to New Hampshire in 1982 at the invitation of Senator Humphrey to play in a golf tournament in Portsmouth for the benefit of a daycare center.

On October 10, prior to the general election of November, 1982, the vice president was the principal draw for a fund-raiser in Manchester on behalf of our Republican gubernatorial standard-bearer, John Sununu. Sununu had never been a known Bush supporter. It was his first run for governor and he was grateful, calling it "the most successful single fund-raising event ever put together in the state of New Hampshire."

It was the first show of unity between the two men, and one wag warned George to check Sununu's loyalty, because if you spell his name backwards, what patriot would put the UN twice ahead of the US?

During the 1980 presidential primary Nancy Sununu, John's wife, had served as state Republican party chairman and in that position had taken a stance for Reagan. Her action seemed so inappropriate that I wrote her an unfriendly letter for which I have not been forgiven. Perhaps at that time it also reflected on Bush, as I felt she strongly influenced her husband's choice of political associates.

Following a strategy session with Judd, Bruce, and Bush "Zekes," Will Abbott and Joel Maiola, I summed up the consensus of the meeting with a memo to George on November 29, 1982. We advised that "with only fourteen months" until the next presidential primary, Bush should accomplish two important, immediate objectives: First, he should cement a relationship with the Sununus. In December, Barbara invited them to Kennebunkport. Second, he should build a bridge to Nackey Loeb, who succeeded her husband as publisher of the Manchester *Union Leader*.

Bush obviously began making headway with Nackey, for shortly after my memo she wrote an editorial saying she understood that when he played tennis, Secret Service agents had to stand at the four corners of the court with their backs to the game, "looking resolutely off into the distance keeping an eye out for intruders." We thought she was being polite in not writing the true story. His tennis game was so bad even the Secret Service couldn't bear to watch.

We further suggested that Bush congratulate both the state's new Speaker of the House, John Tucker, and Senate President Vesta Roy. The phone call came as a total surprise, directly to the podium while the House was in session. It received great press when Tucker asked how George knew about his election and received George's amusing answer, "I didn't spend all those years with the CIA for nothing. I know what goes on everywhere."

In 1983 Barbara attended two events in Portsmouth, touring the Aldrich Memorial House and joining in the twenty-fifth anniversary dinner at Strawbery Banke. George returned to the scene of the 1980 crime at the Nashua High School. Smiling confidently, he said to the audience, "Just want you all to know that President Reagan assured me he was not paying for the microphone this evening."

Then, in his introductory remarks he neglected to recognize the city's mayor, Maurice Arel. After that goof, the vice president was probably sorry he had a microphone.

In mid-August of 1983, Bob Monier, who had been rewarded for his help to Reagan in the Primary with an appointment as special assistant to the General Services Administration in Boston, called for a reunion of the "Reagan alumni" at Howard Johnson's in Manchester. He had also invited me to attend as a representative of the Bush organization. Most of the chairmen there were those I'd assisted in finding for Reagan eight years earlier. The meeting was constructive, with Lane Dwinell presiding over a brief business session to discuss regrouping for the next Primary.

It was none too early, as Nackey had already started gently chiding the president for being too much of a "nice guy" while "George Bush sits under an umbrella and watches the storm clouds, hoping to come out with neither rain on his face nor clay on his feet."

Whenever the Bushes went to their summer home in Maine, Air Force II landed at Pease Air Base in Portsmouth, from which they were motorcaded to Kennebunkport. Mike Dagostino, the respected "Mr. Pease" (a civilian adjunct in an otherwise all-military operation), routinely greeted the vice presidential party upon disembarkation.

On Labor Day weekend Dagostino snared the vice president and Mrs. Bush for a quietly planned "thank-you" reception with the Bush civilian "insiders" at the Officers Club. To this day there might be some question as to the legality of his maneuver, using the club for this political purpose, but no Air Force general would ever dare question Machiavellian Mike.

By late November Monier had been announced as the professional campaign coordinator of the Reagan-Bush forces, although the Bush leaders had not been consulted. In a sense it was ironic that Bob should have been selected, as he had been singularly strident in his anti-Bush bias, both during the Primary and at the convention. But, after a private interview which we arranged for him with George in Washington, his rancor was fully diffused and I signed on as his volunteer co-coordinator.

We immediately began to energize our respective political associates who, by then, were ready to join hands. But, because there was virtually no opposition in the Primary, we were fighting apathy. Still, there were enough perennial workers in both crews to open a headquarters in Manchester by mid-December. It was an easy campaign, as all elements of the Republican party were united.

Our listless efforts were buoyed by other major political events. The Sununu committee grossed a half-million dollars at a second fund-raiser. A series of Lincoln Day dinners was held and a testimonial for Probate Judge Bill Treat brought Senator Dole as the banquet speaker.

Our shot in the arm came eleven days before Primary Day when the vice president returned for a show-the-flag speech at a major rally in the New Hampshire Highway Hotel. Two thousand people turned out, representing all cliques of the party in a convention-type atmosphere, many wearing paper top hats festooned with tiny flags, beaming and cheering to a background of country-and-western music.

Lou Cannon, reporting the rally, said Bush had given a more effective defense of administration policies in the country of Lebanon than Reagan was able to do five days later. He added that Jim Lake had called Bush "the main surrogate, who will be on the cutting edge of all our efforts." Lake further gave George credit for healing intraparty wounds, resulting in less divisiveness among Republicans than ever before.

The Primary vote on February 28, 1984, was, as predicted, overwhelming for Reagan at 65,033. His nearest Republican competitor was Harold Stassen at 1,543.

C-Span president Brian Lamb, in a nationally televised interview a few days earlier, had tried to pin down Mrs. Loeb on her choice for president in 1988. She praised Bush for being "a good boy" but didn't think he had the leadership ability to hold the nation's top office.

In May of 1984 Barbara Bush attracted an overflow crowd to the annual Lilac Luncheon of the New Hampshire Federation of Republican Women. In June, former president Ford came to Bedford to speak on behalf of Senator Gordon Humphrey.

On July 5, Bush was scheduled to fly from Kennebunkport on a one-day round trip to Chicago for an appearance at the American Legion's national convention. Out of the blue, he decided to invite the Kennebunkport Legion's post commander and two of his officers to be his guests.

A stunned Henry Beauvais, the commander, had never spoken with the vice president except "once, our poodle was out and his poodle was with he [sic] and his wife, and his poodle came up and rubbed noses with ours." C. Fred Bush, Barbara's proud cocker spaniel, would have been quite offended at being taken for a poodle. En route to Chicago, George phoned the employer of one of the men to verify his excuse for not being at work. The employer hung up four times on the vice president, insisting he had no time to talk to some joker claiming to be Bush, with his mythical story that both were aboard Air Force II flying to Chicago!

That same weekend, Bruce Rounds had been visiting the Bushes, and George had suggested that he, too, should accompany him to Chicago. Bruce had declined, citing his leading the annual Fourth of July parade in his hometown of Bristol. "Why didn't you invite me?" asked George. "I'd much rather lead a parade in Bristol than in Chicago." Rounds replied, "How about next year?" And Bush accepted.

Later, Bruce wrote to the vice president's office in Washington to confirm the date commitment. A curt, snobbish response advised that the vice president is never scheduled for commitments a year in advance, and further, the chances were slight that the vice president would ever appear in a parade in Bristol, New Hampshire.

Bruce scrawled across the letter, "See how much influence you've got?" and mailed it directly to Bush. Within three days a call came from the White House, confirming the date, time, and place.

A month prior to the Republican National Convention in Dallas the Loeb publications continued their resentment of Bush, this time by editor Joe McQuaid urging Reagan to "dump the aging preppie, George Bush," in favor of UN ambassador Jeane Kirkpatrick.

I attended the Convention as a delegate with Cay, then we flew back to Pease in Air Force II with George, on the day following his renomination as vice president. The same evening he attended Sununu's third major fund-raiser at the University of New Hampshire in Durham. It attracted massive press coverage, as it was Bush's first appearance following his success in Dallas.

One relatively unknown contender, who had filed against Governor Sununu in the gubernatorial Republican Primary, protested strongly when the vice president gave a pre-primary endorsement to Sununu. He felt, as do many Republicans, that the vice president had no business endorsing anyone until a nominee was chosen by the party.

It has always seemed an enigma to me that George Bush, of all people, having served as chairman of the Republican National Committee, apparently has no problem with the party apparatus playing favorites in contested Republican primaries. George himself, as president, has done the same thing in actively endorsing his personal selection in contested gubernatorial races, even in major states. As titular head of the party, he apparently does not object when the RNC does the same thing.

In August the *Boston Globe,* with substantial circulation in New Hampshire, ran a column by Mary McGrory which was very critical of Bush. It elicited an indignant reply from George's sister, Nancy Ellis, which the *Globe* also published: "I just can't sit here and see him so totally misrepresented in my hometown paper, so, Mary, lemme tell you a thing or two," and she did, in spades. Nancy often came to New Hampshire events. George had no stronger supporter.

Bush's only other visit prior to November's general election occurred in mid-September when he landed at Keene for a quick round-trip by motorcade to Brattleboro, Vermont, where he participated in a Reagan-Bush rally on The Green. John Croteau, Andrea Scranton, and other Bush diehards had littered both sides of the highway with a profusion of "Bush for President" signs which had been left over from the 1980 effort and were an embarrassment to the second member of the two-man presidential team.

On December 14, 1984, I wrote a memorandum to the vice president outlining a strategy for covertly reactivating his "original trusted loyalists" to update him on the local political situation directed toward his running for president in 1988. Initially, approximately twenty of us met secretly in a series of dinner meetings which I hosted at the Red Blazer in Concord, during the first six months of 1985.

These meetings offered an opportunity for the lively interchange of ideas, keeping the "Bush spirit" alive in anticipation of his 1988 run for the presidency. After each session I sent a summary of its conclusions to the vice president. We forwarded some such grass-roots advice: "Still perceived as a Brahman with little appeal to the blue-collar voters. . . . Fails in effort to come off as 'one of the boys.' . . . Not accepted either as a true moderate nor as a true conservative. . . . Total loyalty to the president misconstrued by some as submissive and excessive."

Each of us took the responsibility of monitoring the activities of the other potential presidential candidates as they made their frequent forays into the state. The purpose of their trips, the people they contacted, the length of their stays, and the enthusiasm they engendered were all details furnished in my extensive reports.

Also developed from these conferences was recognition that for the forthcoming campaign, computer systems used at the national headquarters should interface readily with those selected for use by each separate state organization. This was a potential problem which Bush's Washington operatives had not considered!

To study the subject I employed the services of Paul Paquin, a local computer expert, and took him to Washington to work out solutions with Roy Tandy, Jr., who was responsible for beginning the establishment of their computer programs.

Curiously enough, our first meeting was at the headquarters of the Health and Human Services Department. The location was selected because there was then no Bush political office. Ron Kaufman, who had led Bush's Massachusetts effort in 1980, was our intermediary, and he was temporarily on loan to that department. (Margaret Heckler, the Secretary, was another loyal Bush Massachusetts ally.) Roy Tandy came over from his job at the Republican National Committee. Both men assured us, however, that they were doing their respective "things" for the vice president on their own time.

Another early consensus was that a Bush "organized nonorganization" should be formed which would include former key Reagan workers from the 1980 Primary. Dwinell, Monier, and other candidates' representatives from the earlier race joined our group in May.

Shortly after we got under way, George's national strategists introduced a PAC, "The Fund for America's Future." As described in Lou Cannon's column, it allowed "friends of the vice president to gather outside the office of the president and establish a political organization." Its stated purpose was fund-raising, to help elect Republicans nationally in the 1986 elections.

Though fervently denied, the Fund was actually a cover for Bush's 1988 candidacy. It was under the direction of Fred Bush (not a relative), who had administered George's fund-raising campaign when he ran against Reagan.

The money-making machine eventually poured millions of dollars into obtaining political IOUs all over the country. It was highly successful in New Hampshire, providing approximately $50,000 to candidates running for office at all levels, from county offices to the Congress.

Our venture meshed harmoniously with the Fund's objectives, except for fund-raising. Will Abbott, former Zeke and thereafter a New Hampshire congressional field director for Judd, signed on as its northern New England executive director, with his office and concentration in our state. Ron Kaufman of the Washington staff was its New England liaison. Ron practically lived in New Hampshire thenceforth to steer all subsequent Bush activities in what was hoped would be a cohesive manner.

Other presidential aspirants were simultaneously showing up all over the political landscape. I met Pat Robertson in April for the first time as a guest of Bob Monier, at a round-table session in Manchester. What impressed me more than the measure of the man were the size and demeanor of his three rugged aides. They looked more like bodyguards than disciples. Here was a preacher, a man of God, yet another Eli! He would have been better off with three angels.

As early as the spring of 1984, former governor Pete DuPont of Delaware had formed his GOPAC to assist other Republicans running for office. He had tested the waters here as the honored guest at the 58th annual dinner of the Southern New Hampshire Association of Industry and Commerce. Already he had a solid and respected team at the helm. His persistent campaigning against the odds over a three-year span earned him the eventual endorsement of Nackey Loeb.

Lew Lehrman, 1982 gubernatorial nominee of the Republican and Conservative parties of New York, had addressed our state convention the previous October, later forming the national group, Citizens for America. He promoted a highly successful succession of breakfasts, appearing to use the mantle of CFA as his own springboard for the presidency.

Another early starter was Congressman Jack Kemp, who was making frequent forays into the state from early March 1985, saying, "New Hampshire is the state where it happens." He was a big hit with the influential Gun Owners and keynoted a "freedom rally" in the fall on behalf of the entire New Hampshire Republican slate.

The Federation of Republican Women's Clubs hosted a dinner in Manchester for Jeane Kirkpatrick. She stated that though she did not intend to play a part in the 1988 primaries, she had switched parties because the Democrats were "out of step with rank-and-file Americans." In 1987, when she reappeared in New Hampshire, she had changed her mind and was considering a run—but she never filed.

Senator Bob Dole was also kindling those loyal friends he had fired up in the previous go-round. He had given Sununu $2,500 through his PAC and attended the governor's fund-raiser on October 10, 1982. He also had headlined a testimonial dinner for Bill Treat on February 24, 1986.

This time he was substantially assisted with several appearances by his attractive wife, Elizabeth, who was serving as U.S. Secretary of Transportation. Both made excellent presentations, resulting in Dole's being the semifinalist when it was all over in 1988. Much of the credit for his good showing should be shared by his strong backing from Senator Warren Rudman and former attorney general Tom Rath.

A wealthy local businessman, Max Hugel, who had resigned as deputy chief of the CIA under cloudy conditions, was circulating "The Hugel Report," elucidating his own brand of Republican leadership. By the end of 1985, he was the proprietor of a new political organization, Project '88. According to Max it was designed to monitor the campaigns of all presidential candidates to assure that the "next president is a true soldier of the Reagan revolution."

The former secretary of state, General Alexander Haig, did not formally join the contenders until the following year, 1986, on the theory that campaigns start too early. He was known to approach his major opponent's supporters with head lowered, scowling menacingly with a piercing blue-eyed stare. "Careful you don't get bushwhacked," he'd say. His style was unique. Under the auspices of the Committee for America, he invited the public through newspaper ads to share free hot dogs, popcorn and soda in downtown Manchester, all to the rhythm of a ragtime band.

Just before Election Day in 1988 Haig switched his support to Dole. This wasn't a bad deal for Bush, because we picked up Haig's two cochairmen, Ed Bennett of Bridgewater and Dave Banks of Concord. Haig had been so caustic in his criticism of Bush that his two leaders reacted by ignoring Dole and signing on with Bush.

It was further proof of the political axiom that if a political leader supporting a particular candidate decides to transfer his loyalty to a different candidate, his followers will not automatically follow.

On February 5 the vice president and Mrs. Bush invited Cay and me to attend a state dinner in honor of Prime Minister Hawke of Australia and his wife. It was an elegant affair held in the Thomas Jefferson Room of the State Department. Attendees included cabinet officers, congressional leaders, and others from the private sector such as Reverend Billy Graham and Lane Kirkland, president of the AFL-CIO. The United States Army string quartet and chorus provided a musical background.

My wife and I arrived early and were captivated by the display of American antiquity in the Jefferson Room, including his personal desk, fascinating paintings of historical events, and striking portraits of early American patriots. The antiques and artwork had been largely contributed to the U.S. government by the Annenbergs, the Claneil Foundation, and other generous Americans.

It occurred to me that we could strikingly enrich the portrait gallery by adding one of our own New Hampshire patriots. With that generous thought in mind, I later wrote a letter to George thanking him for the memorable evening, along with an unusual enclosure.

We had doctored up a black-and-white photo so that it looked exactly like the copy of a portrait (ca. 1776) of one of our own heroes. We used the physiognomy of Bruce Rounds in suit and necktie, adding eighteenth-century eyeglasses and a long white beard, which made him look like a distinguished statesman of yore. Wouldn't the president be proud to add the original of this remarkable painting to the Early American collection of the Jefferson Room? asked my letter. I imagined myself making the presentation to the president and first lady amidst the sound of bugles and much fanfare.

Alas, George did not respond too favorably. In a hilarious, three-page, self-typed reply, he advised that he had discussed my offer with a Clem Conger, curator of the fine arts exhibit, and a Winthrop Humelsine-Jones. Winthrop, he wrote, had advised State on most of their major acquisitions.

George continued to relate a remarkable story which never made it to the pages of American art history. Apparently, circa 1792 Gilbert Stuart had gone through a very trying period, suffering from influenza. To comfort him his solicitous twenty-one-year-old nurse, Rachel, introduced Gilbert to her funny friend, "the village reprobate, Ezekiel Rounds."

Winthrop's research had further revealed that an unsympathetic Ezekiel dared to resist Gilbert's advances and the latter took revenge. He drew an ugly face, put spectacles on it, and added a futuristic striped tie. "Not satisfied he splashed white paint on Ezekiel's head—Rounds having lovely flowing blond hair in those days," Bush writes.

This being a most embarrassing memento of an otherwise illustrious artist, the bottom line was, wrote George, that Winthrop declined the Gregg offer. The vice president, whose love for provocative art works is not widely known, was obviously disappointed but went along with Winthrop lest there be a serious confrontation with Rounds' progeny.

(Because of the vice president's annotation on his letter that it be classified as "Personal - Unofficial" with "No release under Freedom of Information until 2085" and out of respect to my good friend, Rounds, the exchange of correspondence between Bush and myself has not been reproduced per se.)

––––––––––

Even though he couldn't get Rounds' portrait hung with the Revolutionary patriots, on July 4, 1985, George kept his earlier promise to his old buddy, adding an offbeat first to the vice president's worldwide wanderings by serving, one day after leaving Paris, as Grand Marshal of Bristol's (population 2,000) annual holiday parade. Ten thousand people (not counting what seemed to be an equal number of security personnel) converged on the one-mile queue, led on foot by George and Barbara. It was superb Norman "Rockwellesque" drama in the tradition of small town America, with the most urgent, pressing problem being: What do bystanders do when the town's public restrooms are limited to three gas stations?

Immediately after the jubilant Bristol celebration the Bushes found themselves on "The Mount," a shiny white excursion vessel on Lake Winnipesaukee, for a ninety-minute crossing of New Hampshire's largest lake. Five hundred convivial Republicans had paid $150 a head for this fund-raiser to benefit our two congressmen, Judd Gregg and Bob Smith.

Between thirty-second shifts of shaking hands with all aboard, George and Barbara waved constantly to an accompanying fleet of speedboats, cabin cruisers, and anything that could float, including a motorized sea dragon with its green hind end decorated with a "George Bush for President" banner. George called out, "Hey, you guys, you've got the flag on the wrong end."

During Bush's 1980 campaign George had enlisted Ben Thompson. Ben had served as a Hanover police officer in the

Barbara and George Bush share a quiet moment.

fifties and as its chief in the sixties, was a confidant of Senator Norris Cotton in adjoining Lebanon, and was a widely respected citizen of the area.

Even now at Dartmouth's four annual home football games, Ben still dons his police chief's uniform, which has enough gold braid for him to be mistaken for an overly decorated admiral of the Queen's Naveee, to direct traffic at the busy intersection in front of the Hanover Inn. In today's strange, unfamiliar liberal and coed environment, he gives the old grads a comfortable sense of security because they all remember him with a nostalgic "Hi, Ben."

One morning during the 1980 campaign, we had asked Ben to procure a copy of Cotton's book, *In the Senate,* which Bush wanted to autograph and present to Norris. Ben bought the twelve-dollar edition at the Dartmouth bookstore but George had only two bucks in his pocket for reimbursement. Ben didn't seem worried about the other ten, though it did get mentioned occasionally during the intervening years.

As George got off the boat after the Winnipesaukee trip, he handed Ben eleven dollars with a note: "In Paris these last two days, I spent the last of the $10 you loaned me (Hanover '80?) I may need another loan in 1988. But for now here is $11. $10 plus $1 interest. Thanks for helping a friend in need."

Barbara attended a second fund-raiser the following month, this time a fashion show in North Hampton to benefit the Exeter Hospital. She was always so unanimously well-received, it often raised the question, "Why do we need George?"

On September 8, Judd and I were flattered to receive honorable mention in a Loeb paper editorial which took notice of the " . . . fact, it has been clear since the 1980 New Hampshire Primary that the Greggs, father and son, have been Bush tribesmen (spear-carrying division)." The editor was not aware that we were about to turn in our spears for a computerized weapon.

———

Those of us who had steered his 1980 campaign were pleased that George had been actively cultivating a friendship with John Sununu, as we had initially recommended in my memo of November 1982. We felt there was a need for a close relationship between the two men—a conviction which we frequently reinforced with both George and his key staff strategists.

After meeting with all the other candidates and recognizing the opportunity offered him by joining the Bush team, in October of 1985 Governor Sununu secretly advised Ron Kaufman of a willingness to commit for 1988—but not until sometime after his November election of 1986. Publicly, however, he reserved the right to play the field as "uncommitted" until that date, to safeguard his own chance of reelection as governor, and perhaps for an indeterminate period thereafter.

Meanwhile, he would allege neutrality in the presidential primary race.

It was subsequently determined that for the future, Governor Sununu would be the perfect choice as the 1988 Bush campaign chairman, with a deferred public announcement to follow at an appropriate date.

The eventual appointment of Sununu was a wise maneuver for several reasons: First, he was a three-term governor of the all-important first Primary state; second, he represented a significant new face in the Bush organization; third, he was expected to be the incoming chairman of the National Governors' Conference, thus having current gubernatorial contacts in all fifty states; and fourth, his office readily influenced certain authoritative state personnel and the use of their facilities.

I was pleased to step aside for a new leader and so convinced Kaufman. Because Ron had been running the Massachusetts organization in 1979, he knew I had dedicated a sizable amount of time and money over the six-year span toward the objective of electing George to the presidency, and that my investment in the cause was substantial. I intuitively sensed that Sununu was the man for the job and I needed to have my investment pay off.

Having served as state chairman several times, I looked forward to playing a major role in a different campaign exposure. Modus operandi had changed radically during my political career. I was eager to participate and observe from a fresh perspective.

Nonetheless, Ron was anxious that I remain involved, at least indirectly, at the policy-making level, and requested that the two of us talk with Sununu at his home on October 13, 1985. The meeting was most congenial. To keep Sununu informed, it was agreed the three of us would review all pivotal planning by getting together as needs required.

Yet the three of us, acting alone, never sat down together again during the three years that followed.

Many times during that period Ron and I discussed the governor's secretly avowed commitment to Bush. We were both skeptical of it as we could not understand why, if he really wanted to be on the team, he never helped our ongoing efforts during the next two years, prior to his eventual announcement in February of 1987. We didn't even get surreptitious participation, which meant there was no help from his own gubernatorial organization. As Ron said afterwards, "We didn't trust him."

Bill Cahill, a former executive councilor, undertook the position of volunteer chairman for the Fund for America's Future. Working with me, Will Abbott, and many others, we were busy hiring staff and naming committees to gather lists of Republicans for future mailings, creating a newsletter, handling publicity, planning scheduled visits for the vice president, establishing a budget and organizational plan.

Our objective was to develop a game plan whereby the PAC would lend an effective boost to all Republican candidacies during the 1986 election season while, at the same time, building a base for George Bush in 1988. The Fund served as a legitimate cover for reactivating, once again, the persevering, loyal Bush workers, along with their Reagan converts from the 1984 Primary.

1986 could probably be dubbed "the year of the Fund," as technically that was all George had going for him in New Hampshire.

It began with ridiculous "guidelines," more like directives, from Washington, asserting that the vice president had made no decision as to his political future. We were warned we could not refer to him as a candidate for president, nor could we imply the Fund was a campaign committee or that a contribution to the Fund could be a contribution to any future candidacy he might have. The Fund seemed to be running for the presidency.

The Fund had raised and spent far more than the money available to the other candidates. Additionally there were the vice president's official activities paid for by the taxpayers. It was a fine line of distinction, often blurred. George could readily fly in and out of Pease Air Force Base but his competitors, even those serving in Congress, were denied the same privilege. He could also visit the Portsmouth Navy Yard. Incumbency had its distinct advantages.

On March 28, 1986, twenty-seven key members of the New Hampshire steering committee for the Fund boarded a bus for a splendid afternoon and evening with the Bushes at their summer home in Kennebunkport. Also present were Marlin Fitzwater, Bush's press secretary, and Craig Fuller, his chief of staff. Wine and hors d'oeuvres were served at the house, after which the entire party went to the Village Cove Inn for a lobster dinner.

One of the more adventurous guests, exploring the house, had sneaked into the master bedroom and observed what he thought was a pornographic tape beside the vice president's bed. During dinner he began whispering his shocking discovery to others. Fortunately the wicked gossip was repeated to Bruce Rounds, who had just returned from an African safari with a tape for George on rare jungle animals. True to his practical joker's bent, Bruce had mischievously stored the animal tape in a suggestive cassette cover and slipped it into the Bush bedroom. Neither George nor the press ever knew how close George came to being caught in a one-up on Gary Hart.

Meanwhile, on November 28, the unorthodox Max Hugel reappeared, promoting a memorial fund-raising tribute to Bill Loeb in Washington for his Project '88. The list of sponsors was a "Who's Who" of the nation's conservatives, including Bush's presidential competitors and a large New Hampshire delegation.

Though it was a decision fraught with hazard, George agreed to be the principal speaker. Unfortunately, in accepting the invitation it was not made clear that the vice president was recognizing Loeb's colossal influence rather than respecting him as a journalist.

The announcement of Bush's appearance at the dinner provoked a rash of unfavorable reaction from the local press. The *Keene Sentinel*, for example, wrote that he was "associating himself with Loeb's shabby legacy. We wish him all the luck he deserves." Even James Reston, in the *New York Times*, perceived the occasion as "Bush's voodoo politics."

But George Bush put on a spectacular performance before a full house, humorously noting that he had always put down Bill Loeb as "doubtful." Nackey agreed he did an excellent job. She also drew a few guffaws of her own from the press table when she stated her husband had never confused editorial columns with news columns, as she said is the case with much of the media. Considering the reputation of the *Union Leader*, no regular reader would ever say they were seldom confused.

In March of the following year, Max Hugel and John Sununu, again under the banner of Project '88, sponsored a reception for Pat Buchanan, then assistant to the president and director of communications, at a time when Buchanan was being talked about as another possible presidential nominee.

Due to his image of "money" created by the Fund and "imperiousness" created by the office of the vice presidency, the Fund's scheduling committee felt that George should be making only non-fund-raising, people-to-people visits under its aegis.

It was a profitable strategic decision when he spoke before a joint convention of the New Hampshire House and Senate on April 17, 1986, its members being an assorted collection of typical Granite Staters. (He had previously addressed them in 1979.) Each member was given an individual free photo opportunity with the vice president, which nearly everyone accepted. Even the Democrats humbled themselves to take advantage of the occasion.

During the photo reception Senator Bartlett led Barbara Bush over to old friend Bruce Rounds, who was wearing a ladybug lapel pin. "I believe you know Rounds," said Bartlett. Barbara, not responding, was looking at Bruce's ladybug. "What's that?" she asked, with a twinkle of mischief in her eyes. "It's a ladybug, the state insect," beamed Rounds. "I always thought you were the state insect," she said with a sardonic smile . . . and walked away without saying another word.

That same night there was a poorly timed commitment for Bush to address the annual meeting of the New Hampshire

Association of Business and Industry at Manchester. This well-financed group represented the elite of the state's commerce which, again, tended to identify George with the moneyed interests.

Judd and I were invited in late June to the vice president's House in Washington for lunch with George, Barbara, and his staff of campaign strategists to express our views on how the 1988 campaign should be run.

We recognized that security logistics integral to the office of vice president in 1986 contrasted dramatically with our presenting him as a free agent in 1980. Nevertheless, his recent appearances here had been geared primarily to the "kingmakers," that is, "fat cats." We stressed our conviction that the vice president sorely needed more direct, hand-to-hand contact with the voters of the state, as he had done so successfully during his first campaign.

While Bush and his advisors were gracious and attentive to our admonishments, they were buoyed by favorable national polls, sacrosanct in the Bush camp, and it was obvious our concerns were not taken seriously. Somehow the guys in Washington never seem to recognize it's the locals who win elections. At least we had a good meal and did not get bitten by C. Fred (Barbara's cocker spaniel) or any of the other guests.

September 21 was "New Hampshire Smorgasbord Day," four events with something to please everybody. Unfortunately the first left a bad taste in everyone's mouth. The Bushes had been scheduled to helicopter from Kennebunkport to Whitefield, to participate in a morning mock press conference with selected students from regional schools and attended by local Republicans. At the last minute bad weather grounded the choppers. It was too late and too far to motorcade.

At the event, meanwhile, Dr. W. H. Gifford, the beloved North Country personality, was regaling the audience with Yankee humor while Judd worked with White House Communications to set up a loudspeaker telephone patch. Eventually George answered the questions from Maine over the system, but his replies were rambling and dull, to the bitter disappointment of the eager students. When word leaked out that Bush would motorcade to the next event at Dover, the adults were also grumbling, "If he can get to Dover, why couldn't he have come here?" (A round-trip to Whitefield would have taken an extra four hours.) One funny aside at the Whitefield meeting was a radio call from Sununu that he was en route, passing through North Woodstock. The governor had been advocating a fifty-five-mile-per-hour slowdown program, even though he had been stopped for speeding, to our embarrassment, in Massachusetts. Judd announced Sununu's call, saying that at fifty-five miles an hour the governor could be expected to arrive in a half-hour. Fifteen minutes later Sununu walked in, totally unaware of why the crowd was laughing at him.

The second event was the dedication of a new hospital wing in Dover. The vice presidential party (it was an official affair) arrived by motorcade to ruffles and flourishes for a nonpolitical speech in a huge orange and white tent. It had taken nearly two weeks of White House planning by the Secret Service, Bush Advance, and White House Communications for less than one hour of content.

The beef of the day came in midafternoon when three thousand people were fed and entertained, as guests of the Fund, at the Gunstock Recreation Area in Gilford by twenty members of the Bush Barbecue Brigade and another two hundred volunteers under its leadership. Free invitations had been extended to all GOP candidates, party workers, and their families. Security was relaxed, enabling George and Barbara to move unrestricted and greet everyone.

It was traditional grass-roots campaigning: the tastiest recipe for New Hampshire. The planning and staging were directed in a simple, homespun style by a political neophyte, Roger Godwin, who sagely reflected: "We, the willing, led by the knowing, are doing the impossible for the ungrateful and have done so much for so long with so little, we are now qualified to do anything with nothing."

The last event that day was another evening fund-raiser for Governor Sununu, which overcame the scheduling committee's reproof when he conceded to make it private and small. About one hundred couples paid $500 each for a cocktail reception at the Manchester Country Club. It was a fitting windup for a full day, which truly ran the gamut of everything from sweet to sour that is presidential campaigning.

This was the type of day that underlines the required physical endurance and impeccable appearance of both the candidate and his staff. At every event, 8:00 A.M. or P.M., the audience is fresh, but the candidate and the rest of us are more likely to be sour than sweet.

In concluding this chapter and the saga of the vice president's Granite State adventures in 1986, it would be a dereliction of this writer's duty not to record a December editorial prediction from his favorite newspaper: "More Mush from the Wimp . . . That's why this newspaper thinks George Bush will never be President."

The advance team that always stayed ahead! (left to right) Joel Maiola, Bill Golding, Hugh Gregg, Bill Cahill, Kelly Walker, Steve Edwards, Ed Lecius, and Dan Durkin. (Dave Valdez)

CHAPTER 5

Bush Races
to the Presidency
1987

The final phase of the preliminaries for the 1988 Primary had begun in early February of 1987, two weeks prior to George's filing his "George Bush for President Committee" with the Federal Election Commission. A fully staffed New Hampshire campaign office, under the direction of Will Abbott, was already operating out of Concord. Abbott said the Fund's functions had ceased and his focus had shifted to determining the depth of the vice president's political support.

Simultaneously, Governor Sununu continued to keep his distance and told the press he had not decided which candidate he would endorse—Dole, Kemp, Bush, or DuPont. His top aide, David Carney, noted that Sununu shared a special "camaraderie" with Governor DuPont, and tongues began to wag when Sununu's principal fund-raising director, Howard Keegan, and three of his influential loyalists signed on with the governor of Delaware.

But on February 16, 1987, thirteen Granite State Republican activists, including John Sununu, met with George, Ron Kaufman, and Lee Atwater, Bush's national campaign manager, in Kennebunkport. The governor then outlined an organizational plan to be implemented upon his formal acceptance as New Hampshire's chairman.

Four days later he addressed a letter to sixteen thousand of his supporters, giving them advance notice of his public announcement of February 16. The letter read: "After many weeks of thought and review of the candidates, I have decided to support Vice President George Bush for President"—a slight understatement inasmuch as he had told us he would commit sixteen months earlier.

Andy Card, later George Bush's deputy chief of staff, was sent up from Washington to coordinate Bush's campaign in northern New England. His primary responsibility, however, was to run the New Hampshire effort for Sununu.

Committees were formed covering a wide range of activities: Strategy, Advisory, Scoop (to intrigue or outwit the press), Executive, Finance, Scheduling, Advance, the Freedom Fighters (to harrow the grass roots), Volunteers, and Materials Distribution. I chose Advance.

The significance of my role was noted early on when Barbara Bush commented on my ineptness at parking cars. Little did she realize the importance of my assignment as chairman of Advance. But before the year was out she must have been impressed that I had graduated to riding in cars, rather than parking them.

The Advance committee would perhaps have been better termed the "turf" committee. From the beginning to the end it was a constant clash of concepts between how we thought things should be done in New Hampshire and how it was decreed from Washington they would be done. Until Bush's defeat in Iowa the following year, the script was always written from the national rule book.

A problem we encountered with the "youth corps" servicing the Bush operation, both the vice presidential staff and the campaign personnel in Washington, was that most were uncommonly aloof and politically inexperienced. This was especially true when they traveled with the vice president here in New Hampshire. There were unpleasant episodes, lapsed public relations, with too many fresh and different faces taking their turns at commanding the locals.

To exacerbate the mismatch, the procession of new hires in the Bush offices apparently resulted from the spiraling velocity of his turnstyle policy which spun and shifted the management of both the official and campaign offices.

New players from out-of-state show up in every presidential primary. They fail to understand that because New Hampshire is a small state, it has a homogeneous population with greater citizen participation in government than other states. Thanks to the concentration of national media the candidates traditionally devote an inordinate amount of their time to personal canvassing. That's one of the reasons why our voters are so well informed. Yet, every four years, it takes precious months to educate the newcomers that our political folkways really are different, and sophisticated—though rustic.

This dichotomy was a constant irritant between Kelly Walker, who was the lead agent of the Washington Bush Advance, and the Granite State team. He had his own typical, preset, Washington-trained view of how to do Advance. It took him a while to recognize the value of the "local people" factor—the same old persistent problem.

At one point we arranged a dinner meeting at the Cat 'n Fiddle restaurant in Concord with Kaufman, Card, Kelly Walker, Georgi, and Bob "Landslide" Turner (so-named because he won then lost a recounted election for the legislature by two votes), when we defined a structure to which all would agree on how the Advance operations would be run in the state. This meeting was a real awakening for Kelly as he felt initially it was a personal attack on him, but eventually he came to realize its value and that he would have to work politely with the locals to get votes.

Meanwhile, our Advance group of very talented volunteers acted independently of the Concord campaign headquarters. We were charged with implementing the vice president's schedules in conjunction with the Secret Service, White House Communications, State Police, and local law enforcement agencies. Our responsibility also encompassed all matters pertaining to his appearances, from coaching greeters, preparing the "first name" lists for George's notes of appreciation, and providing blue drapes

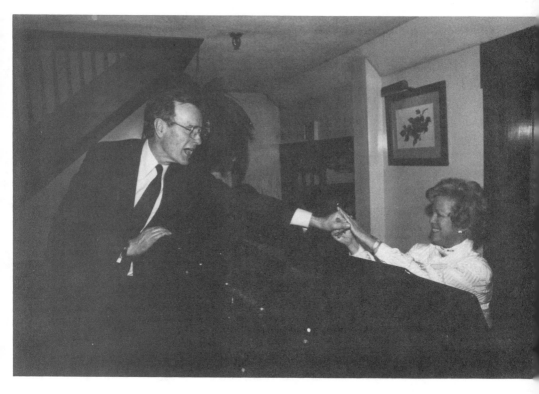

Vice President Bush greets hands-on director, Georgi Hippauf.
(Dave Valdez)

for TV aesthetics, to providing food for and cleaning up after the traveling staff.

For each visit we set up separate one-week, fully staffed, yet temporary offices in various locations under the direction of Georgi Hippauf. Specific site managers were designated by Steve Edwards and Bill Golding; Bob Turner solicited the vehicles for the motorcades which were organized by Jon Osgood and John Meserve, supported by Jon Burbank, Alan Sewall, and Mark Thurston. Augmenting this structure were press and technical advisors sent from the national headquarters to support Kelly Walker, all working out of our offices.

Advance was predicated on scheduling. Dates were either requested by Concord for existing state events or free days would be allocated from the vice president's national itinerary. While Lee Atwater was in charge of a separate national campaign office, the vice president's travel was directed by Craig Fuller, Bush's chief of staff, and John Keller, in charge of Advance—both of whom were White House personnel. Final determinations, including minute details, appeared to be commanded by faceless fax machines from somewhere in Washington.

Some trips, or even parts of trips, were official; others were classified as political. The expenses of an official trip were absorbed by the taxpayers, whereas a political sojourn was charged against the candidate's campaign funds. Also, different Washington personnel were used when the advance team was present for an official visit.

A week to ten days before each scheduled stop a preliminary inspection of the physical premises was conducted by both the security and political advance teams, including the installation of phone lines to the White House. In addition to specifying motorcade routes, a facility for direct communication with Washington had to be established for every inch of the traveled roadway, which frequently meant backpacking antenna equipment to mountain summits.

But Bush's most favorable exposures were unscheduled stops, absolutely verboten by the faceless faxes, and anathema for the Secret Service. Yet, as long as they were "spontaneously planned," we were sometimes able to free our vice president from this bureaucratic authority. It was ironic that only after Iowa did unscheduled stops become heralded as the great strategic invention.

————

The job description of an advance man does not mention the physical risks required. At one luncheon Kelly had positioned the TV cameras for a direct shot at George while he was speaking when, to Kelly's horror, a waitress placed a coffee pot on a tray directly in the line of sight. Nearly crawling on all fours to keep his image below the raised head table and podium, Kelly quietly sneaked up to the offending kitchenware.

Then, with a not-too-deft, quick-handed sweep, he grabbed the pot, only to upset it onto the leg of a lady listener at the adjacent table. The coffee was hot, the screech was hotter, and Kelly hid under the table. When he came out, one speech later, he had cost the campaign one pair of L'Eggs.

In early March a three-day meeting of the Northeast Regional Republican Conference, hosted by former New Hampshire state chairman Elsie Vartanian, was scheduled in Nashua. All the potential 1988 presidential candidates had been invited. Initially it was promoted as "An EVENING with the next President of the United States," but Bush, using the power of incumbency, refused to appear jointly with the others. Instead, he did a solo at lunch and the tickets were reissued, "A WEEKEND with the next President of the United States."

While the competitors were crying foul, Kaufman was explaining that until George made a formal announcement of his candidacy (which subsequently he did in Houston on October 12, 1987), he preferred not to do a "cattle show."

Dole jabbed, "I got a telegram just as I walked in, saying, 'I can't be there this evening. Nobody told me.' Signed, George Bush"—and then the senator left. Meanwhile the rest joined in an impromptu chorus singing, "Where's George? Where's George?"

But maybe George had the last laugh because upstairs in the hotel I had assembled some key "doubtfuls" for one-on-ones with candidate Bush and thereafter he motorcaded to Hudson for a jammed reception at the home of state senator Rhona Charbonneau. There he was introduced by Governor Sununu who said this was the kind of crammed room where you can see him, feel him, touch him, and smell him. The event, at least, left a pleasant odor.

A motorcade that snarls traffic is as big a curse for Advance as it is for those who curse it. Between vehicles for Advance, Security, Control, and a couple of vice presidential limos (one is a spare), we were lucky when there were only a dozen units, not including press vans or buses and the helicopter flying overhead.

A bewildering amount of planning precedes every vehicular movement, from the guarding of overpasses and the blocking of access ramps to preparing alternative routes for the nearest medical facilities in the event of accident. Still, the trappings of a regal presidency do not make friends when a worker is frozen in traffic trying to get to work on time or hurrying home after a tough day.

On Bush's Memorial Day weekend visit to the Nashua/Salem area many drivers, unaware of what caused their delay, got out of their cars to question other drivers: "What's going on?" The Nashua *Telegraph* reported that one spectator, presumably from Massachusetts, replied, "It's silly season in New Hampshire. That's what's going on."

Timing is the essence of scheduling. Every schedule is meticulously time-studied by Advance's walk-through several days prior to the vice presidential visit. Events are then so closely interrelated that it's critical there be no slowdowns. On the same trip the State Police suffered the ultimate embarrassment when the cavalcade was held up for five minutes so they could jump-start the lead cruiser.

To obtain a liquor license for a private club, it is a requirement in New Hampshire that admission be restricted to members and their guests. This is usually accomplished by keeping the entrance locked. Its opening is controlled by the bartender, who responds to a doorbell on the outside, thereby identifying visitors before letting them in.

A week before the vice president's trip to Salem, the advance team had to inspect the Elks Lodge, a private club, to arrange for his appearance there. The password to gain admission was "ER"

(Exalted Ruler), but we had not been so informed, nor had the club officer who authorized George's appearance advised the bartender of the impending advance visit.

When the Secret Service showed up in their dark suits and sunglasses, the members, playing cards and shooting pool, must have assumed it was a raid. The agents were refused admission because they didn't know the password, and "Open Sesame" didn't work. Eventually an arriving member sized up the situation and in confidence shared the secret: "ER."

On the following day, to avoid further Memorial Day traffic congestion and because it was an official visit, George was helicoptered from Kennebunkport to Durham for the commencement address at the University of New Hampshire. It was a spectacular arrival, with the four choppers of his fleet putting down within sight of the ceremonial crowd at the stadium.

As in the shell game, we hazarded guesses. From which one would he emerge? What's more, due to the publicity surrounding the event, when he finally did appear George probably felt a little bit like the nut under the shell. After the landing, adjacent to the stadium and about a hundred yards away, in full sight of everyone seated, Bush and the entire staff were actually motorcaded across the field.

The student paper had chastised the college president because the students were not privy to the selection of their commencement speaker, implying they might have chosen "better speakers."

Worse yet, several faculty members, troubled by the Iranian situation, vowed to boycott the exercises. One of them even wrote in the *Boston Globe*, "A commencement speaker should be an inspiring role model. Instead we have a man who looks at black and calls it white. Either he is consciously withholding the truth or engaging in self-deception bordering on the psychotic."

Except for a few graduates who turned their backs to the podium, and others wearing orange-colored fluorescent arm bands, the day was totally unexciting. In fact, George's speech was so heavy-going that no one applauded until the end. I suggested they were just happy that he was finished, but he proffered that perhaps he should have paused longer now and then, in the hope that someone might have gotten the urge to clap.

––––––––

Volunteers were always needed in the Advance Office such as receptionists to cover phones and perform a myriad of clerical tasks. Proprietary tensions often arose when dedicated local people detected arrogance from insensitive paid Washington personnel who next week might be working for another candidate. Better still, if Bush made it, then perhaps a position would open in the White House. Many of our volunteers had been working since 1979 to get George Bush elected, a distinction not recognized by the transient Bush staffers.

Friction was inevitable, yet understandable. Our volunteers were motivated by a deep dedication to the cause or from personal loyalty to the candidate. Few expected any financial reward for their contributions of time and energy, whereas with most of the professionals, many of whom were less competent than some of the volunteers, it was a job to be done.

Irritability was also generated from a perceptible spirit of exclusive fraternity among the Washington professionals which disdained the political loyalties of the volunteers. This behavior was exacerbated when senior staff accompanied the vice president, as then the professionals would become preoccupied with providing needless amenities for their bosses. Furthermore, the national staff was primarily concerned with Bush's national image, giving little consideration to local impressions or impact.

Suspicions regarding George's connection with the Iran-Contra scandal were always with us. Vincent DeNobile of Rochester had never met Bush, and his doubt was one of two hurdles that had to be overcome before he erected a giant yellow tent on his lawn and invited two hundred friends for a reception. He was satisfied that there were no Iranian skeletons in George's closet by an unequivocal "no" from a respected Bush spokesman.

But then, Secret Service ascertained that the bridge on the main road to DeNobile's house was possibly not sturdy enough to support the VP's armored limousine. They found this out by driving huge dump trucks loaded with gravel, weighing three to four times more than the VP's limo, over the very bridge they feared would collapse under its weight.

The event site was still in doubt until someone prevailed on the city to do a grading job on a dirt road which approached his home from a different direction. In the end it was a happy compromise, as the giant shrimp served there were the best in the whole campaign.

———

All of George's arrivals into New Hampshire were by air, except for an occasional motorcade from Maine. It was customary upon debarkation for six to ten greeters to shake his hand at the foot of the ramp. Occasionally some would be elected officials who, never having met the vice president, were initially pleased to have been selected. They were asked to be at the airport nearly an hour before flight time.

Trouble was that George would move quickly down the reception line with a pleasant "Nice to see you," and dash off into his limo before the greeter had the slightest chance to tell him about his Aunt Nellie who knew George when he attended the Greenwich Country Day School.

A former combat pilot, George was anxious to become a greeter himself when he learned from Don Davidson that the last operable B-17 Flying Fortress from World War II was being flown to Nashua for servicing, en route from Europe to a museum in Houston. A sizable crowd of veterans and flying buffs had assembled for the landing, but there was no vice president at touchdown. Instead he was sitting in a disabled limousine on a Manchester street.

"Mommy, they have guns!" a wide-eyed four-year-old told his mother as he peered out of a neighborhood window and saw flashing lights, State Police, and Secret Service agents leaping from their cars with weapons showing.

What he really saw was a $100,000 car with a dead alternator. And, ironically, it was eventually started by the battery cables from his mother's Chevrolet. Meanwhile George was off to the Nashua airport in the spare limo, no doubt commiserating with the B-17 pilot on the unreliability of ground transportation.

Sharing a typical campaign day with the vice president and Barbara was an exciting experience, as on August 15, starting with an early-morning landing in Manchester. Greeters were Governor Sununu and Manchester's Republican mayoral candidate, Ray Wieczorek. Ray wanted a photo with Bush to improve his chances. He lost. Two years later he tried again, without the picture, and won.

Five minutes before Air Force II hit the tarmack we were advised by the Secret Service that our two press vans were not cleared to go on the runway, and thus could not join the motorcade. The volunteer van drivers, expecting to be in the motorcade, had not been taught the route to Londonderry, site of the first event. Consequently they took a wrong turn and arrived fifteen minutes after the vice president. The reporters were not pleased, so for the balance of the day we agreed to send them ahead of the motorcade, giving the drivers road maps!

For the first time in the event's 87-year history a vice president and his wife participated in Londonderry's Old Home Day. The Bushes led a short parade on foot, before five thousand onlookers, followed by twenty-six units and five marching bands, smiling and shaking hands all the way. It was blisteringly hot. Everyone was grateful that instead of making a speech from the reviewing stand, George waved a small American flag and said, "Great to be with you. Thanks so much."

With a three-quarter-hour trip on interstate highways to Hopkinton, the next stop, the procession was traveling in the left passing lane at speeds between sixty and seventy miles per hour, thus obviating the usual ramp and bridge guards. By the use of sirens and lights, traffic in the left lane was directed to move further toward the left median strip and motioned to slow down or stop, thus allowing passage of the motorcade vehicles.

It was not only a dangerous practice, but also against New Hampshire law, as motorists are supposed to pull over to the right and stop. Just another detail we subsequently compromised with national procedures.

There were always two State Police cruisers in front of the motorcade to double-check security and traffic density, one fifteen minutes ahead and the second five minutes in advance. I always rode in the five-minute car, along with a Secret Service agent, in order to reach the site just ahead of the vice presidential party and to insure the preplanned greeting ceremonies were fully set and ready for its arrival.

On this particular day we did not make it to the event before the Bush party. After exiting Interstate 89 and driving up Maple Street in Contoocook en route to the Hopkinton Fairgrounds, we spotted a man walking on the site with a rifle under his arm.

It took the Secret Service agent less than thirty seconds to jump from the cruiser, draw his revolver, and accost the pedestrian. The suspect was a typical native gun owner out for target practice. He had no idea the vice president of the United States was about to pass by and could have cared less. He just wanted to go shooting in our "Live Free" lifestyle.

Because the rifleman had to be restrained for proper identification by the State Police and until the motorcade had passed, by the time we reached the fairgrounds the program was well under way. It was a potluck lunch for three hundred specially invited Bush organizers.

George addressed the crowd from a dais in front of a barn, decorated with red, white, and blue banners, speaking under a sign: "Hopkinton State Fair Poultry and Rabbit Department." Both Bushes had to shake hands with everyone who stood in a long receiving line, which included trunk grips with our campaign elephant, Tanya, and her constant companion, Bob Steiner. Bob and his wife, Lee Ann, never missed a Bush event, though their guest did not always fit in at cocktail receptions.

Inasmuch as the Bushes had left Kennebunkport at eight o'clock and it was to be a long day, we needed to schedule a brief rest top in a secluded place to give them a few minutes of privacy. The small town of Webster seemed to fit the right timing, so I had quietly requested an old friend from Yale who had an attractive home there, which had been the Tasha Tudor farm, to host the stop-by.

George had been forewarned to be on his best behavior as the wayward Yale family members were liberal Democrats, but I don't think he ever realized you can't find many Republican houses on the back road through Webster where he could relax.

The motorcade was split on leaving Hopkinton, with only the Bushes and Security stopping at the home of our friends. Staff and press were escorted to the next scheduled stop in Salisbury. While George and Barbara were inside, I learned from the fifteen-minute car that a crowd was gathering, right on our route to Salisbury, to watch a softball game as part of Webster's Old Home Day.

I contacted Chief Aime Roy by radio, for permission to add a quick vice presidential "hello" to the occasion. Though another staunch Democrat (which is hard to understand because Webster votes Republican), he was thrilled at the idea and agreed to forewarn the throng and have it assembled at roadside. Thus, we connived an unscheduled stop, unfortunately without press.

The spontaneity of the visit took everyone by surprise. The Bushes were warmly received and George even sat in a 1907 Stevens Durea so that its owner could get a picture which he'll treasure longer than the Durea. By coincidence he also had a photo taken with one of Jack Kemp's honorary chairmen, the inimitable state senator Happy Jack Chandler, who was sacked a few weeks later for telling a distasteful joke.

We had spent several weeks maneuvering to share Salisbury's Old Home Day with its 842 residents. Unfortunately, the news of our intent leaked indirectly to the chairman of the board of selectmen from a Bush supporter attending a funeral. When the selectman received our formal request for an invitation, he was not fervently receptive. But eventually, on the theory that if you don't like the man, you can at least honor the office, we were accepted, provided we did not politicize the sanctity of their traditional affair.

The preparations that took place thereafter were noted by Peg Boyles in the *Boston Globe*. Concerns about restroom plumbing reminded one resident of "the year the water pump was out and we had to run a garden hose over from Mildred Noelte's barn." Another citizen spotted the Secret Service, exclaiming, "Nobody around here wears ties. Those guys must have all come up from Concord." But the greatest indignity was, "I'd like to remind those Advance men it's been prophesied that the first shall be last on Judgment Day."

Initially the agreement for our participation in the festivities resulted partially from a promise that the vice president would recognize the young local winner of a national DAR Good Citizens Scholarship prize, and present Citizen of the Year awards. At the last minute the Secret Service decided George could not be properly protected at the exposed spot beside the library, where tradition required the ceremony take place, so Governor Sununu substituted to make the presentations. Again, Security ranked Advance to the detriment of the political objective.

Meanwhile, George was behind the town hall attempting to exercise an antique fire pumper as a participant in a firemen's muster between Salisbury and the neighboring town of Andover. As an additional amenity a dunking booth had been ordered, but it was delivered to New London instead, our next stop for the day. It didn't make much difference, as it turned out, because by the time George got through pumping everybody was soaked—including a Secret Service agent who was assigned to stand in an overgrown field fifty yards from the event!

On leaving the town hall in his limousine, he used the car's loudspeaker to good advantage, as he was wont to do. Particularly surprised was Lucy Cudhea, whom he spotted in the crowd and joshed by name. He already had Lucy's support, but after this personal recognition he'd have it thereafter, in perpetuity.

Arriving in New London we were first welcomed at a small reception of civic leaders at the home of former congressman Jim Cleveland. Jim was in the hospital for a hip replacement but Hilary, his wife and 1980 Bush finance chairman, was a most gracious hostess for an elegant affair. Her only mistake was also welcoming the press, which promptly cleaned out the hors d'oeuvres table and depleted the beverages.

The final activity of the day was walking a rope line on New London's Main Street, lined by several thousand people attending the town's annual Hospital Day. A rope line is usually avoided by the Secret Service as there is no certainty regarding the motives which may drive some of the constituency on its other side. Yet it's the quickest way of shaking hands with a maximum number of voters, though the agents must surround the vice president so closely that it makes handshaking and photo ops difficult.

Nonetheless it was an overwhelmingly successful venture. One lady was having trouble taking a picture while her son watched. Bush had a better idea. He handed her camera to his aide who captured a shot of the vice president and the boy together. When asked for autographs he would present a business card embossed, "Vice President of the United States," with his signature swirled at the bottom. Two youngsters were heard to comment, "He's cool. He's hip."

When we arrived near the dunking booth George challenged me to sit in the chair, with a wager he'd hit the bull's eye with one throw; otherwise I'd get a shot at him. How could I lose? He had been a first baseman, not a pitcher. What I hadn't considered was velocity. He missed the small target, the ball hit the machine with the speed of a Rocket Roger pitch, and shook the whole contraption so hard that it dumped the entire reservoir all over me.

As the vice president and Mrs. Bush moved slowly down the long rope line at the right edge of the roadway, the limo kept pace abreast of them to shield against possible intrusion from the left

Vice President Bush always knew I was all wet. (Dave Valdez)

side of the street. When they finally reached the end, they stepped into the limo and were off to the Lebanon airport for their return to Kennebunkport. As the car rolled away, from the loudspeaker in the vehicle George called to the crowd, "Great day. So long. Bye, bye." It reminded me of Santa Claus: " . . . and to all a good night."

Bush was forever unperturbed. Always thoughtful, he felt his frequent use of Pease Air Base was imposing stress on its normal routines. He wished to demonstrate his personal appreciation to the personnel who were actively involved in servicing both Air

Force II and his presence on the base. Thus, about two hundred airmen accepted an invitation from the vice president and his wife for a fall picnic on the grounds of the Officers' Club.

Even Duky and a couple of his German Shepherd colleagues, security dogs, showed up, as they were constantly borrowed by the Secret Service throughout the campaign to sniff out buildings before George's arrivals. From a safe distance they received very special thanks from Barbara.

George is always at ease with the military. He displayed an intimate understanding of their frustration when he whimsically suggested advocating New Hampshire legislation to legalize the shooting of pigeons in the state in order to keep them from messing up his plane when it was stored in their hangar.

As an expedient way of introducing influential people to George, we would request his permission to invite them to ride with him in the vice presidential limousine. There was flexibility in the program with a change of passengers on each leg of the journey.

During a September trip from Pease to North Conway, for example, Bill Bartlett, president of the New Hampshire Senate, and his wife, Lee, shared this privilege. Bill had not been enthused about Chairman Sununu nor his legislative program, yet two days earlier Bill had publicly announced his support for Bush, thus the drive was a very practical way of expressing our appreciation.

Washington speechwriters would occasionally work up a series of "talking points" for George when he was to appear at some specific New Hampshire event, and would ask us for items of local color. We had told them that the promoters of the Conway area had invented mud football and had just completed the first world's mud football championship. When George arrived at Fox Ridge Resort to address business people, this is the kind of stuff he had in his briefcase:

"I heard about your mud football championship game last weekend. Mud football seems kind of like politics. You need to watch your step . . . after a while everyone starts to look alike . . . and as much as you might want to fling mud at your opponent, it's unsportsmanlike if you do." Needless to say, he didn't use any of it.

Another line from the briefcase which might have been used: "I just came from Yield House, just down the road. I thought back to 1980 when I campaigned there, standing in the parking lot shaking hands. There's a difference when you're vice president. Today they let me inside."

Fortunately, his extemporaneous opening went over well, and he was presented with a scroll by Carroll County Bush chairman Bill Zeliff listing the names of five hundred committed voters.

After leaving North Conway the motorcade halted to greet children on the lawn of the Bartlett elementary school. A second stop was brief and also "spontaneous," though preplanned, in front of the fire station at Twin Mountain, where seventy-five curious citizens had assembled. George was given an autographed copy of the town history from its author.

After we left, a bystander commented to a reporter, "I wasn't particularly impressed by the vice president, it was those Secret Service guys that really blew my mind, with their machine guns and all." This comment reflected what was more often viewed as an unfavorable public image.

The vice president's large traveling retinue contrasted sharply with Bob Dole's, who was usually accompanied by one or two assistants, driving off in a private five-passenger sedan.

Whitefield and the White Mountains Regional High School was our destination on that trip. Even if he had to "come by dog sled," the vice president was fulfilling, at last, the commitment made a year earlier when poor visibility had grounded his "Huey" helicopter. This time he completed an "Ask George Bush" with the students and then led them in the Pledge of Allegiance, all part of a national TV hookup, with millions of Americans across the country marking the U.S. Constitution's 200th birthday.

Schools provide attentive and inquisitive audiences. High schools make especially good environments for political candidates, as frequently the students will influence their parents. Further, they can be done in the morning, before large, captive congregations. This is why so many schools can get presidential candidates so easily. It has always been a mystery to me why the national press has never picked up on the fact that some candidates would have trouble showing activity during those early hours, were it not for the schools.

The perennial Bush-watcher which never neglected Bush in that preelection year of 1987 was the *Union Leader*, spieling forth a series of editorials. On October 9 Nackey Loeb summed them up by regurgitating many of the nasty diatribes her husband had written over the previous several years, adding her own acerbic comment: "George Bush is not a leader now, just as he was not in the 1980 campaign."

On a crisp, brilliant autumn afternoon in October, two days before the formal announcement of George's candidacy in Houston, the Bushes attended my son Judd's and his wife Kathy's annual Family Day in the fields of their home in Greenfield. It was a spectacular event, attended by 3,500 invited guests, and organized exclusively by Judd's own political henchmen, with no intrusion from the Bush Washington Advance.

Over two miles of rope were used to secure the field and over seventy-five Gregg volunteers helped run the event. In preparation it had taken Joel Maiola, Judd's aide, a couple weeks to mow the grass, remove rocks and tree stumps, meanwhile getting stung by bees from Judd's cornfield. Maiola's myopia messed up everything when he drove the tractor onto a stump. It took two hours to prop it off.

The accolade of the day went to Judd's brother Cy, who organized and supervised parking arrangements for the multitude. His team worked like a pack of beavers, immersed in a stream of more than a thousand cars, except nothing got

George addresses the "outrageous mob" at Greenfield. (left to right) Neil, Lauren, and Sharon Bush, Congressman Judd Gregg, Vice President Bush, Kathy Gregg, Nancy and Governor Sununu. (Walter Hippauf)

dammed up. The fields, once bestrewn with withering corn-stalks, were now jammed with far less appealing radio antennae, lined row after row in compliance with Cy's customary mathematical acuity.

The Secret Service got a jolt when they requested twenty members of the Greenfield Police Department to help for the day. The force consisted of the chief and two part-time officers.

Though covered by the three national TV networks, *Time, Newsweek,* many of the nation's leading newspapers and local press, the media was restricted to interviewing only guests, not the vice president.

The arrival was dramatic. Five marine helicopters swooped in over the hilltop ferrying the vice president, his staff, Secret

146

A small segment of the "outrageous mob." (Walter Hippauf)

Service, and national newsmen. Surrounded by a throbbing throng of eager well-wishers and handshakers, he slowly inched his way from his chopper past brightly colored tents, hot dog grills, and kiddie rides to a podium built of hay bales, corn stalks, pumpkins, and a profusion of yellow chrysanthemums.

With ruffles and flourishes from the "Yankee Strummers," it was a festive, enthusiastic audience which he addressed as "an outrageous mob." Then, in a more serious vein, he spoke the truth: "New Hampshire can make or break you."

A perfect day, by all accounts, organized with no Washington control—a tribute to local expertise. Only the inimitable Merle Burke, with his crew of volunteers at the "crisis tent," was unhappy. There was no crisis. "What shall I do with all my people?" he queried disconsolately at one point. "There's been no crisis!" Merle is the consummate overgrown Boy Scout, always

Cy Gregg still directing the last to leave! (Zachary Gregg)

ready to lend his outsized helping hand—the epitome of New Hampshire volunteerism.

Thank-you notes and accolades from our New Hampshire friends poured in for days afterward, with one discerning woman commenting that it's still very special to have an elective process which prompts the powerful to foray into small towns like Greenfield, asking for votes.

———

One of the time-honored deceptions practiced in most campaigns revolves around letters to the editor. In our case the national technocrats dummied up suggested drafts to be signed by Bush supporters, then mailed to local newspapers, leaving the false impression that they were spontaneous thoughts authored by the senders. Some of the proposed scripts were pretty far out, like one which ended,

"Long live the next President of the United States—George Bush!" A sympathetic Bush stalwart would probably have consigned it to the wastebasket, but sloppy Washington procedures thwarted the scheme anyway by addressing one to a key DuPont partisan.

Also on the subject of letters, apparently the professional political fund-raisers have demonstrated that the more pages borne by the appeal, the more money the letter will raise. Former governor Mel Thomson received a six-paged epistle from George Bush, addressed to the "Governor-Elect," some ten years after the title applied. Mel was particularly enticed by the promise, "Your advice now, in the days to come and in the years after our victory, will be critical to the success of my presidency."

Governor Thomson commented, "I can just see the average Joe, who received a similar copy of the vice president's letter, envisioning himself as standing on Pennsylvania Avenue waiting for a call from the president to come into the Oval Office and give his advice." For my money, the governor sized it up just right, and it baffles me that such nonsense can enhance the image of a candidate.

Trivial matters, like attaching the vice presidential seal on the front of the podium, can get an advance man in trouble. In the middle of George's rousing speech at the annual banquet of the New Hampshire Municipal Association, he banged the podium with his fist and the seal, to the embarrassment of the audience and consternation of Steve Edwards (who had mounted it), fell to the floor with a loud thud. Without missing a beat, Bush said, "We're making room for the new seal, here." The crowd loved it.

Although Bush had raised nearly thirteen million dollars by 1987, his frugal Granite State handlers got the bright idea of bidding for a buck apiece from his followers to cover the $1,000 filing fee.

The program worked pretty well except that one of our postage-free return envelopes came back with a brick attached, postage due.

In return for the dollar, contributors were invited to join

George on filing day. They would accompany him as he strolled along Concord's Main Street en route to the State House.

Two days before the filing, we had chosen an assembly point for our street walk in Concord. A short press conference had been planned in an outdoor public courtyard which contained two live maple trees. The Washington Advance representative requested the trees be cut down for unobstructed TV viewing. One local wag observed, "There ain't that much sap in them trees."

The day of the filing was bitterly cold. Amid the shivering crowd the vice president spotted my wife, Cay, and asked how long he should speak. She said: "Anything more than a 'good morning' would lose the election."

He complied. It was the shortest speech of his campaign.

Fortunately we had been able to advertise that Ted Williams had paid his dollar and would join the march. Even George agreed that it was thanks to having the 400-hitter there to sign autographs that a respectable crowd showed up.

It is to the credit of our state that in Bush's myriad appearances here there was never a time when he was in physical danger. On New Year's eve at Concord's First Night celebration we did get a fright. George and Barbara had been in a "living room" setting for three hours, greeting over three thousand revelers who passed through a reception line. The surroundings were safely controlled, as every visitor first had to pass through a metal detector, and carried items were inspected.

Suddenly, we heard a loud bang, like a revolver shot. "Oh, God," exclaimed George as he ducked, instinctively. Secret Service agents moved instantly to shield him. Yet, almost as quickly, it was apparent a child's balloon had popped. Everyone relaxed and the festivities continued, all of us alerted to the dangerous world in which we live.

CHAPTER 6

Bush Tops the Field
1988

The absurdity of restrictions imposed by the Federal Elections Commission was magnified when we had to arrange billeting for the Bush entourage at White River Junction in Vermont. The ploy allowed his campaigning across the Connecticut River in adjacent New Hampshire, thereby taking advantage of loopholes in the FEC regulations which limited the expenditures permitted in New Hampshire.

The spending maximum in the Granite State, due to our small population, was approximately $444,000. This was a ridiculous restraint. Even local statewide office-seekers spend at least twice that figure. Thus, ways are sought to circumvent the restriction. When advertising is done on Boston television, for example, it reaches the largest population area of New Hampshire, yet the greatest percentage of cost is charged against the Massachusetts limit.

Thus, the eighty-three rooms and attendant expenses for four nights, from January 13-17, 1988, at Howard Johnson's in Vermont were not added to our budget. An additional benefit was the FEC provision that allows any day of campaigning taking place in more than one state to be charged against the candidate's national account. To comply, George visited the Veterans' Hospital in White River, then spoke to a combined meeting of the Woodsville, New Hampshire, Lions and Rotary Clubs which conveniently met at the Happy Hour Restaurant in Wells River, Vermont.

At the Happy Hour luncheon Jim Walker, our Woodsville chairman, was set to introduce the vice president, who would thereupon emerge from behind a blue curtain where he'd been stashed away in a holding room. But Walker froze and became momentarily speechless. Finally, to his embarrassment, he cleared his throat, gathered himself together, and announced, "Please join me in welcoming the next president of the United States, George Marshall."

Walker instantly turned red and the crowd was stunned. Nobody knew what to do. Out came George Bush. In what was probably a minute, but seemed like an hour, the audience broke into simultaneous laughter and applause. George Marshall, our Lisbon chairman, was sitting in the front row. He tells all who joke about it that he still intends to be the next president.

Lodging at Howard Johnson's had another twist. As former governor Lane Dwinell was a part owner, not only did we get exceptional attention, but after our departure the Bush rooms were rededicated as the "George Bush Suite," then rented at a special price. Users were also warned that if it became the "Presidential Suite" in November, the price could become even more special. Probably we could not afford to go back there now.

During our four days there one of the escapades from the hotel included a luncheon address at the Sunapee Country Club. It resulted in a letter to the local weekly from an irate lady whose cat was allegedly disturbed by the low-flying helicopter which circled her house "for hours" while the vice president was speaking.

She claimed it was so noisy her cat did not dare venture outdoors all afternoon. "What did the helicopter crew expect to see?" she asked. "Perhaps a column of tanks rumbling up Interstate 89?" She attacked the whole performance as a totally unnecessary taxpayers' expense and wanted the vice president to reimburse her for the cost of a bag of kitty litter.

On January 16 the first New Hampshire debate for all the presidential candidates was scheduled at Dartmouth. Bob Goodman was the seasoned professional used by the Bush staff to take complete charge of all debates. Bob phoned me to suggest that in our advance walk-through with Secret Service, we should attempt to arrange for George to sit stage-right on the platform because he is left-handed.

Goodman thought there was a fire door on that side, which would make it simple to convince the agents that the potential of an emergency evacuation of the vice president would preempt his occupying a stage-right position, in spite of the sponsors' intention to assign seats by lottery. Apparently Goodman had successfully worked out a similar deal at an earlier debate in Houston.

Unfortunately, our inspection of the premises disclosed there were entrances from both sides of the stage and Professor Richard Winters, who was running the show, remained adamant that seating would be determined by lottery. George ended up with the short straw and sat stage-left.

Following the debate came New Hampshire's first overt exposure to the relatively new profession of "spin" protection, that is, the handlers' interpretation of the meaning of the events slanted in favor of their candidate. It provides amusement for the media who are otherwise perfectly capable of making their own analyses.

After the debates, the television sets were still running in the press room when in plunged Governor Sununu, Pete Teeley who was Bush's press advisor, and Craig Fuller, Bush's chief of staff. It was obvious to these staffers, if not to the two hundred media representatives, that Bush had won the debate going away.

Each spinmaster was thoroughly briefed on unequivocal, favorable rebuttals to any disparaging queries or remarks from the reporters. Immediately thereafter they were followed into the room by deputies of the other candidates, each of whom was also supporting a "winner" of the debate.

On a northerly swing we hit Berlin, a pulp and paper city which sometimes effuses a sultry sulphur smell. We were amused when a staff briefing paper took note of it. But we were stunned when a Washington staffer, offering an in-town limo ride with the vice president to a pair of local supporters, observed, "It's got an air filter so you won't have to smell this sh_ _." He had misprized the community's lifeblood scent.

On January 28 Bush was scheduled to visit the Portsmouth Navy Yard as the first stop of a full day of New Hampshire campaigning. The visit was somewhat suspect, as political aspirants are not permitted on military bases to further their political objectives. In fact, on the previous evening, former governor DuPont had stood outside the gate greeting thousands of workers at shift-change.

George's stop at the Yard was to be different. It was an official vice presidential inspection of a nuclear submarine. As coincidence would have it, he did casually drop in at the cafeteria and saluted several hundred workers from a hastily arranged staging (planned and prepared several days earlier). He complimented them on being one of the finest work forces in the world.

Just concluding his nonpolitical remarks, he was about to leave to fulfill a commitment as the featured speaker for an expanded meeting of the Portsmouth Rotary Club when he received an urgent call from the White House. The president requested his immediate return to preside over a critical vote in the Senate.

It should have been a great day for me. George handed me his Rotary speech with a note, "Hugh—thanks for filling in—if they give you a 'standing O,' please don't run against me."

I had the fifteen-minute drive time between the Navy Yard and Yoken's restaurant to digest his material. But en route, the State Police driver, Lt. Walter Morse, had to stand by at the scene of a traffic accident until the local police arrived. Although we were delayed, I was fortuitously allowed more time to collect my thoughts.

His scripted opening lines weren't too bad: "I understand Gorbachev got into a bit of hot water when he returned to Moscow after the summit. He was accused of promoting his breakfast with me for domestic political advantage."

Or, he could have used the second suggestion about the Texas rancher and the New Hampshire farmer, where the Texan bragged he had a truck he could drive all day and still not get from one end of his ranch to the other. The farmer replied, "Yep, I had a truck like that once."

Yet, somehow neither story fit my style and besides, I'd never met Gorbachev. Upon arrival, with the audience advised of my being substituted for the vice president, it was as though they had been promised Arpege and were getting Vigoro. Some walked out; others stayed for the door-prize drawing.

Fortunately the day was saved. Once again White House Communications rigged up a direct link to George from Air Force II and he talked to the audience while in flight to Washington.

Recollection of Bush's relationship with Gorbachev reminds me that at Judd's Family Day, the vice president said he had been the first American to meet the Soviet leader. Later, when Gorbachev was in Washington to sign the INF Treaty, George had invited Governor Sununu and two representatives from Iowa to that exclusive breakfast at the White House. The tactic was attacked by Dole for politicizing, and by Haig for "trivializing" a serious encounter of the two superpowers, imposing his own "petty political ambitions" by selecting the two early election states.

Alexander Haig, of course, never did like Bush and was very colorful in expressing his disdain. One day when he was shopping for votes at the New Hampshire Mall he castigated the vice president for not speaking out on tax and budget issues, saying "Why haven't we heard a peep, not even a wimp from him [Bush]?" He called George a "turkey" whereupon I wrote the VP a note to cheer him up ... at least he had not been dubbed a "pigeon."

On February 2, 1988, accompanied by General Chuck Yeager, Bush made his third appearance before a joint session of the New

Hampshire House and Senate. This time the photos taken thereafter were limited to identified Bush supporters. We had learned these giveaway premiums get more votes than banks do by offering free dishes for new accounts.

Following their legislative appearance, Bill Bartlett, then Senate president, hosted a reception in the executive council chamber for the two men. When Bruce Rounds came through the line, the vice president asked him to tell the general the joke about the Yankee couple visiting in Texas, "'cause I don't remember it." Bartlett was dismayed because the line was held up while Bruce did as ordered, even though George had advised Bartlett it was worth a chuckle to the general who hailed from Texas.

The story bears repeating. A Maine couple traveling in a motorized home stopped for gas at a Houston filling station. The wife was in back making a sandwich while the husband was outside talking to the attendant. The Texan, noting the license plates, commented that Maine was the greatest state. He had served there in the Air Force.

"What did he say, Herbie?" the wife questioned from inside. "Said he liked Maine," came the reply from Herbie.

The attendant continued to laud Maine for its rocky shoreline and great lobsters.

Again, from inside, "What did he say, Herbie?"

Again, in reply, "Says he likes our lobsters."

Finally Herbie asked the attendant why he'd come back to godforsaken Texas if he liked Maine so much. "Well," said the Texan, "I had an awful sexual experience there."

"What did he say, Herbie?"

"He said he thinks he knows you."

––––––––

The editorial views of local newspapers are influential in most statewide campaigns, but their effectiveness in presidential primaries is considerably less—the Manchester *Union Leader* excepted—due to the saturation provided by the national media.

Thus, through the first several chapters of this book relating to Rockefeller, Reagan and Bush, I have chronicled the candidates' activities as reflected in the *Union Leader*. This seemed appropriate both because this paper is the only statewide daily, and it boasts the editorial flair of the Loebs, who are universally acknowledged as confrontational catalysts.

Obviously any presidential candidate must focus on the national press. Still, one of the necessary tribulations of running here is to befriend the New Hampshire dailies. A good example of the challenge for Bush in 1988 was the Nashua *Telegraph*, which had been favorable to him in 1980 . . . at least before his infamous debate which it had sponsored.

The publisher at the time, Herman Pouliot, enjoyed a personal relationship with George, had a summer cottage nearby on the Maine coast, and has traditionally promoted Republicans. In deference to this association Bush had given the paper two opportunities for editorial board interviews, whereas no other paper received more than one.

The day after the second interview, George was speaking to the Gun Owners of New Hampshire when he used a toy plastic pistol as a prop, to demonstrate how easily a terrorist could subvert airport security checks.

Two days later the *Telegraph* editorialized that George was "fast becoming Mr. Slick—avoiding the issues and concentrating instead on what will give him the most and best exposure." There was no comment whatsoever that George had already spent over two hours in private discussions with the publisher and editors of the newspaper for open questions on any subject of their choice.

A week later the *Telegraph*, as the crowning irony, endorsed two candidates: Governor Michael Dukakis, a Democrat, or, if you preferred, Senator Robert Dole, a Republican!

How could this have happened? Were I to speculate based on my acquaintance with the characters involved, I would presume that when it came down to the bottom line, personal contacts made the difference. I believe Pouliot had a closer personal connection with a key supporter of Dole, Gerry Nash, than with a Bush counterpart, John Stabile. Moreover, by playing it both ways the Telegraph counted on having at least one sure winner.

After George won the Primary he received and tolerantly complied with a request from the *Telegraph's* publisher to have President Reagan personally autograph a photograph taken of Bush and Reagan at the 1980 debate. Thereafter the paper described George as "that drugstore cowboy whose legal residence may be a Houston hotel suite, but who knows so little about the state he thinks the Alamo is pastry topped with ice cream." A curious way of thanking Bush for his tolerance and cooperation.

––––––––––

George spent the first few nights of February at a new Clarion Somerset Hotel in Nashua, as its very first guest. Except for two nights during the final week before the Primary, the entire Bush entourage took over the two top floors of the same hotel. On one of the excepted nights the group stayed in nearby Lowell, Massachusetts, to avoid charging all the sizable expenses of the touring party to New Hampshire, as allowed by the FEC regulations for extended stays.

The top floor of the Clarion included the vice presidential suite and accommodations for senior staff. Access was secured under the direction of the Secret Service. We, in turn, had moved into the hotel with our advance office, on the floor below, almost three weeks earlier. From that post we previewed and advanced round-trip schedules from Nashua for each day of the final week.

Whenever the vice president and his coterie stayed overnight anywhere in the state, each of thirty to forty key-staff rooms had to be checked by the advance team to remove all promotional materials, test every light, turn all TV sets to CNN Headline News, check the heating system, and place a sticker in the right-bottom corner of the bathroom mirror announcing baggage call for the next morning.

We also had to prepare a kit which included room assignments and pertinent phone numbers, area information, and other vital data. This comprehensive packet was left on each bed. It was a sad day indeed when one forgetful aide at the Clarion failed to unlock the "senior staff lounge!"

The highest priority was perfect readiness of the vice presidential suite—not to forget the popcorn, Diet Seven-Up, and his favorite bran cereal, preferably with fruit, for morning breakfast.

On Monday, February 8, the night of his defeat in Iowa by Dole and Robertson, the Bush group arrived at the Nashua Airport. George was characteristically upbeat, but some of his key staff members were perceptibly bewildered. The press was writing him off.

Weeks earlier, on the assumption he would be exhausted from victorious caucuses in Iowa, yet wanting to demonstrate he was not taking New Hampshire for granted, we had planned an intensive twelve-hour, event-filled day. It would begin the morning of February 9; he would leave for Washington the same evening. The intent was to give him a brief rest before starting the tour, thus the motorcade would not leave the hotel until 9:30 A.M.

The first sign of the senior staff's significant distress was a call from upstairs on the evening of their arrival from Iowa, to arrange for a 6:30 A.M. plant-gate appearance "somewhere in Nashua" the next day to prove that the vice president was fighting back. Fortunately we had already set one up for later in the week at the Nashua Corporation. We simply rescheduled.

Further evidence of the crisis was apparent shortly thereafter from orders for a series of changes in the scheduling policy. It was directed that only essential commitments would be honored, leaving a maximum amount of free time for other use.

Roger Ailes, Bush's communications advisor, had arrived and was working on new radio and television commercials. The vice president, Ailes, Bob Teeter, Bush's pollster and political confidant, Lee Atwater, the National Chairman, and Governor Sununu began a succession of strategy sessions on the top floor. They had even summoned Peggy Noonan, who had been Reagan's favorite speechwriter, to help Bush recast his image.

Fortunately, these meetings resulted (to a degree) in the Bush campaign's adoption (at last) of some of the suggestions that many of us had been constantly recommending since the start of the campaign.

One good example: We knew that former senator Barry Goldwater was a Bush supporter and we had strongly urged that he write a letter evidencing his conviction to his New Hampshire mentor, Nackey Loeb. Such an endorsement published by her paper would have exerted early and effective influence on the conservative voters, and put the paper in a compromising position.

Instead, as a panic-button afterthought, Goldwater was flown from Arizona in Bob Mosbacher's jet (Bush subsequently appointed Mosbacher as Secretary of Commerce) to the Clarion for a press conference—after most of the right-wing voters had committed to Kemp, Robertson, or DuPont. It was a generous thing for Senator Goldwater to have done and certainly received media attention.

The best decision coming out of these strategy sessions was to muffle the structured vice presidential image and place him in spontaneous situations where, from direct personal contact, citizens would feel he was one of them. From the beginning our advance team had sought autonomy in arranging such exposures. Authority was never granted on the theory that every movement of the vice president's travel had to receive the explicit approval of the Washington staff. Now his senior advisors were in New Hampshire—desperate and willing to try anything.

One innovation was to send out scouting teams on our travel routes to hunt down places where quick, unplanned stops would permit maximum handshaking with attention-getting photo ops. The horde of accompanying media was not forewarned. Initially, even the Secret Service was not privy to the artifice.

Before leaving the hotel, we suggested some potential places the scouts might reconnoiter. On the first day the scouting team was only a few hours ahead of the main body. Riding in the five-minute car I was able to notify the motorcade in advance of each

Bush brings in the heavy artillery. Former senator Goldwater, Vice President Bush, and Hugh Gregg. (Dave Valdez)

unplanned stop. That day, we hoped it would be at a Salem mobile-home park, which would have been a slight diversion from our published route.

Within ten minutes of the turnoff point a scout radioed to scratch the idea, because they had knocked on several doors and found no one at home or had received ungracious comments about Bush—hardly an attractive situation in the final week of the campaign, with two busloads of media and a long line of private press vehicles following along!

Other deviations, however, worked out extremely well. The

best photos were instantaneously contrived right at the site, with whatever props were on hand. At a lumber yard, after greeting numerous employees and customers, I arranged for George to climb aboard a 24-ton Kalmar forklift and drive it, both to his amazement and that of the onlookers. It was an on-the-spot maneuver which got us top of the television news for the day.

On another occasion, without his flinching even the slightest bit, I persuaded him to drive a mammoth semi-trailer at a truckers' rest stop, with a Secret Service agent hanging on to the cab. All such photos made George a TV star on the national news and provoked local comment reflecting a new George Bush. In this case it was even better because Sununu showed up during the exercise in time to tickle the press: "Wait till you see the sky diving."

Meanwhile, Dole had been using a very effective Doonesbury television ad, which pictured George walking off into the horizon without leaving any footprints. Over the weekend, prior to Primary Day, Ailes designed a powerful response. It was a "straddle" ad, contrasting the Bush and Dole positions on a number of major issues.

The two-faced exposure of the straddle ad was the first of what was conceived by many as the beginning of negative campaigning by the Bush forces. It so embittered Dole that subsequently, in a live interview with Tom Brokaw of NBC, Dole responded to the question, "Is there anything you'd like to say to the vice president?" with the acerbic, "Yeah, stop lying about my record."

The crowning glory from the Bush family's most dedicated, longest-working member in the Granite State campaign bloomed on Election Day. For months, John Bush, George's nephew and a college student, had been organizing young people in the high schools and from college campuses, both in- and out-of-state. These students would show up routinely as organized cheering sections at all Bush events.

The night before the Primary, they peppered major thoroughfares in the more populous southern tier with small blue Bush signs attached to four-foot stakes and stuck them into snowbanks, like blossoming daffodils in early spring.

Hugh Gregg, Vice President Bush, and Ed Jordan. "General" Jordan kept us in touch with the White House. (Dave Valdez)

It was a sudden, startling contrast, happening overnight—a mind-boggling show stopper. There had been no signs the day before!

On election morning John's troops were standing at high-volume intersections holding similar signs and chanting, "Bush! Bush! Bush!" It had a startling and potent effect.

On election night before they went to Manchester for the victory celebration, George, Barbara, Marvin and his wife, Margaret, were at our home for dinner. Also in attendance were those hardworking, otherwise unheralded members of the New Hampshire advance team, including motorcade drivers. Several of these guests, because they had always worked behind the scenes, had never met George and Barbara. Ostensibly it was a gracious show of appreciation by the Bush family for these dedicated people who had played such an important background part over the previous several months.

What the Bushes didn't know was that our home phone line had been on the blink for several weeks and New England Telephone had been unable to remedy the problem. I knew if we had the vice president at the house we would get the benefit of White House telephone expertise, as it requires workable communications—and for free.

We had been working at the Clarion with Ed Jordan from the Office of White House Communications, a delightfully cooperative and jovial gentleman whom we fondly nicknamed "The General." Always dressed in civilian clothes, Ed was, in fact, an Army Signal Corps enlisted man.

He came, repaired our phone, and had the opportunity of having his photo taken with the vice president, as did our other friends. He insisted that I stand beside the two of them for the picture, so I introduced him to the vice president as "General Jordan."

Subsequently, as Cay and I left the house in the limo with George and Barbara, George inquired: "By the way, who was that general?"

———

On Election Day George Bush upset the professional pollsters with a stunning fifteen-point victory margin (Bush 59,290; Dole 44,797) over their predicted winner, Senator Dole. Credit for this achievement was attributed to a mix of many factors, but the debate continues on which was the most prominent.

The national media brainwashed itself into mass conclusion that Bush's unique belated advertising turned the tide, but I think it failed to recognize that New Hampshire voters have consistently demonstrated that personal contact and pressing the flesh scores highest here, as opposed to the audio or printed message.

The last-minute appearance of Goldwater, the one-on-one unscheduled handshaking of the final week, and the photo ops of a reanimated George Bush undoubtedly contributed to the Bush triumph, as did the ingenuity of John Bush's direct appeal to a limited number of voters. Then, too, inherent to the overall envi-

ronment was the generic association ingrained in some conservatives of the relationship between George, the loyal soldier, and
their popular hero, Ronald Reagan.

In my view, it was none of those things which counted most.

It was ten years earlier that we first met George Bush in New
Hampshire and established an organizational effort which, indirectly, resulted in his being chosen as vice president. During the
intervening years he visited the state more than any other
national figure and developed innumerable lasting, personal
friendships with more New Hampshire people than probably any
other out-of-state government official in its entire history. In
fact, I would wager George now knows and recognizes more of
our citizens by their first names than anyone living in our state,
other than our currently elected politicians and perhaps a few
former ones.

His transient residency in nearby Kennebunkport, with his
frequent commute from Pease Air Force Base, and the perks of the
vice presidency whenever he traveled in New Hampshire had
given him name recognition far beyond that enjoyed by any other
candidate during my forty-year involvement in politics.

Besides, the Manchester *Union Leader's* unfavorable publicity
was ever-present, keeping his name before the public. Even after
he had won Nackey commented: "Obviously, in our eyes George
Bush is not the right candidate. If he is being supported as the
new Reagan, it is the case of the wrong candidate being supported
for the right reason."

I draw a parallel between Bush's defeat by Reagan in 1980 and
Bush's victory in 1988. Reagan beat Bush basically because
Reagan had built a loyal organization in 1976 when he was nar-
rowly defeated by President Ford. Bush won in 1988 basically
because he had built a loyal organization in 1980 when he was
upstaged by Reagan.

Peter Goldman and Tom Mathews, *Newsweek* reporters,
were dead wrong when they wrote in *Quest for the Presidency*
that "Bush's lost souls had come back in the fold." Bush had not

lost any souls. They were there all the time—albeit perhaps breathing inaudibly.

The personal loyalties of a strong political organization extend very deep, particularly with a candidate like George, who constantly nurtured those who had helped him. The main reason George Bush won in 1988 was because he parlayed his initial one-on-one relationships of the 1980 campaign through ten years of thoughtfulness, and he cultivated new friends in the same fashion.

R. W. Apple, Jr., of the *New York Times* was way off the mark when he wrote that Governor Sununu "personally recruited Bush 'captains' for most of the state's 221 towns." The implication was that these were all new recruits which Sununu had laboriously enlisted. The fact is, more than half of the 378 local chairmen were either previous Bush chairmen from the 1980 effort or came from Judd Gregg's congressional/political organization, which had always been supportive of Bush.

In the euphoria of his victorious Primary night, George told his supporters, "Thank you, New Hampshire," and pledged it was something he would never forget.

It was a moment of mixed emotions for me at the Manchester Airport later the same evening. Finally we had accomplished what we had set out to do ten years earlier. But there was an emptiness in saying goodbye to the Bushes, knowing a wonderful experience and relationship were over. Barbara summed it all up with a gracious note to Cay: "George and I had a tear in our eye as we flew off from New Hampshire and saw Hugh standing there alone."

Of course I was not alone. There were hundreds of loyal volunteers throughout New Hampshire, many of whom had dedicated themselves to the Bushes for more than ten years. We all celebrated. A good job had been done, although it took somewhat longer than we first expected.

George did not forget. Nine months later, on election night in Houston, expressing his gratitude to the nation he concluded his speech with a sincere "Thank you, New Hampshire."

THE WHITE HOUSE

WASHINGTON

January 13, 1989

Dear Hugh:

As I prepare to return to California, I wanted to take a
moment to tell you how much I've appreciated your support
and help all these years. In 1980, you and I, with the help
of the American people, started a prairie fire that has burned
with ever greater intensity, sparking one of the greatest
political movements our Nation has ever known.

With the election of my trusted friend George Bush, you and
I can rest assured that the revolution we've created and the
great victories we've won during these past eight years will
not be undone. Rather, they will provide a solid foundation
for his administration to build upon.

Yes, we've done wondrous things together. We've cut taxes,
revitalized our Nation's defenses, spurred the economy into
the greatest peacetime expansion in history, and restored
confidence in our Nation and the principles it embodies.
America is back and standing tall again. Nothing we've done
on my watch makes me happier than to see the renewed pride
in our country and optimism for its future.

While I'm looking forward to spending more time around the ranch,
I know that there are battles yet to be fought and -- you know
me -- I'll be out there speaking my mind as I always have.

For now, just let me say that your tireless contributions
to my many campaigns for office have provided Nancy and me
with fonder memories than you will ever know. It was your
unwavering support, enthusiasm, and commitment to our cause
that sustained us through many a long and difficult hour.

God bless you, and God bless America.

Sincerely,

Ronald Reagan

The Honorable Hugh Gregg
RFD 5, Gregg Road
Nashua, NH 03060

Ronald Reagan's letter.

Part Two

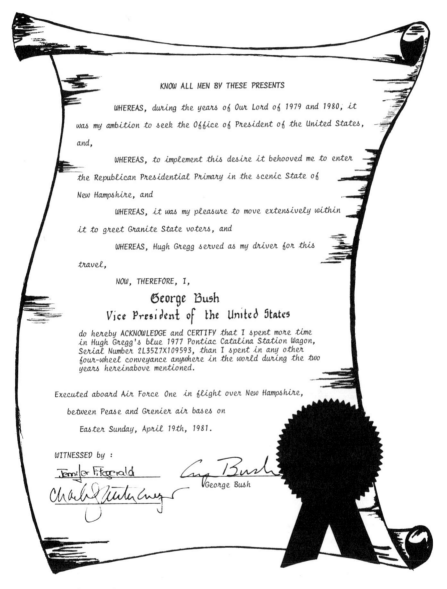

KNOW ALL MEN BY THESE PRESENTS

WHEREAS, during the years of Our Lord of 1979 and 1980, it was my ambition to seek the Office of President of the United States, and,

WHEREAS, to implement this desire it behooved me to enter the Republican Presidential Primary in the scenic State of New Hampshire, and

WHEREAS, it was my pleasure to move extensively within it to greet Granite State voters, and

WHEREAS, Hugh Gregg served as my driver for this travel,

NOW, THEREFORE, I,

George Bush
Vice President of the United States

do hereby ACKNOWLEDGE and CERTIFY that I spent more time in Hugh Gregg's blue 1977 Pontiac Catalina Station Wagon, Serial Number 2L35Z7X109593, than I spent in any other four-wheel conveyance anywhere in the world during the two years hereinabove mentioned.

Executed aboard Air Force One in flight over New Hampshire,

between Pease and Grenier air bases on

Easter Sunday, April 19th, 1981.

WITNESSED by :

Jennifer Fitzgerald

Charles Hunter Gregg

George Bush
George Bush

The roads well-traveled by George Bush.

CHAPTER 7

The Bushes
Remembered

My relationship with George Bush has been closer than any
I have enjoyed with many of my other lifelong political friends
here in New Hampshire. Considering the amount of time—the
long and strenuous days we spent working together from the fall of
1979 through his election in 1988—some ten years of my life were
interwoven with his in our mutual pursuit for his presidency.

This intense period included countless exchanges of calls and
correspondence. The friendship was reignited every time we met,
in New Hampshire, Kennebunkport, or Washington. Our communications were regular right up to the time when John Sununu
took over as New Hampshire chairman for the 1988 campaign. I
was relieved when he finally announced publicly that he would,
in fact, support George Bush.

To avoid any possible jurisdictional conflict with Governor
Sununu during the 1988 campaign, I chose to remain as active as
before, but in a more hands-on capacity, at a subsidiary level. The
assignment I undertook required more travel, physical exertion,
detail, and on-scene action than when I served as George's campaign chairman. My direct contacts with Bush during this critical
year were limited to his visits in the state when I was always at
his right hand, working with the New Hampshire advance team.

What I've learned of him over the years, his personality and
habits, could fill a separate book. But my first, foremost impression of George Bush is that he is selfless. This trait is so unique in

politics that it may be the reason why public perception of the whole man was so confused. In no way did this attribute diminish his self-confidence and sense of purpose.

At the same time, he is generous in spirit and so naturally gallant that he could be misperceived as perhaps too deferential and almost patronizing. His demeanor is such that even as vice president, strolling around the White House with President Reagan, his deference was readily perceptible. This old-fashioned, almost obsequious, behavior results from his fine upbringing.

His sense of noblesse oblige was generated from his family background, where his father had served as a U.S. senator and both his maternal and paternal antecedents had been philanthropic in their community activities.

Amusing, perhaps his good manners do not measure up to George Washington and the cherry tree. George's sister once told me that her brother did, indeed, hide broccoli under his other vegetables so that their mother wouldn't see it.

He has one distinction of which few congressmen can boast: he has never taken an honorarium. Considering his lifelong political career, from serving in that august body to ambassadorships at the United Nations and China, along with heading the CIA and RNC, this conduct should not go unheralded.

In keeping with strict etiquette, his custom of scrupulously writing personal thank-you notes turned into proliferative political profit. If there is anyone in the country who doesn't have a personal autograph from George Bush among their memorabilia, it's only because they never met him.

The Doonesbury cartoonist, Garry Trudeau—hardly George's best friend—even suggested a format for citizens writing to him as president: "I think you're doing a great job at (insert a compliment). Please send me a handwritten note thanking me for writing you." As Trudeau suggested: "Hurry! Don't be the last in your neighborhood" to get your personal thank-you note.

A modest man, it was not until he had been many months into the 1980 campaign when I learned the full details of his extraordinary war record. He had never told me about being in a submarine for a month after being shot down in the Pacific. He was reluctant to discuss that incredible story and it took considerable prodding from his managers to permit its publication and use of the film taken at the scene of his dramatic rescue.

Nor did I ever doubt his personal bravery. Even when his friend and security guard, Bob Gambino, advised there might be some security threat, resulting from his having directed the CIA, he never appeared apprehensive about his personal safety.

A physical fitness buff who exercises regularly and plays all sports, he is indefatigable. Even after a long, hard day on the campaign trail, he would appear as alert and vigorous as he did at daybreak.

No matter how unfair or unpleasant criticism might be directed against him, he's outwardly unflappable. I've never seen him show displeasure in public. Still, to insiders, especially on down-time, he was always intense, never losing sight of what he was doing here. He would vent his anger privately, and there would be no question as to how he really felt about an individual or situation that upset him.

He was also given to the fun of exchanging risqué jokes with close associates. Sharing the same penchant with Reagan, I'm sure that Tabasco was not the only saucy spice passed across the table at their weekly luncheon meetings. In fact, Bruce Rounds used to provide the vice president with material to keep the president entertained.

Both George and Barbara are two of the most gregarious people I've ever known. Certainly, son Neil, whom we knew best, has inherited the characteristic. They never seem to have any time for themselves. There's always a houseful of friends, some from the happy, early times in Texas, or worldwide acquaintances cherished over the years, and the guest list is ever-increasing. Those of us who had been his loyalists in the early days had almost free access to their summer home at Kennebunkport, like good neighbors.

In the off-season when the summer home was not staffed, he would give us a call to suggest we drive up for a visit. After a brief social hour we would casually go out for dinner at a local restaurant.

The Bushes are a very close-knit clan, of which he is the respected patriarch, subject only to his mother, an exceptional woman with whom he has always been remarkably tender and solicitous. When assembled there are probably over forty of them, including children and grandchildren, without including George's and Bar's relatives. Each of the separate family units visits frequently both in Washington and Maine. One of the truest pictures of the real man was depicted by an ad which showed him completely absorbed in the joy of lifting a granddaughter up in the air, with obvious mutual affection.

For a man who has participated regularly in the pomp and circumstance of international ceremonies, he adjusted readily to the unpretentious New Hampshire ambience. Sometimes it's hard to conceive that this regular guy was yesterday having lunch with the king of Saudi Arabia or playing croquet with the queen mother of England. His informality with us is such that it's almost awkward to address him now as "Mr. President."

He has an uncanny ability to remember names and faces and seems to recognize more people by their first names than anybody in the country. He has a delightful habit of picking up the phone, at random, and calling anybody he knows to keep in touch, and sometimes some he doesn't know, to wish them well or congratulate them on some accomplishment.

In the White House this same natural penchant for informality and for spontaneous telephone calls has nurtured close personal associations with world leaders, from Gorbachev to Pope John Paul II. Gerald Seib of the *Wall Street Journal* labels the evolution of style as "Dialing for Diplomacy." Actually it is an outgrowth of the same character trait that has always inspired the sustained loyalty of his political followers.

In turn, he has been easily accessible to those he has known. I've always felt that no matter what the time of day or whatever the problem, he would be receptive to a phone call. This sense of closeness is shared by a multitude of others who have reached him even when he was traveling in Air Force II or his limousine.

Even since he became president, New Hampshire's supporters have been granted reasonably free access when they've gone to Washington for some special purpose. This is in considerable contrast to the routine by which Reagan conducted his Oval Office agenda. This difference was demonstrated on the morning after George's inauguration, when both he and Barbara rose early to welcome the waiting crowd of ordinary citizens to whom they had opened the White House doors.

His recognition as a "consensus" president reflects the fact that he has always been a good listener. I've observed that he was unique among politicians in that, rather than telling you how he felt about things, he was always asking how you felt. When a controversial issue was involved, it was his style to solicit the opinions of as many experts on the subject as possible. From their diverse impressions, he would formulate his own position.

One notable occasion when, in my view, George Bush did not accept a consensus of opinion was at the Clarion Hotel during the last week of the 1988 Primary campaign, when all of his advisors, including Barbara, encouraged him to run the negative ads against Bob Dole. Even after several days he never really agreed to it; rather, he just let it happen.

"I don't have any kind of a textbook management theory. The main thing is to surround yourself with men and women of excellence—bright, able people. Don't worry if they have significant differences of opinion on the issues. Get the best and then lead them to solve problems." This self-description of his style is a capsule of the way he administers, though some of his subaltern selections may appear to be based more on politics than ability.

Still, according to *The Winning of the White House 1988*, written by the editors of *Time*, "To candidate Bush, paid political operators were strictly hired help. Volunteers, on the other hand, won his admiration."

Except for volunteer John Sununu, it was a handful of paid political survivors from the Bush campaign of 1988 whom he retained to run the White House. Volunteers who primarily contributed huge sums of money were abundantly rewarded with ambassadorial and diplomatic assignments. Other unpaid advisors were given cabinet posts.

As vice president, George appeared to have a disposition for rotating key personnel. It has never been clear in my mind whether this was a deliberate administrative practice. But as happens with all of us, when a person moves on in life, places, people, and things are bound to drop off along the way.

A few high-profile aides like Dave Bates, Pete Teeley, and Chase Untermeyer left the Bush forces for a time, then resurfaced in other roles later on. Others, like Jennifer Fitzgerald and David Sparks, received new assignments. Then there was Craig Fuller, who appears to have departed permanently.

David Keene, who had been Bush's chairman in 1980, signed on with Dole in 1988 and campaigned against his former mentor. According to Dave Broder, Keene "supplied reporters with an endless stream of quotes suggesting Bush was easily swayed and weak in conviction." The open fashion with which he conducts his personal life, surrounded with people, parallels his method of governing. His facile relationship with so many affords him a bottomless pool of personal and professional resources and advisors.

In fact, one could say that he detests confrontation and is only at ease when arriving at a consensus with those expressing adversarial views. But once a direction has been chosen, he expects full cooperation from everyone involved.

Obviously any publicly elected person needs to reflect the sentiments of those who put him in office, lest his political life be over. When he became vice president, perhaps abetted by his staff, George seemed to develop a fetish for favorable approval ratings. To a reasonable degree a vice president or president must strive to maintain broad applause from the electorate. With Bush, however, excelling in opinion polls became a raison d'être.

His participation in many extraneous events appears more like grandstanding than the traditional itinerary of a White House occupant. Since becoming president I suspect he has spent more time out of the Oval Office than any of his predecessors. His managers seem obsessed with the perpetual photo opportunity.

Granted, it was such vivacity and vigorous campaigning which elected him in the first place. But his postelection scheduling is often interpreted as playing more to popular perception than rendering substantive service. Now that he is the chief executive his schedulers should no longer need to focus on the photo op or prime-time TV news.

The secretary of state illustrated this plight when Bush was being criticized for the handling of the General Noriega situation in Panama. Jim Baker felt that, notwithstanding this disapproval from opponents, the important argument was that the president's overall approval rating was in the 70% range. As Lou Cannon wrote, "Polls are notorious seducers of Presidents."

Bush detests dissension. A quick example: I had called to his attention, after he became president, that we had a Republican housekeeping problem in our New Hampshire family because Governor Sununu's wife would not shake hands in public with one of our congressmen. As evidence, I personally gave to him a *Union Leader* editorial which read, " . . . it wouldn't be too surprising if the president himself finally insists that this stupid feud end before it gets so far out of hand that it affects the office of the presidency."

In his typically responsive fashion, he subsequently wrote me, "I hope that matter is now under control. John & I have talked about it. He certainly does not want it to linger on."

Later, when he was asked by a reporter whether he had talked to Sununu about the matter, he replied, "Well, there may have been a word about it. That was before his kinder, gentler days. I don't recall any weighty discussions about it at all." He did not acknowledge I had ever contacted him.

Meanwhile, the press was having a field day with the issue, implying that the president had not spoken to Sununu about the

1979

Candia — Norman Maiden (483-2011)
Canterbury — Oliver Fifield (783-4321)
Carroll — Hilda Winn (846-5714)
Center Harbor — Col. Lewis Hanson (253-6953)
Charlestown — Walter H. Palmer (826-6277)
Chatham — Mrs. Woodrow (Abby) Munroe (694-2063)
Chester — Luther Grimes (887-3202)
Chesterfield — James E. O'Neil, Jr. (251-6365)
Chichester — Pam Binning (798-5044)
Claremont — Mrs. Howard R. (Virginia) Anderson (542-4339)
Clarksville — Mrs. Donald (Evelyn) McKinnon (246-8235)
Colebrook — Granvyl Hulse (237-4039)
Columbia — Frederic Foss (237-4993)
Concord — Robert E. K. Morrill (224-9650)
Conway — Frederick E. Leighton (356-3122)
Cornish — Stephen P. Tracy (675-2892)
Croydon — Jules Pellerin (863-2472)
Dalton — David Dana (837-2552)
Danbury — Donald J. Cook (768-3450)
Danville — Mrs. Paul F. (Elizabeth) Gustavison, Jr. (642-8747)
Deerfield — Col. John L. Sherburne (463-8382)
Deering — Jeremiah A. Donovan, Jr. (464-3841)
Derry — Ed Anderson (432-7055)
Dixville — Mrs. Gail Barba (255-3981)
Dorchester — Robert W. Thayer (786-3392)
Dover — Geraldine Sylvester (742-1522)
Dublin — Ralph Perkins (563-8653)
Dummer — Mrs. Raymond A. (Diana) Holt (449-3488)
Dunbarton — Mrs. Kenneth (Terry) Busick (744-5361)
Durham — Hon. Francis Robinson (868-7412)
East Kingston — Bruce N. Levis (642-3113)
Easton — Mrs. Vincent (Shirley) Place (823-8596)
Eaton — Harry Fowler (447-2828)
Effingham — Paul Menard (539-6053)
Ellsworth — Mrs. William J. (Kay) Deachman (726-3329)
Enfield — Kenneth Wheeler (632-7010)
Epping — Mrs. Richard (Noreen) Travers (679-8118)
Epsom — Ashton Welch (736-9961)
Errol — Robert W. Bean (482-3328)
Exeter — Mrs. Alfred E. (Anne) Beck (772-3458)

Farmington — Mrs. Norman E. (Jane) Fall (755-2271)
Fitzwilliam — Mrs. Faith Trueax (585-9028)
Francestown — Robert B. Parker (547-2749)
Franconia — Mrs. Dwight K. (Mary) Taylor (823-7740)
Franklin — Henry B. Trachy (934-5182)
Freedom — Elizabeth A. Acton (539-6614)
Fremont — David Lafayette (895-3388)
Gilford — Herbert G. Ingram (524-2055)
Gilmanton — George W. Bingham (267-6565)
Gilsum — John Calhoun (357-3311)
Goffstown — Mrs. Suzanne Bean (497-3403)
Gorham — Leo P. Gagnon (466-5010)
Goshen — George A. Dorr, Jr. (863-1075)
Grafton — Leonard A. Guaraldi (523-4895)
Grantham — Philip Allen (863-3567)
Greenfield — Mrs. Judd (Kathy) Gregg (547-3452)
Greenland — Frank F. Richards (436-8590)
Greenville — Mrs. Robert (Beth) Taft (878-2433)
Groton — Alexander Lennox, Jr. (786-2371)
Hampstead — Mrs. Louis (Margaret) Griffith (329-5274)

Hampton — Penny A. Hamilton (926-5190)
Hampton Falls — Francis Ferrera (926-2606)
Hancock — Mrs. Vinton A. (Jane) Cartmell (525-3302)
Hanover — Philip G. Krueger (643-2509)
Harrisville — John Colony, III (827-3010)
Hart's Location — Frank B. Patrick, Jr. (374-2715)
Haverhill — Mrs. Paul (Beth) Mayette (787-6270)
Hebron — Paul Hazelton (744-8918)
Henniker — David Currier (428-7619)
Hill — Joyce Colby (934-5249)
Hillsborough — Frederick H. Vogt (478-3255)
Hinsdale — Michael Lyster (256-6590)
Holderness — Mrs. T. Desmond (Dorothy) Butler (968-3591)
Hollis — Mrs. Joseph E. (Shirley) Cohen (465-2323)
Hooksett — Cheryl Bennett (668-4163)
Hopkinton — Edward Leadbeater (746-4943)

Hudson — Richard E. Dolbec (889-6722)
Jackson — Mrs. Alfred (Judy) Fuller (383-4462)
Jaffrey — Oren J. Bellerete (532-6693)
Jefferson — Peter Guest (586-7795)
Keene — Andrea Scranton (352-1722)
Kensington — Clark Jacobs (772-2615)
Kingston — Richard Meehan (642-8711)
Laconia — Edwin Chertok (524-5538)
Lancaster — William Ingram (788-2214)
Landaff — Mrs. M. Knapp (838-2815)
Langdon — Hayes Sager (826-7758)
Lebanon — Lorine M. Walter (448-3746)
Lee — Richard Doherty (659-5338)
Lempster — Gilbert Pinkney (863-2434)
Lincoln — W. Murray Clark (745-2262)
Lisbon — George Marshall (838-6740)
Litchfield — Mrs. Demarest S. (Sara) Cassidy (882-7753)
Littleton — Brien L. Ward (444-6945)
Londonderry — William Lievens (432-9644)
Loudon — Mrs. Roger A. (Sandy) Stillman (783-4479)
Lyman — Mrs. John H. (Beverly) Reynolds (838-5507)

Lyme — Robert MacMillen (795-2522)
Lyndeborough — Edward M. Abbot, Jr. (654-9663)
Madbury — C. Thomas Crosby, Jr. (742-7411)
Manchester — Randall F. Cooper (356-9357)
Manchester — Frank Wageman (622-5719)
Marlborough — David Cheney (876-3318)
Marlow — Ronald E. Gorges (446-3345)
Mason — Mrs. Richard (Shirley) Morley (878-2941)
Meredith — Josiah Fisher (279-4677)
Merrimack — John O'Leary (424-3896)
Middleton — Star Snyder (473-2166)
Milan — Louis E. Gallant (449-3355)
Milford — Mrs. Bart V. (Lorraine) Prestipino (673-2911)
Millfield — Mrs. Hartley L. (Erta) Sweatt (482-3273)
Milton — Richard L. Kibbe (473-2829)
Monroe — George Tyler (638-2524)

Mt. Vernon — Handolph J. Reis (673-6180)
Moultonboro — Murray Nickerson, Jr. (476-5624)
Nashua — Mrs. Howard (Mary Jane) Wing (883-4809)
Nelson — Mrs. Roberta Tolman Shea (847-3285)
New Boston — Mrs. Mary Anne Chittim (487-2641)
Newbury — Mrs. Horace (Carrie) Whitcher (763-2176)
New Castle — Esther Roberts (436-4223)
New Durham — Mrs. William B. Cullimore (859-5891)
Newfields — Mrs. John R. (Dorothy) Evans (772-9728)
New Hampton — Laurence A. Blood (744-3073)
Newington — Norman W. Myers (436-5817)
New Ipswich — Marvin E. Salmonson (878-2784)
New London — David Kidder (526-4767)
Newmarket — Charles Wayda (659-5748)
Newport — Joel W. Maiola (863-3307)
Newton — Thomas Grogan (329-5775)

Northfield — Mrs. Peter (Donna) Zeras (286-8431)
North Hampton — William Cahill (964-5448)
Northumberland — Clyde Fiske (636-1202)
Northwood — Martha M. Abbot (942-7755)
Nottingham — Mrs. Robert (Ruth) Morris (942-5242)
Orange — Gwynne Prosser (523-4897)
Orford — Mrs. Clifford (Julie) Fifield (353-4881)
Ossipee — Mrs. Gerard E. (Christine) Powers, Jr. (539-2252)
Pelham — Philip Currier (635-7212)
Pembroke — Edward J. Allgever (485-3076)
Peterborough — Robert Grip (924-3027)
Piermont — James L. Wilson (272-5839)
Pittsburg — Mrs. Marjorie H. Barry (538-6688)
Pittsfield — Bruce Pethic (435-8266)
Plainfield — Sara M. Townsend (469-3313)
Plaistow — Mrs. Henry J. (Devana) Szmyt (382-4736)

Sutton — George G. Wells (927-4472)
Swanzey — John Croteau, Jr. (352-8355)
Tamworth — Charles Aspinall (323-7242)
Temple — Kenneth B. Saunders, Jr.
Thornton — Mrs. Gunnar (Heather) Baldwin (745-8959)
Tilton — Mrs. Christopher R. (Jean) Batchelder (524-4962)
Troy — Mrs. Herman K. (Elaine) Schierioth (242-6641)
Tuftonboro — Mrs. Susan Ramsbotham (544-3053)
Unity — Mrs. Vernon R. (Doris) Taylor (542-5972)
Wakefield — Herbert F. Mackinney (522-8804)
Walpole — Tucker Burr (756-4228)
Warner — Clarence Pushee, Jr. (764-9463)
Washington — Ronald Jager (495-3618)
Waterville Valley — Ralph H. Bean (236-8640)
Weare — David B. Schartner (529-7390)
Webster — Mrs. William (Karen) Joslin (746-3332)
Wentworth — Milo H. Cheney (786-9945)
Wentworth's Location — Nelson Ham (483-3225)
Westmoreland — David G. Adams (399-4366)
Whitefield — Coram Bond (837-9953)
Wilmot — Susan Rayno (526-6105)
Wilton — Philip C. Heald, Jr. (878-1321)
Winchester — Mrs. William (Betsy) Ladd (239-4468)
Windham — Edward Cormier (898-9647)
Windsor — Ronald A. Houghton (478-3137)
Wolfeboro — Nancy G. Palmer (539-6510)
Woodstock — Mrs. Dalton (Mavis) Avery (745-2548)

Chairman — Hugh Gregg (882-4763)
Operations — Bruce C. Runds (744-3636)
Coordinator — James C. Chamberlin (868-9623)
Administration — Lucy Muller (669-9373)

We invite our neighbors who wish to support or take an active part in

The GEORGE BUSH Presidential Campaign to contact any one of us

A PRESIDENT WE WON'T HAVE TO TRAIN

New Hampshire Highway Hotel, Concord, New Hampshire 03301

(603) 224-6911

matter, and questioning outside parties as to whether or not the exchange between Bush and myself had actually occurred. Both Lee Atwater and Sununu aide Dave Carney were quoted. Atwater said, "To say that the president told John Sununu to cool it is just not right."

I let the matter drop rather than allow it to be blown out of proportion by the media. But Atwater's statement was misleading in its implication. Neither Dave Carney nor Lee Atwater has ever been privy to my private communications with George Bush, nor could either of them possibly know anything about our confidential relationship or that the president had written me a personal note on this particular matter.

As might have been anticipated, communication between me and the president has diminished since John Sununu joined the organization as its front man.

It began during the last week of the 1988 primary campaign when the senior staff lived on the top floor of the Clarion Hotel. Sununu was their exclusive consultant on the local situation. The views of those of us who had been in the field every day for months, supervising the on-site operations of the campaign, were not solicited.

Thereafter Judd succeeded Sununu as Governor of New Hampshire and Sununu was appointed Bush's chief of staff. Neither the Bush staff nor the governor appeared to remember that it was Judd who had assisted in leading the Bush forces for ten years, having turned over his own political organization to Bush in 1979.

It was the original Reagan crew of 1976, added to Judd's workers (he was an executive councilor and four-term congressman before being elected governor), plus all the new supporters we had enlisted in the 1980 and 1984 efforts, which formed the basis of what eventually developed into a combined force for Bush in 1988.

More than half of the full-time volunteers came from these sources. Bush's comeback after Iowa was largely due to the exertion of such long-term stalwarts as Rita Palmer, Ruth Griffin, Cathy Cummings, Kim Zachos, Davy Gregg, and Dave Currier.

On the professional side, my personal assistant, Georgi Hippauf, was a full-time member of the traveling staff in charge of our temporary offices, located all over the state. Judd had provided his top field organizer, Steve Edwards, to guide the advance group—also on a full-time basis.

Obviously, because Sununu never informed the media of these contributions, it has been assumed he was the one-man show who rescued George after the Iowa debacle.

Atwater inadvertently exacerbated the situation at a huge Republican event in Manchester on June 13, 1989. He referred to Judd Gregg by praising the "three years" Judd had "worked hard" for George Bush. Long-time Bush supporters were upset that Atwater did not know it was Judd who helped lead the troops for George Bush a whole nine years before Sununu conceded to board the burgeoning bandwagon.

But, such perturbations are within the normal perils of politics. Some critics may interpret the above as sour grapes or irrelevant. But that's the way it was and John Sununu was an important player.

President Bush returned to New Hampshire the month after his inauguration on the pretext of addressing a business group, but in fact "to thank you, New Hampshire," once again, for its part in his good fortune. It was as though I'd come full circle, invited as one of the greeters lucky enough to shake his hand as he moved toward the VIP's sponsoring the event.

"Hugh," he teased, "never thought I'd see you in a greeting line. It's come to this?"

George Bush and John Harrigan jogging in Jefferson, 1979. (Coos County Democrat)

CHAPTER 8

Image: "Mirror, Mirror, On the Wall"

This chapter re-examines and analyzes some of the circumstances and conduct that affected the public images of Rockefeller, Reagan, and Bush.

The success of a winning candidate is predominantly based on his image as a "winner." Some individuals are sadly labeled "losers," probably because they look or act like losers.

It is one's perception of people or events which creates that initial positive or negative image in our individual or collective minds. Through whatever occurs after this first impression is made, we tend to perpetuate a negative or positive instinct, or feeling, which deepens into what we come to believe is pure fact.

Campaign planning begins by analyzing the candidate's strengths and flaws, then devising a strategy based on the presentation of the candidate in the best possible light, literally and figuratively. What can compound the challenge is the correction of any public misperception of a well-known candidate, in which case there may be a lot of image rebuilding to do before an agreeable persona can be fabricated.

Winning is the goal of a political campaign. Image is what makes it happen. The citizen's perception of a candidate, often deliberately created or modified by events, publicity, or propaganda, determines how he or she will vote.

It's not necessarily the best aspirant who gets elected; rather, it's the one who makes the best impression. Spontaneous events and packaging frequently decide presidencies.

An example of unanticipated circumstances changing the course of history was Rockefeller's undoing in New Hampshire. He was defeated by an invisible candidate. The oddity of that episode was its dependence upon our write-in system which, while workable at that time, is no longer practical. The case also differed from 1952 when Eisenhower, in absentia, beat Taft because the general's name was on the ballot and he was a national hero.

The clever crafters who sponsored Lodge had taken advantage of public sentiment that sought an alternative to both Goldwater and Rockefeller. While obviously serious in their endeavor, their venture was undertaken partially as a fun exercise, never really anticipating victory.

It was generally agreed by Ted White and other authoritative observers that most of the votes for Lodge would otherwise have gone to Rockefeller, which would have given him a comfortable margin over Goldwater. Instead, the ghost of Lodge disappeared and Rockefeller's loss here allowed Goldwater to emerge as the front-runner for the presidential nomination.

Goldwater went on to a bad defeat in the fall. We'll never know how Rocky might have done had he been the Republican nominee, but his knockout in New Hampshire by a nonparticipant was a singular phenomenon which no one could have predicted when he announced his candidacy. At that time he even had Lodge's pledge of support.

The Nashua debate was another occasion when an event might have influenced the outcome of an election. In my view Reagan probably would have defeated Bush in 1980 anyway, because his exertion was buttressed by the loyal remnants of his campaign organization from 1976. They simply had lain back until he returned to the state after the Iowa caucus, at which time he personally rekindled their enthusiasm.

George Bush had been totally unknown, an asterisk, when he began. Had it not been for the disastrous effect of the Nashua debacle he probably would have come much closer to upsetting Reagan. A near-finish by Bush might well have been interpreted by the media as a win, like it did for McCarthy in 1968 and for McGovern in 1972. A perceived win by Bush following so quickly the "Big Mo" from Iowa could well have spelled curtains for Reagan.

The prime example of perception gone awry was Reagan's misfortune in his 1976 contest against Ford. Again, it was a classic case of an underdog running to unseat a powerful incumbent. Reagan probably would have garnered more votes than the president if the last-minute 55% prediction from Governor Thomson had not received such wide publicity and credibility. If Reagan had numerically defeated the president or was even perceived as having won our Primary, possibly Ford would have withdrawn as President Johnson had done when he saw the handwriting on the wall in 1968.

Until the 55% margin prophecy, our plan of building a solid case with the political analysts that we did not have to get more votes than Ford to be called "winner" was working well. In fact, it was substantially strengthened when I upped our original estimate of 40%, which had been somewhat suspect, to what most reporters believed to be a more realistic 45%. It was then conceded to be a generally fair appraisal, supported by some of the polls.

Thus, before Thomson got into the act the media had indicated that anything within a few percentage points of Ford's total would have been viewed as victory for Reagan. Yet, because of Thomson's untimely sophistry, when Reagan came within two points of beating Ford, the Californian was written off in the press as a loser. The depressing effect of that impression carried over to the succeeding Florida Primary and effectively put a damper on his national effort.

The warning from this lesson is that no matter how successfully one may have framed the candidate's profile as a campaign tactic, it can be squashed overnight by a shift of media consensus.

Today, candidates, in some cases perhaps unknowingly, are more subject to the whims of their professional managers than they were in the freewheeling days of Rockefeller. Rocky's New Hampshire travels were not accompanied by a big staff, nor did any of them appear concerned with his demeanor, dress, or dramatizations.

Rocky's style was singularly Rocky's, and he did things as they came naturally. Even in dealing with the issues he was atypical, intimately familiar with how state government was run. In 1962 he had given three lectures at Harvard entitled "The Future of Federalism," in which he said, "The preservation of states' rights depends upon the exercise of states' responsibilities." He needed no help in promoting this philosophy.

His recent remarriage was something he could not handle by himself. Happy's having left her children rankled many people. It became a cloud over his every activity. When we tried to dispel its unfavorable aspects by presenting them in joint appearances, the disapprobation persisted. As cooperative and congenial as she tried to be, it did not seem to work. When she became pregnant the problem intensified.

Rocky's domestic situation had created an unfavorable perception of the man which neither he nor we could dislodge. It had nothing to do with the candidate's qualifications to serve as president, yet it was this imperfection which became a major stumbling block in 1964. Ten years later, when Ford chose Rockefeller as his vice president, the doubt was no longer a paramount issue—a good demonstration of how fickle the public mind can be.

Meanwhile the four parents of the Lodge movement didn't bother to create any images. They didn't have to. Their candidate was remembered for his service as Ambassador to the United Nations under Eisenhower and as a disciple of the popular president. He was then a Republican serving in a Democratic administration. New Hampshire didn't want either Rockefeller or Goldwater. It was the rare political circumstance where no packaging was necessary. He got the votes just by not being in the right place at the right time.

When Governor Reagan first came to New Hampshire he was received as a Hollywood celebrity. His recognition for years of service as governor of California was overshadowed by his reputation as a movie actor. The average voter knew little of his record in government nor about his views on national issues. They knew even less about Ford, who, from nowhere, had suddenly vaulted to public attention by assuming the presidency. Probably both started out pretty much in the same playing field.

Basically, the Granite State has always reflected a conservative political philosophy. Reagan's persuasions fit the same pattern. Thus, it was easy for Sears to connect the candidate to our ideology. For contrast he seized upon so-called liberal tendencies in Ford's record. The campaign was to be a model of a conservative running against a liberal. Ford played into the strategy by attempting to paint Reagan as being too far to the right to be electable. These perceptions of the two candidates persisted throughout the campaign, though Ford's managers tried to present their man as a moderate.

Senator Cotton had been elected to Congress at the same time as Ford. Because they were good friends, Cotton agreed to be the president's honorary chairman. Still, Cotton was an acknowledged conservative. His statement about Reagan being "his kind of fellow" played right into Sears' hand—precisely the message Sears was trying to convey.

In the end it was only the power of the incumbency which prevailed over New Hampshire's conservative impulse.

President Ford was reputed as having a boy-scout-like political style. Though people knew little of his background, many were sympathetic to his sudden succession to power. He was not likely to disparage any opponent in his reelection effort. For an adversary to be critical of Ford's short and unanticipated term in office could backfire.

Thus it was determined that Reagan's campaign likeness would be that of a "Mr. Clean." This theme fit well with the governor's basic conviction that one should speak no evil of another, particularly in the interest of party solidarity. Thus had emerged Reagan's Eleventh Commandment, "Thou shalt speak no ill of any Republican."

This one sentence created a kindly image which served Reagan well throughout his subsequent political career.

———

The images of both Rockefeller and Reagan were few and straight-forward as compared to the innumerable varying perceptions people have of George Bush. It's doubtful that any candidate for the presidency of either party has been seen from as many conflicting viewpoints when trekking the campaign trail here. Opinions have been formed from malicious rumors perpetrated by antagonists; other views evolved reasonably from George's own background and demeanor.

Bill Loeb was the master at painting his adversaries with a tainted brush. He marked Bush with all kinds of unfavorable traits, but probably his culminating success was his stroke with the Trilateral issue. When he first tagged George as a Trilateralist, I and many others had never heard of the association.

As the Manchester *Union Leader* news stories began to run, the question most consistently asked of Bush was, "Who are the Trilateralists?" Then, when Bill's editorials began to heat up the issue by defaming the organization, the question became, "What was your affiliation with the Trilateralists?"

In the final phase Loeb matured the perception to the conclusion that the Trilateralists represented an anti-American clique and Bush was an active advocate. No matter that George had resigned from the group before coming to New Hampshire and that its membership included such conservatives as Caspar Weinberger, who was Reagan's state director of finance.

Bush claimed Texas as his residence, but he never came off to us in New England as our vision of a John Connally or a hard-riding Texas Ranger. In fact, Reagan was closer to our vision of the Marlboro Man—at least he could ride a horse.

Fortunately or unfortunately, as the case may be, Bush was

the product of Phillips Andover Academy in Massachusetts, Yale University, and a socially prominent family in Connecticut. Furthermore, the family summered in Maine, where George was most happy when relaxing at the family's expansive Kennebunkport estate.

It was this background which logically gave rise to his "preppy" image, a denotation adopted for quick characterization by the press. The candidate himself, in the early days, made no effort to shake off the impression. Being familiar with its genesis, we were not much bothered by it either and certainly no one here took seriously his claim of being a Texan. At the same time he never quite qualified as a New Englander. He was almost a man without a state.

His casual demeanor, sporty dress and Ivy League mien were both familiar and tolerable. Being aware of his extensive record of public service we recognized Bush's rather homespun modesty as the nature of the man. But when the national media began paying attention to our campaign and interpreting "preppy" to mean "lightweight," it became obvious that the definition or the candidate would have to change.

George, sensing the criticism, converted his style to a more dignified approach. In public appearances his dress was more formal, off-the-cuff remarks were more carefully considered, and he projected himself with greater stateliness. By the time he reached the White House the columnists were no longer using "preppy" to describe the vice president. Had this alteration not been brought about, his political career might well have ended right here in New Hampshire.

Images are sometimes also manufactured as the objectives of long-range strategy. The 1980 Reagan-Bush contest lent itself ideally to such an opportunity. Author Richard J. Whalen wrote in the *New York Times* Sunday magazine that there was a question of whether Reagan would apply himself hard enough "because of his 9-to-5 routine as governor and his undisguised enjoyment of loafing." We had learned from working with the governor in 1976 that his inclination to work short hours might be promoted into a campaign vulnerability.

There was the additional potential liability of age. In 1979 Reagan was sixty-eight years old, which meant he would be seventy-three at the end of his first term as president and seventy-seven at the end of his second. This seemed to us a good issue, particularly if combined with a fatigue factor. But these were distinctions of a very sensitive nature which, if attacked directly, would have generated calamitous backlash. In 1980 I had already put my foot in it with the Reagans when I'd earlier suggested that maybe he was shopworn from earlier campaigns.

Luckily, we had a sharp contrast with George Bush who was an exceptionally vigorous fifty-five. Our plan was to take no public cognizance of Reagan's age or his work habits. Rather, we would overaccentuate the vitality of our candidate. All of his schedules were prepared to emphasize the robustness of his physical stamina. He traveled tediously long hours with strenuous exercise whenever feasible.

This explains the early-morning departures, aerobics at the Concord YMCA, and routine jogging. The photo taken of his sprinting with John Harrigan became a trademark of the campaign. We had it cropped and reproduced on a 3 1/2-by-4-inch handout card entitled "Join a Front Runner" and distributed it with George's every handshake.

The voters perhaps knew little of Bush's stand on the issues, but everyone was aware that he was a mighty healthy character fully capable of undertaking the strenuous schedules and tensions of the presidency. Whether they ever made the comparison to Reagan was questionable.

In 1988 the Bush handlers introduced a form of disinformation to create a negative impression of his opponent. Radio and TV ads were designed to insinuate that Senator Dole was sympathetic to tax increases, a position opposite to that of Bush. It was not true, of course.

This form of maligning his foes was sharpened in the fall of the year when the vice president fused the perception that his democratic adversary, Michael Dukakis, was unpatriotic, soft on crime, and indifferent to the environment.

Lying about an opponent was perhaps commonplace back in the rough-and-tumble political days at the turn of the century. More recently, candidates had become more respectful of each other. But again, there appears to be developing an increased trend for one aspirant to attack another with a great degree of acrimony.

I don't suppose bitterness between contestants is any worse than it ever was, yet it now seems more visible. While such truculence may make headlines, it demeans the process and turns off large blocks of potential voters. A far call from Reagan's Eleventh Commandment.

———

A candidate's image must relate positively to the electorate which determines his fate. This can give rise to a troublesome dichotomy for the presidential aspirant who starts his campaign trail here, then continues in other states. The importance of media perception in this first Primary means the candidate must concentrate on appealing to the concerns of our voters, which may not necessarily be reflective of the country as a whole. He or she might say, like Goldwater did in appealing to our conservative bent, that Social Security should be voluntary, whereas such a statement would be fatal in the broader national arena.

It is therefore essential in designing a campaign plan first to understand some of the problems of a state before making the rounds. For example, because of our reliance on natural resources, we are worried about the specific environmental effects of acid rain. The experts tell us this curse is ruining our lakes and forests. They say the damage comes from the industrial smokestacks of the Midwest. If a candidate promises to make us happy by muzzling those pollution-producing plants, he or she may become mired in controversy later on in Michigan, Illinois, or Ohio.

As the home of the Seabrook nuclear power plant, New Hampshire places a special significance on the universally controversial issue of nuclear energy. For nearly two decades it has been a major bone of contention between the proponents and detractors. Located on the Massachusetts border, its safety has been a thorn in the sides of many out-of-state neighboring communities. While violently opposed by the government of the Bay State, it has been encouraged by ours.

The candidates campaigning here have been unable to dismiss the nuclear plant as a purely local problem. When Massachusetts Governor Dukakis ran on the Democratic ticket in 1988, his stance against Seabrook was clear-cut. Conversely, Bush was perceived as favoring nuclear energy, though not the Seabrook plant specifically unless it established foolproof safeguards. Again, it was a case of what plays well in one state and not in another.

Because New Hampshire is the Primary state where the greatest percentage of its citizens meet the candidates face to face, it's also important for the contestants to know something of its ethnic and economic base, from which political opinions are formed. It is true, for example, that we have a small number of blacks and hispanics, although these and other minority groups are rapidly increasing. Time spent in defining issues of concern to them is not likely to receive much attention from our voters.

When Rockefeller ran in the sixties, our labor force was primarily employed in the relatively low-wage textile and leather industries. Today these factories have been replaced by computer-related and high-tech firms. By 1988 the state had the lowest rate of unemployment in the nation and ranked fifth in per capita income, resulting in a more sophisticated population which seeks greater substance in its candidates for any office.

Woe to the speaker who does not endorse a sincere belief in the value of the New Hampshire Primary system. Should he make it to the White House and thus become titular head of the Republican party, it is imperative that he accept this tenet if he expects our vote. Besides, it gives status to our political job-seekers when they go to Washington.

We are fortunate that Reagan and Bush, perhaps inspired by the euphoria of New Hampshire victory, have pledged their support to the continuance of our Primary. All Democratic winners have made the same commitment.

A candidate can also self-destruct if he shows the slightest inclination of considering new taxes. We're proud to join Alaska in being the only other state without a sales or earned-income tax. It's a death warrant for a candidate to come here with any opposite views on either of these two issues.

Of course images could be easily created and retained if candidates never had to react to controversial subjects not on their primed list. But it doesn't happen that way. There's always someone on the stump who will ask some obtuse question which is not deftly handled. Or there's the careless or fuzzy answer to a thoughtful inquiry which gets blown out of context by the press. These situations concoct unintended, instant images which often harrass the candidate henceforth, such as Dole's "Stop lying about my record" remark.

It is political legend that politicians kiss babies to demonstrate their love for children. But today this deportment has snowballed into a wide variety of carefully structured scenarios to assert the depth of the candidate's interest in all things.

To illustrate, a sampling of Bush's travels in 1987-88 took him to Hubbard Farms Chicken Hatchery in Walpole, the General Electric meter plant in Somersworth, a demonstration of the Air Force Thunderbirds at Pease Air Base, an Old Home Day parade in Londonderry, a Franco-American reception at the Alpine Club in Manchester, the Apollo Computer Company in Exeter, a student assembly at Berlin High School, the submarine USS Groton at the Portsmouth Naval Shipyard, the East Coast Lumber Company in Hampstead, Lane House Senior Center in Littleton, the Exit 3 Truck Stop in Greenland, First Night festivities in Concord, and a graduation at the University of New Hampshire in Durham.

In each of these diverse surroundings the candidate must profess both knowledge and concern in the profession or activity of the people involved. Usually the facility or the event is well cased by Advance to ascertain there will be no surprises and that the candidate knows exactly what to expect. How well he performs in these situations sets the image for the day and sometimes, maybe, even for the entire campaign.

Jean Davidson of the *Los Angeles Times* concluded, "Americans choose their elected leaders, in part, the same way they buy vegetables—by appearance." She's probably right. Just think of how many times you've been fooled by a melon.

It's probably unjust that a man's natural stature and appearance can affect votes. Republican presidents elected of late tend to be tall. Senator Howard Baker, a short man, was somewhat disadvantaged when running against Bush. We were always trying to snap a good photo of the two men standing next to each other to exploit the contrast.

Though beards may be popular again, you will note that all Republicans have been clean-shaven. The last major candidate to sport even a mustache was Tom Dewey—and he lost. Notably, Lyn Nofziger didn't look like a Fuller Brush ad until after he had been around the track as a smooth-faced cherub in Reagan's first campaign.

The candidate's wardrobe also sets a tone. I don't recall any Republican candidate regularly appearing on the trail here who did not wear a suit, usually dark, and the customary necktie. They do dress down for such events as parades and outings, to look down-home. But between the Secret Service, when involved, and the candidate's aides, who are usually similarly attired, it sometimes looks as if the Mafia had arrived. I have always enjoyed Democratic Senator Paul Simon's unorthodox bow tie,which set him apart. But, to be fair, he never ran well.

Wives and family probably take as much abuse in a campaign as the candidate, yet they must not be too outspoken lest they upstage or embarrass him. It is rare that an elegant, eloquent

Elizabeth Dole appears as reserve firepower, and uncommon to have a bevy of articulate, congenial children, as is George Bush's good fortune.

A candidate's wife, in particular, shares the spotlight with her husband in the mind of the public. In Reagan's case, it made no difference. With Rockefeller, it probably cost him the election. In Bush's situation, family was a distinct advantage. The active participation of Barbara and their children added new constituencies of their own.

Religious affiliation, or at least the appearance thereof, is also necessary. A candidate for the U.S. presidency must have a fundamental belief in God. They've all made it a practice to attend church services on the Sabbath, whenever possible. Reverend Pat Robertson brought a new dimension to this identification when he said, "This is God who's commanding me." In his case, his preoccupation with the ministry probably frightened many of those concerned about preserving the traditional separation of church and state.

The number and attitude of the staff surrounding the candidate may take a toll on well-wishers. Anyone running in our Primary needs at least one aide by his side at all times to assist in recognizing and recording names of greeters, supporters, and incidents of special significance. If this aide is totally unpretentious, it strengthens their joint acceptance. Bush has been very discerning in his choice of men like Dave Bates and Tim McBride for this responsibility.

If other attendants mix into the reception routine, I've watched voters turn away in disgust, as they sensed it wasn't worth trying to reach the candidate himself.

When a voter meets a candidate, there's something very reassuring about a good, firm handshake. It may have something to do with our lineage as rugged New England settlers, or perhaps from our zesty, continued independence in matters of state, but our impression of vote-seeking foreigners can go sour if they don't come off as solid as "The Old Man," the rocky profile which is our state symbol.

Nor are Granite Staters suckered by shams like Bush's attempt to adopt Kansas-born-and-raised Dole's "I am one of you" winning slogan used in Iowa. Humorously referring to Senator Biden's purloin of another's rhetoric, George tried to prove he was "one of us" by citing his birth in Massachusetts, education in Connecticut, and summer home in Maine. He dropped the idea after a couple of test runs.

Convincing evidence of a candidate's popularity is for many people the relative size of the crowds that turn out for him. For observers it is often proof of support, even though curiosity may be the only motive for many attendees. So, it usually always pays to entice as many listeners as possible whenever the office-seeker appears in public. That's why well-organized student groups such as those enticed by John Bush, moving from meeting to meeting, chanting and carrying placards, are effective in generating fervor. If the clamor is well staged, the candidate's image is aggrandized.

In addition to gathering good crowds for Reagan's Citizens' Press Conferences in 1976, we often found people were embarrased to ask the first question. Reagan, after waiting a few seconds, would say, "If you don't ask me some questions, I'm likely to make a fifteen-minute speech!" Then we'd have a shill pop up from the audience with a loaded inquiry on subject matter Reagan knew well. Just like warming up the audience for a TV quiz show, the ploy got the meeting off to a good start and made him look especially well-versed.

Humor can be a beneficial ingredient, too. Reagan was the pro, even using old saws: "It's been said that government is the second eldest profession, but I sometimes think it bears resemblance to the oldest."

The Canadians are the real masters of political parody, as their Rhinoceros party adheres to no national boundary and has run its own candidates for the U.S. presidency. One plank of its platform required driving on the left-hand side of the road as in England, but the new regulations would be edged in gradually, applying only to trucks during the first year.

Regardless of what their schedules may prescribe, there is always the dilemma of whether a candidate should appear rushed or relaxed when moving through a crowd. Sometimes it helps to project the image of "our man on the move." Yet, if he doesn't stop long enough to answer Granny Gert's query on Social Security, she may not vote for him.

The one thing the candidate cannot afford is to give the media any opportunity of inferring that he's not terribly busy. This is why we always publish tight schedules. The candidate's down time is carefully hidden within the surplus time allowed for some events.

Ground transportation for one candidate may contrast dramatically with another's. A White House incumbent is automatically locked into a long motorcade. But the degree to which this cumbersome procession is allowed to interrupt normal traffic flow can test the tolerance of other motorists. In almost every campaign it becomes a sure matter for negative editorial comment. Yet, considering the security precautions required, there is little a president or vice president can do to alleviate the disruption.

In the early stages of a campaign or when a candidate does not have Secret Service protection, there is the Hobson's Choice of arriving with the whoop and holler of a large entourage of aides and henchmen, or rather modestly stepping down from his car with one or two supporting vehicles behind. For a major candidate with a large press following, traveling by bus is the most practical solution.

The contrasts of these varying patterns must send a message to the bystander, though I have never concluded how it should be interpreted. In 1980 Reagan had the retinue and Bush did not. In 1988 Bush had the retinue and Dole did not. In both instances the long line won. Maybe that should tell us something.

For me, however, it has always been an amusing aside that it's standard practice to use exclusively dark-colored sedans and vans in these caravans. With their lights on, the cortege can be taken for a funeral which, in some cases, it turned out to be.

A standard orthodox practice of bolstering one's image is to play off the reputation of another respected person. Rocky never felt he needed to bask in the reflected glory of anyone else. Other aspirants have felt their prestige in New Hampshire was enriched by importing notables to buttress their cause. It's a "good guy by association" theory frequently followed when a face lift is needed. Reagan used Lloyd Nolan, Ford called upon Elliott Richardson, Rogers Morton, and Henry Cabot Lodge, while Bush brought in Senator Goldwater, Ted Williams, and Chuck Yeager. It's my guess they were dreaming if they really believed the popularity of one person could be transferred to another.

It is conceded that more often than not the big names draw a larger crowd than the candidate would have attracted by himself. Of course, free lottery tickets would probably do the same thing.

In summary, favorable public perception is the lifeblood of a successful candidate. The ultimate objective is its transfusion throughout the whole network of his or her electioneering anatomy.

The next three chapters will illustrate how it is pumped into the campaign bloodstream through organization, the professionals used, and media.

How much are these elements influencing the electorate?

CHAPTER 9

Ode to the Organization

(Author's comment: Unless the reader is interested in the nuts and bolts of how a campaign is managed in New Hampshire, I would suggest skimming this chapter.)

The organization can play a vital role in a candidate's success, though it's not a necessary ingredient to winning. As previously mentioned, Rockefeller and Goldwater, both of whom were well organized in 1964, were defeated in New Hampshire by Henry Cabot Lodge, who had no organization whatsoever nor a pretense of one.

The mechanics of an effective, well-oiled organization normally function quietly and with discipline, the administration privately devising a plan and implementing strategy, without fanfare. It is frequently ignored by the media, except for passing observation, because newsmen have no way of measuring the experience or potential effectiveness of the people involved. Also, reporters are naturally skeptical of the leadership's boastful claims.

In 1976, for example, we established Reagan's credibility as a candidate running against an incumbent president by publishing the identity of a chairman in every community. The recruitment of such a statewide network was a noteworthy accomplishment, yet the sole concern of the media was to verify the list's accuracy.

The press never attempted to discern its impact on or importance to the overall effort.

Conversely, the organizers themselves may choose to keep secret the extent of their efforts, in order to surprise the opposition on election day. All of which leads to the conclusion that favorable public perception of campaign organizations, per se, is generally not the most important factor in the image competition.

Nonetheless, in many campaigns it is the candidate with the strongest organization who comes out on top, as with the Bush campaign of 1988 in New Hampshire. In 1980 Bush had drawn together a dedicated group of loyalists whose sphere of influence grew larger in the Reagan/Bush reelection effort of 1984, and thus was firmly in place long before 1988. None of the other major aspirants came close to the Bush grass-roots groundwork.

The ultimate objective of the organization is to get out the vote on Election Day. This requires building a framework of dependable political workers in each community who take responsibility for determining the voting preference of every voter within their respective jurisdiction and, more importantly, being certain that the favorable ones cast their ballots. It usually operates similar to a military hierarchy under a general chairman and a steering committee, with regional or county chairmen supervising town and ward chairmen.

A victorious organization depends heavily on extensive door-knocking. Its members must personally proselytize the voter at his home, on the street, or at his workplace. Support cannot be accurately measured from the numbers who may or may not turn out for a candidate's appearances. A good organization has no need for random professional polling as it is aware of its strength from its own sweeping canvass.

Traditionally, a state chairman is chosen from recognized political leaders who themselves have been candidates in statewide campaigns. Assuming the presidential candidate is not an incumbent or a vice president, the local state chairman is given considerable autonomy in the operation of the campaign.

The contrast was evident between the authority we had in directing Rockefeller in 1964 and the lack of absolute authority given to the leaders for President Ford in 1976, or to Vice President Bush's leaders in 1988.

The interplay between the candidate, the campaign director, and the local staff provides an interesting contrast from one campaign to another. Rocky was unusually solicitous, Reagan was not, and Bush made little effort to intermingle unless it was integral to a specific campaign maneuver or an activity arranged by the campaign director.

The styles of the three candidates contrasted most interestingly at the beginning of their campaigns. Rocky would pitch right in, whereas Reagan kept a studied distance. Bush was more reserved, less effusive. He seemed a private man pivoting in a public place. All three were keen competitors, though Bush was less tough-skinned (though undetectably) than Rocky. Reagan was generally slick as veneer, Teflon-coated, rarely showing a blemish.

The local chairman's team is the personal network that extends his energy, multiplies his contacts, and broadens his reach. The loyalty of this team and its esprit de corps are what make a headquarters radiate an external energy and optimism—contributing to the positive image of a winner!

A dynamic, competent staff generates enthusiasm and attracts new participants to the cause. Amicable relations between this group and the candidate's imported professional staff can greatly enhance the effectiveness of both.

This theory is proven by the practice of members of Congress who succeed in serving their constituencies by enlisting an in-state staff which is trusted, respected, and well known to the citizens of the constituency. It is not customary to bring in the Washington professionals to support New Hampshire aides. As confidence in the surrogates grows among the populace, so does local satisfaction.

Considerable effort is always made to enlist civic leaders as cochairs at every level, people whose good names lend credibility to the candidate. Another goal which has not changed in forty years is the assignment of popular, identifiable chairmen in every precinct of the state.

In the national picture the influence of Granite State delegates to the Republican National Convention is miniscule as, at maximum, we are entitled only to a couple dozen of the over two thousand delegates in attendance. Back in the Rockefeller days, delegates were listed on the ballot independent of their preferred presidential nominee, and thus were of direct assistance in getting out the vote, both for themselves and their candidate.

Under current procedures, delegates are no longer on the ballot; rather, they are handpicked exclusively by the winning presidential candidates in proportion to the number of votes received. This system offers the opportunity of enlisting politically influential citizens to fill the delegate slots while not requiring any substantial contribution from them. The organization gets the benefit of an impressive VIP list to enhance its candidate's credibility.

Volunteers at every rung of the hierarchy are attracted to a campaign for various reasons. Some join up out of sincere, dedicated principle, or loyalty to the cause, to the candidate, or to the party. Others look upon it as an opportunity to extend social relationships, or perhaps with a self-serving objective of furthering their own professional or political interests.

In New Hampshire the majority of volunteers seem genuinely interested in good government and consider their services as a contribution to it. Others are political animals—quadrennials who don't want to be left out of the excitement, though extremely valuable for their experience and hard work.

In 1979 we introduced the "Zekes," extraordinary young men and women, most of them recent college graduates, who sought active participation in the Bush campaign. They began applying for positions early in the year, some from out-of-state, some with limited experience in local or congressional races, all earnest to learn more about hands-on campaigning. Unlike all other volunteers they were given a nominal salary, to cover only their most basic expenses.

The Zekes served as personal contacts between the campaign director and his chairmen at all levels. They became the field workers, with a variety of responsibilities ranging from the recruitment and nurturing of local chairmen and key volunteers, to all sorts of support services including responsibility for supervising local events where the candidate was to appear. Blowing up balloons, setting up signs, and organizing cheering sections for enthusiastic welcomes were only a few of the tasks they undertook.

Having served well in their novitiate, many of the Zekes who have been mentioned in this book are now successful political operatives in both New Hampshire and Washington. With the developing sophistication of staging presidential candidate appearances, some of the duties the Zekes performed are now executed by more professional advance personnel. Nonetheless, ambitious apprentices have been used in every campaign since 1979 and are now essential to a well-rounded operation.

The recruiting, assignment, and control of the vast number of volunteers which make up the core of an effective organization statewide, require a multitude of support services. The basics have changed little since 1950, but some procedures have been eased and expedited by today's technology.

Names, addresses, phone numbers, and other pertinent information of all supporters and workers were previously recorded on 3-by-5 or 5-by-8-inch index cards, filed alphabetically in steel or wooden drawers. Different colors were used for quick delineation of assignment categories. These files were the crux of the organization and were continuously annotated and updated.

Maintenance of these records required hands-on, personal attention from the staff, and constant reference thereto reinforced familiarity and recognition with both the names and the individuals involved. When lists of participants were needed, appropriate cards were culled and information was hand-typed. This antiquated process of inventory was far more personal than today's computerized input, and it is much more difficult to memorize computer codes.

When I served as governor, copies of all letters from the State House were made on carbon paper. Copy machines were not in routine use, even during the Rockefeller campaign. General mailings were first prepared on nonelectric typewriters, then sent to the printer for typesetting and reproduction.

Later, in the Reagan-Ford race of 1976, many of these manual steps were replaced by the use of electric typewriters and copiers. Now, with the introduction of computers and laser printers, supporter information is coded and production is instantaneous. Computerized graphic capability allows for promotional pieces and newsletters to be generated in-house.

Today, direct mail is limited only by the financial resources available. It is used both for fund-raising and as a vote-getting device. The professionals insist that a six-page letter is much more effective than a one-pager. For my part, the more verbose the letter, the quicker it gets to the wastebasket.

Nonetheless, a new industry was born, with the post office being the indirect beneficiary. Also, direct mail is one method of avoiding campaign expense limitations, by printing and mailing materials from out-of-state. While it is an expensive way of raising funds, it has proved profitable. When a person contributes money to a candidate, the donor will presumably support the investment with a vote. On the other hand, a letter devoted exclusively to soliciting votes is speculative as to its effectiveness.

Another useful offshoot of the general mailing is a personal letter signed by the officers of a particular trade association, civic group, or fraternal organization, directed to its members. Obviously when a particular group has a one-issue cause, such as the NRA versus gun control, a strong letter from its executive supporting the views of the group will definitely produce votes.

The need for more office space has grown commensurate with the increasingly large volunteer and professional staffs with sophisticated office equipment. When Rockefeller was the candidate we started out with four staff members, operating out of two obscure, converted bedrooms at the New Hampshire

Highway Hotel. None of us was professional, except for the two typists.

By the time we conducted Reagan's campaign twelve years later, we had graduated to easily accessed public rooms in the same hotel, with a staff of ten. Most were still volunteers, but both office and media professionals had been added.

In 1988 the Bush headquarters took over an entire house and served as the base of operations for dozens of workers, both volunteer and professional, including assistants from Washington. For the first time, the availability of the Fax machine offered lightninglike communication with the national headquarters and elsewhere. Portable lap-top computers offered flexibility on the road.

The telephone remains the staple of communication. No longer are several standard business and WATS lines sufficient for the task. Rather, intricate phone systems, complete with intercom and privacy buttons, with calls directed from a skilled receptionist, are imperative for meeting the demands of today's electioneering.

The growth of telemarketing, unknown as such twenty years ago, now plays an important part in a campaign. It is standard operating procedure for every presidential candidate to purchase lists of potential voters with their phone numbers. Telephone banks are set up in central locations, manned largely by volunteers, for several hours every day. Each operator is given a script, with thorough instructions on how to make cold calls to targeted households. How different from the "old days," when telephoning was also popular, but from quite a different approach. It was more friend to friend, neighbor to neighbor.

We used to set up phones in the private homes of certain individuals. The hit-and-miss approach was no less time-consuming but frequently more effective, for two reasons: 1) scripts were unnecessary as contacts were usually between individuals who were already personally or professionally acquainted with each other; 2) the people interviewed were less likely to be peeved by what is now regarded as an impersonal and intrusive marketing method.

Some professionals still theorize that if you can get random commitments by phone, from total strangers, such commitments can be considered valid votes counted for polling ratios. It has been my experience that the data collected in this fashion is unreliable, providing only a snapshot in time, especially as they are merely spontaneous reactions likely to change as the election approaches.

All these innovations represent increased costs which, in turn, have raised accounting standards, especially for compliance with ever-changing FEC regulations which were practically nonexistent years ago. Legal and accounting expertise is required for interpretation and control. The full-time raising and spending of larger sums of money also require additional staffing.

The amount of dollars raised in New Hampshire is inconsequential except, perhaps, as a tangible indicator of a candidate's depth of local support. Success in our first primary is critical to favorable national image perception. Thus, no candidate can afford to consider entering the national contest unless he of she has first, at least, funded the campaign here from other sources.

Loosening local purse strings for an out-of-state contenders is difficult to do in New Hampshire, because their viability is untested here. The fledgling campaign must be financially secure, which should not be a serious problem for a substantial candidate, because FEC regulations limit expenditures here to a tiny percentage of his or her national budget.

The allowance to George Bush of $440,000 for expenses in New Hampshire was less than 3% of the total amount that he had raised to finance his entire 1988 campaign. Thus, this FEC restriction to a minimum spending limit is entirely unrealistic, though the serious candidate must abide by it in order to draw federal matching funds.

In the off-years, gubernatorial and senatorial candidates have spent double the amount of money allowed for presidential candidates. In 1988 even the New Hampshire congressional district contenders spent an average of $532,000.

Obviously, this federal miscalculation places ridiculous restraints on the budget of a presidential campaign organization. The treasurer must continuously seek ways of attributing costs to other states or to the national budget, which explains why TV advertising is primarily done in Boston and nearby Massachusetts, or Vermont hotels are chosen whenever possible. A resourceful operation takes advantage of every possible legal loophole, without apprising the FEC of substantial reportable expenditures.

The influence of PACs on campaign fund-raising is controversial, but little has been discussed about the negative impact of certain FEC regulations on spending. With increasing costs for support materials and services, one might seriously wonder how any candidate will be able to conduct a meaningful campaign in the 1990s, unless there is some relief from current FEC restrictions. John Connally tried to free himself of them by not taking advantage of matching funds—an impractical handicap for most people.

Consequently, the current system of federal regulations governing spending as it applies to New Hampshire is also unrealistic and invites subterfuge. The candidate must begin campaigning here sooner and longer than in other states in order to get established, which requires a more substantial initial investment.

Of course, there are clear advantages to running for president as an incumbent. These include guaranteed, instant crowd appeal, along with Air Force I, the armored limousine, flashing lights and sirens of the motorcade, Secret Service escorts, and TV flatbeds. The incumbent has open access to military installations such as Pease Air Base and the Portsmouth Navy Yard. His organization needn't struggle for adequate media coverage, nor should they worry about the schedules of other VIPs or even the availability of accommodations, as most hotels will always find a way to book a presidential or vice presidential party.

There is, of course, a downside to the security restrictions imposed upon the chief executive. He is less able to meet New Hampshire citizens one on one. The voter may make allowance for this circumstance. Yet, perhaps subconsciously, unless the voter had close exposure to the candidate in an earlier campaign, the Granite Stater's opinion will remain somewhat reserved as he or she has been conditioned to the opportunity of talking personally with presidential aspirants.

National statistics disclose that in every election since 1976 when any incumbent sought reelection to the House, it was at least a 90% or higher certainty that he or she would be successful against all opponents. In 1988, 98% were reelected, with only six of the 406 incumbents who sought reelection being defeated, and most of the losers were ensnarled in ethics problems.

Further, as reported in the *Wall Street Journal* from a study by author Larry Makinson, "The average House race was decided by a margin of nearly three to one, or 72.6% of the vote. (George Bush's 53% margin was thought a presidential 'landslide.')"

It's an interesting dichotomy that a similar political theorem does not always apply when presidents run in New Hampshire. Estes Kefauver defeated Truman, McCarthy scared off LBJ from seeking a second term, and Reagan came within one percentage point of beating Ford. This confuses the pollsters, who are so frequently fooled when reading the minds of our electorate.

The pressure and time demands made on campaign personnel who are responsible for the handling of media have also increased substantially. Before television the foremost duty of the campaign's local press secretary was to issue news releases, which were widely distributed and usually printed.

But the day of the news release has passed. The media now demand constant, instant access to the campaign's press director, leaving little time for writing. Today's good newspeople want their phone calls answered. They are also constantly seeking out the privilege of one-on-one interviews with the candidate—a major scheduling problem. Further, the mobility of traveling TV crews has fostered a hunger for instant reaction, requiring constant stroking by the campaign spokesperson.

Within recent years, feeling the effects of TV intrusion, radio has responded with its own version of instant news by the introduction of "actualities." It is the recorded voice of the candidate fed over a phone line to a radio station for replay. Whenever there is something newsworthy to say, the candidate makes a thirty-second statement on a cassette, which is then transmitted to whatever series of radio stations will accept it.

This opportunity for instant verbal communication with the public is very convenient, particularly when the candidate is on the road with a tight campaign schedule. In some instances it amounts to free air time, which otherwise might have been a paid commercial. The judicious use of this medium will continue to be a significant promotional tool for future campaigns.

Another function of the media relations department of a campaign's formal organization is the preparation and presentation of issue papers. While these have always been an integral part of available materials on a presidential primary candidate, the issues have become far more complex, requiring considerably more expert research. The insurgence of one-issue groups has added to the sophistication of response required from a candidate, and ardent supporters of any particular cause can make overwhelming demands which have to be carefully assessed and addressed.

Overall, the demands of a more sophisticated electorate, accustomed to instant gratification, have forced a depth of expanded capability which strains both the breadth and finances of what used to be a much tighter, more centrally controlled operation.

Perhaps the most demanding duty in a headquarters office is that of the scheduler. Any major candidate is customarily besieged with invitations to address various groups or attend assorted public functions. Insofar as such invitations can be logistically slotted into a preplanned itinerary, they are welcomed opportunities for the candidate. The difficulty arises when the dates or times conflict between opportunities.

Simultaneously the scheduler must consider geographic relationships to assure there will be coverage all over the state. He or she must frequently create events in critical areas, either to fill in a time gap or to assure exposure in a community where there otherwise would be no solicited inducement to appear.

The scheduler is constantly pressed to arrange one-on-ones with individuals who have some special project, concern, or even a constructive suggestion which they insist on presenting privately to the candidate. Subsidiary to this demand is the request (often the same people) for an autographed photograph taken with the candidate, especially if he is an incumbent vice president or president. Professional photographers have always been available on contract to catch promotional situations. The recent habit of capturing personal photos of supporters in the act of greeting the candidate has made it essential to have a full-time staff photographer.

When the scheduler has committed the candidate to an appearance, it becomes a further responsibility to coordinate with advance personnel to insure the best possible attendance. Twenty years ago, when media coverage for many events was sparse, the staff did not have to worry about numbers to demonstrate support. Today, the scheduler not only attends to the candidate's itinerary, but must also coordinate with the work of others to gather a crowd and be certain that appropriate VIPs are on hand.

While joint appearances of opposing candidates have been traditional for those seeking state office in New Hampshire, the custom had not been adopted in Republican presidential races until recently. They would often speak before the same groups, but always on different days. Rockefeller, Nixon, Ford, and Reagan never confronted their opponents until 1980 when the national fervor for debates finally caught up with New Hampshire.

In both 1980 and 1988 two debates were held for some of the Republican candidates. Because of intense local interest and in-depth media coverage, these events set a new focus on campaign activity. The Nashua debate, for example, was the highwater mark in the Reagan-Bush race. While they were able to avoid such confrontations in the past, as did Goldwater in avoiding Rockefeller's challenge, the new precedent makes it unlikely that candidates can confidently refuse them in the future.

Debate arrangements place a particularly heavy strain on an organization. The scheduler must be sure that the time and location mesh with overall strategy and can be properly advanced. Formats and rules of conduct must be negotiated with the competitors and debate sponsors. Briefing of the candidate uses up an inordinate amount of time. Some participants have emphasized the importance of debates by complementing their forces with outside consultants. The shrewdest deputies must be available to provide the right postdebate spin for the media.

After almost forty years of the repeated primary process, certain traditions have emerged to which serious presidential candidates must adhere. Various sponsoring groups plan on their appearances, and some events are inevitable, such as the national debates that once were sponsored by the League of Women Voters. The serious contender cannot afford to ignore business groups, Party affairs, the New Hampshire legislature, or other similarly influential bodies. For example, all of the major candidates have appeared before the Southern New Hampshire Association of Business and Industry.

Beyond this, changing trends require the courtship of different factions, whose priorities are likely to vary from one election to another. Nowadays, special attention must be given to the various concerns of our senior citizens, and to the growing problem of child care in a changing society.

The financing of Social Security became a major problem for Goldwater in 1964, but today the funding of the system is not as controversial as are the care, welfare, and medical assistance provided for our seniors. Catastrophic health care, along with who is going to pay for it, has become a major apprehension for the elderly. Their numbers have grown substantially and they are now represented by local chapters of powerful national lobbies, such as the American Association of Retired Persons (AARP).

Little credit has been given to the Republican State Committee and its relation to the several campaign organizations. Its principal contributions during the long months of campaigning are to offer voting lists, generate an event calendar, and maintain its Concord office for the neutral use of all candidates. It also sponsors rallies, meetings, barbecues, picnics—all sorts of affairs which bring together the candidates and party faithful for a show of unity.

Similar activities are launched by town and county Republican committees, providing the rare opportunity for all the activists, regardless of the candidate they support, to join together for a common cause. Large numbers of volunteers come from the Federation of Republican Women, whose unit clubs operate independently under the aegis of the New Hampshire Federation. Were a dollar value applied to the thousands of hours so contributed, the sums would far exceed major media buys.

In those election years when the Republicans are in control of the White House, the national party is better able to allocate support to its subsidiary operations. Thus, the assistance of the Republican National Committee given to its New Hampshire affiliates in dollars, Washington tours, seminars, briefing books, and personnel always seems more effective in promoting our primary system when we have a president or vice president in the race.

The use of surrogates, many of whom are entertainers, athletes, or other politicians, can succeed in drawing a crowd, but few can address the issues. The ploy draws attention to the candidate, if only temporarily, and may work well with ethnic groups when the introduction is made by one of their respected members.

An offshoot of the surrogate practice is third-party endorsement by a prominent public figure, such as Senator Goldwater's appearance for George Bush. Many politicians doubt the value of these schemes since they bring as many enemies (guilt by association) as they do friends. There's also the underlying question of whether personal popularity can be transferred from one individual to another. Still, the organization pursues anyone whose public support may help the overall effort.

Promotional materials remain the staple of an organization. Yet they, too, have changed with the times. During the fifties, bumper stickers were an essential item, though they were then difficult to remove from the vehicle. Now they're made of easily removable plastic, but not so popular because of their profuse usage to promote other causes. Yesterday's pin-stick button also gave way, often to a cheaper stick-on label which has no appeal as a collectible.

The rental of well-placed outdoor billboards was a popular competitive strategy for candidates during the sixties, whereas today, environmental considerations have made them undesirable. Large political signs remain pretty much the same, although smaller ones are gaining in popularity.

Plastic posters ranging from one to three feet, square or rectangular, are now offered to supporters in far greater quantities than ever before. They are sometimes mounted on sticks for rally demonstrations, or stuck in the front yards of private homes. Their proliferation became such that the state was obliged to pass legislation limiting the time periods when they may be displayed. It was this type of sign which President Bush's nephew, John, used so successfully on Primary Day in 1988 to promote his uncle.

Development of videocassettes led to their first widespread campaign use in 1988. Some candidates generated tapes which defined their positions on issues, while others created dramatic biographical presentations. Pat Robertson completed a huge general mailing of his cassettes. The Kemp organization, on the other hand, invited voters to the homes of their supporters to see him on VCRs in a comfortable atmosphere where the merits of their candidate could be discussed informally.

Before the New Hampshire primary system was legalized in 1952, a candidate running for statewide office would talk to the political leaders of each community and they, in turn, would get out the vote. This procedure was obsolesced by Senator Estes Kefauver, who introduced the personal touch from voter to voter. Radio and newspaper advertising were not then commanding the major share of the campaign budget.

Today, the cost of television advertisements added to the use of radio and print media can approximate fifty percent of the total monies spent on a campaign—the largest single expense—and the funds must be apportioned wisely. Thus, the media advisor has taken on an increasingly critical role, becoming an integral part of the campaign structure to assist the strategists in their overall planning. This emergence of media as pivotal to the basic organization is a direct result of television's tremendous influence on political campaigns.

On five occasions the presumed last-minute front-runners in the New Hampshire presidential primaries have been upset by challengers: 1952, General Eisenhower over Senator Taft and Senator Kefauver over President Truman; 1964, Ambassador Lodge over Governor Rockefeller; 1984, Senator Hart over Vice President Mondale; and 1988, Vice President Bush over Senator Dole.

An effective primary organization should have managed to get an accurate reading of how the majority of its own party activists would vote prior to Election Day. The big unknown is the Independents. The number of registered Independents has always exceeded 30% of the Granite State's total voters. It's interesting to note that there are more of them than registered Democrats.

It may be fortunate that the majority of Independents do not vote in primaries. They fear that by doing so they will lose their Independent status. Yet our rules do make it possible for them to re-establish their Independent status by reregistering, after they have voted in a Primary where they necessarily, though temporarily, had to select one of the two parties. There is no way of safely predicting how many of them will pick up a Republican or Democratic ballot or, more importantly, whose name they might select. When an Independent does vote, it's usually "for the man" and not on party issues.

Because of the potential influence which Independents might wield in a Primary, they are aggressively solicited by the organizations of both parties. All of our general mailings and voter identification procedures are directed to them with the same zeal as to

Republicans. Nonetheless, it is difficult to gauge their reaction. Many tend not to be particularly political and seldom even vote in general elections. Others do not decide on a course of action until shortly before the polls open.

In addition to the approximately 100,000 registered Independents who have never voted in a Primary, another untapped, sizable source of potential support are the more than 250,000 individuals over the age of 18 who have never registered. Among them are many young people who can be reached through the high schools and colleges visited by the candidates. But until someone comes along with an overall program to provoke their interest in government, this segment of the population will continue to be absent on Primary Day. A change in their attitude could substantially affect future presidential elections.

Frequently overlooked are the potential votes of those Republicans or Independents who are unable to make it to the polls on Election Day. The bulk of this group are citizens enlisted in the military or business people who are temporarily out-of-state.

A resourceful Vermonter was innovative in using modern communications to secure a last-minute absentee vote. On election eve he faxed ballots to neighbors who were visiting in California. They returned them by overnight Federal Express in time to be counted at the polls. The deputy secretary of state said, "I don't think that the people who drafted the absentee ballot laws in the eighteenth century knew about fax machines," but he believed the faxing would probably be an allowable substitute for a mailed ballot.

Even without armed conflict, thousands of New Hampshire men and women are serving all over the world in government or armed services for our country, most of whom are never approached for absentee ballots. Then, too, there are substantial numbers of handicapped or elderly who are confined to nursing or retirement homes.

Obviously there are great diversities of interest between these groups, challenging a well-run operation to develop issues of appeal for each of them. All candidates normally visit a maximum number of the confinement facilities for the handicapped and elderly, where the aspirants have the advantage of an attentive resident audience which will usually assemble in a community room to hear them.

But the key to securing the votes of our institutionalized citizens is for the candidate's volunteers to ascertain that the favorable ones are properly registered. If they are shut-ins, the organization must arrange for them to vote by absentee ballot. If they are mobile, transportation to the polls must be provided on Election Day. With an ever-increasing elderly population these procedures will demand more attention as we approach the next century.

When responding to solicitations, whether in person or by phone, Republicans who have made a choice will usually admit it. Some, in an effort to demonstrate the strength of their candidate, will name others who are of like mind. Thus, it does not take long to get a sense of how the campaign is going.

It is essential that a successful organization remain alert to what competitors and their organizations are doing. A tougher job is determining the opposition's internal strategies. When their plans can be anticipated, disastrous surprises can be avoided and counteractions prepared. It becomes imperative to have friends in the media who frequently have such information.

Another good source is dissidents who leave other campaigns, either due to disappointment with the candidate or disaffection with their organization. Better still is to have the tipster, or double agent, working from the inside. All of these methods are characteristic of the typical organization, none of which seems to change over the years.

After Election Day the successful campaign's paraphernalia is stored away but its political ramifications are far-reaching. A major task is to satisfy those workers who seek permanent employment on staff. Many New Hampshire personalities have ended up in powerful Washington positions because they worked hard to elect a president.

Governors Sherman Adams and John Sununu became chiefs of staff. Republican activist Gerry Carmen ended up heading the General Services Administration, and as U.S. ambassador to the United Nations' Geneva office. Laconia Democrat Bernard Boutin also ran the GSA on the appointment of President Kennedy.

Hilary Cleveland was appointed to the International Joint Commission-United States and Canada; Betty Tamposi became an assistant secretary of state for consular affairs; and Bonnie Newman was made assistant to the president for management and administration.

These men and women, in turn, expanded their staffs or related public ventures with their own loyal subordinates and family members who had helped them support their chosen, winning candidate. Even back in 1982 the *Baltimore Sun* had counted three dozen New Hampshire-related sinecures for a combined salary of $1.5 million. It would appear that these figures have been dramatically inflated in the Bush administration.

This offers an unusual opportunity for governmental service, especially for young people such as David Carney. Dave started his political career helping Judd Gregg when he ran for the New Hampshire executive council in 1978. Thereafter he became chief political assistant to Governor Sununu in the State House. When Sununu became chief of staff to the president, Carney was named White House deputy director for political affairs. A reporter once described him to me as "the John Madden of politics." There is now no limit to his political horizon. Where else but from our spoils system could such probability arise for an eager, young enthusiast?

Winning the early New Hampshire Primary has been of well-earned and well-publicized benefit to our small state, because its citizens are rewarded with quick access to the appropriate authorities in Washington whenever they have problems with federal executive departments. At the same time, such key staffers are in a position to nurture the president's ties with the state, ready to initiate a possible reelection campaign.

While constituent service is usually practiced from elective offices of lesser level than the presidency, it is also replicated by the White House. Maintaining personal contact with New Hampshire is both good government and good politics. The chief executive communicates occasionally with key supporters. When he visits the state on official business, he often recognizes them in some special way. Or, such citizens are invited to visit the Oval Office to have their picture taken with the president or vice president.

The phenomenon of political reality that requires statewide organization or reorganization of political campaigns every four years is inherent to the unique process which makes the Primary system work. Of course, the anomalous write-in vote which upturned the 1964 Primary election in favor of Henry Cabot Lodge, without an organization, was the exception that proved the rule.

Add to this perplexing exercise the increasing, pervasive influence and influx of media with its prevalence in opinion-making. As Michael Oreskes wrote in the *New York Times*, "Winning elections has become a business, a big business with professional associations and magazines, where volunteers have been replaced by computer assisted polling, the pamphlet by the television spot."

A national candidate can perhaps still win the New Hampshire Primary today without an in-state organization, providing he has a superior media campaign. But if it is run without a local organization, we're getting even further away from the participatory politics on which our elective system was founded.

CHAPTER 10

The Proliferative Professionals

When our presidential primary statute was enacted forty years ago, politics had the earmarks of an art form. Now, like so many other things in this high-tech age, politics is becoming more of a science. Long-range planning and increasing concern for the physical safety of the candidates is displacing much of the spontaneity of those earlier campaigns.

A stringency has crept into the system. Participating is not as much fun as it used to be and soon there may no longer be an important role for the amateur. New classes of professionalism have emerged. Decisions rest on polls, ratings, and self-styled political consultants. Everything tends to run by the book.

Specialists are assigned to each aspect of campaigning—one for issues development, fund-raisers, media advisors, the public-opinion pollster, an authority on direct mail, experienced technicians for running phone banks and Advance. Many such categories are staffed by hired hands who move freely from candidate to candidate in successive campaigns.

Some of these so-called professional strategists not only move from one campaign to another, but sometimes work against a candidate for whom they had previously been employed. David Keene, mentioned earlier, was Bush's national manager in 1980, then served in a similar capacity for Dole when the senator ran against Bush in 1988.

In addition to the top-level strategists, there are innumerable subordinate advisors who are not publicly identifiable. Their roles, actions, or even the material they prepare is not credited to them in any way at all. Meanwhile, much of what is said by a candidate or promoted by his campaign may be produced by these same people who, though competent, do not even have a true commitment to the candidate or to the overall effort. These staffers may be working for a candidate in whom they have little confidence or for positions with which they personally disagree. They may lack both loyalty and accountability to the effect or outcome of their efforts. They are somewhat akin to the well-paid congressional staffers who are the least accountable public servants, yet they actually draft the laws affecting all of our lives.

In the Rockefeller days, such noncommitment among professionals would not have been tolerated.

Over the years, since 1952, New Hampshire has also developed a cadre of its own unpaid, true "professionals." They differ from the casual volunteers by virtue of their experience and political prowess. Most of them have run for and held high statewide elective office or have been on the inside, integral to such efforts. They are not consultants; rather, many are voter-tested, practical politicians. Presidential candidates now recognize that their campaign here must be guided by the advice and visible inclusion of these respected leaders. They add local credibility and direction.

Integrating such men and women with the national staff is frequently difficult. Innate to the democratic process at all levels are constant jealousies involving patronage and who is responsible for what. But harmony in the overall camp is vital for a smooth-running Granite State operation.

Most key players in sensitive positions on the national team of a presidential candidate are earnestly dedicated to their leader and, in many cases, are his most intimate friends. Many assist in-house at the candidate's national headquarters, or serve only in an advisory capacity, thus making it impossible for them to travel regularly with the candidate. My acquaintance with these professionals is therefore restricted to long-distance communication, except for those rare occasions when they've been in New Hampshire on the campaign trail. Those on the permanent traveling staffs we get to know quite well.

Among the many outstanding individuals it has been my privilege to meet in running the successive campaigns for Rockefeller, Reagan, and Bush, several merit special comment. Reviewing these relationships, it seems strange that all of them are men. Maybe this explains why our technique of electing people to the presidency is not "kinder and gentler."

Rockefeller's de facto chairman, George Hinman, comes first to my mind. While he took no part in the daily doings of the operation and rarely left his office high atop Rockefeller Center, he was always available by phone with a solution for any problem presented to him. Though a lawyer, financier, and businessman, a director of IBM, he was held in the highest esteem for his contributions to the Republican party as its long-time Republican National Committeeman for New York.

They don't make them like George any more. His infectious smile, delightful sense of humor, and gracious manner put everyone instantly at ease. In a way he reminded me of the vanishing Yankee—though he was born and lived in Binghamton, New York, and didn't have the twang. In fact, quite the opposite: he was a thoroughly polished, thoroughbred gentleman. Underneath the veneer was a shrewd understanding of people and a politically pragmatic way of dealing with them.

Unquestionably the loyalty of this remarkable man to the Rockefeller family was one of the governor's greatest assets. After Rocky's death, because as Hinman said, "We all loved Nelson," he chaired the fund-raising for a memorial at Dartmouth known as the Nelson A. Rockefeller Center for the Social Sciences. Even then, seventeen years after the campaign was over, George courteously wrote to me, "You stood with him [Nelson] when the going was hard and there were a lot of personal disappointments to you thereafter."

It seems to me that if men of Hinman's caliber were still running national campaigns, the results would be as effective as under today's managers, but they would be conducted with a lot more dignity.

————

John Sears and Jim Lake were fully chronicled in the Reagan-Ford chapter, but they also figured in the subsequent Bush-Reagan campaign. They were a unique duo, both rascals, with Jim the amiable one, yet still very much a rascal. Lake had become personally acquainted with all the important members of the grass-roots organization which had been established for Reagan in 1975-76. Its depth and enthusiasm for the candidate at that time was unprecedented.

When Jim returned in the second campaign, in opposition to me, it was to cultivate the seeds that had previously been sown which, meanwhile, I had been trying to replant for Bush. This led to occasional communication between us and much good-natured jockeying for position with certain workers.

Thus, I was not surprised when one evening Lake called me from a Reagan meeting in Laconia to suggest an exclusive two-man debate between his candidate and Bush. I assumed Jim thought it would be a good way of clearly demonstrating that the two were the front-runners and that "the actor" would swallow up "the preppy."

It sounded great to me, as I was intimately familiar with the styles of both men and was confident Bush would hold his own. But I hadn't counted on the rascals, quietly and without notice to anyone on our side, violating the mutually agreed-upon rules for the one-on-one by inviting the other Primary contestants to join the forum! Not only had they hoaxed us, but subsequently Anderson, Baker, Crane, and Dole realized they had been used, too. After the Nashua debate, as Hannaford observed, Sears "was smiling like a Cheshire cat."

Two days later, when Reagan fired Sears and Lake, it was Reagan who had our sympathy.

By far the most delightful guy from the Reagan stable was Lyn Nofziger, the bantering off-and-on again press secretary, all-time master of the ad-lib one-liner. He was a fervent conservative, staunchly loyal to Reagan, for whom he provided a daily dose of usable quips, along with others which were even better.

Clean-shaven in those days yet often disheveled in dress, he lectured on the merits of the narrow, rumpled collar and the wide tie which he habitually wore loose around the neck. I once suggested to him that if it weren't for the constant chomping on his cigar, he could be mistaken for a bag of remnants. In return, I received the gift of a narrow necktie, with the suggestion that it was good for hanging.

Lyn claimed not to know the meaning of the word "insouciant," but it perfectly describes his normal disposition. He would emit a low growl when upset, set his own rules in dealing with the media, yet was respected by them for telling it like it is. If the candidate made a mistake, Lyn would deflect his admission of it with a pun. He was a pro in his field—not like so many others in the profession who deal with half-truths to shield their candidates' blunders.

There were three other trusted Reagan lieutenants who rode regularly with us on the bus: Marty Anderson, Pete Hannaford, and Mike Deaver. All were good-natured, self-effacing, and unintrusive in the workings of the traveling production. To Reagan's credit, he brought most of his California team with him to the White House.

Anderson was an economist on leave as a senior fellow at the Hoover Institution of Stanford University. He was the "think tank" and research specialist. Marty would listen carefully to Reagan's remarks and frequently conferred with him on positions taken. Occasionally he would leave the tour to develop new material. It was his responsibility to diffuse such issues as the $90 billion federal budget cut. Obviously good at his job, Marty was a most effective member of the Reagan team.

Hannaford had served as the governor's director of public affairs in California. In 1975, he had joined Deaver to form a public relations business in Los Angeles. Reagan was a major client.

Pete was an excellent writer who provided position papers and assisted Anderson in preparing speeches. Consistently low-key and pleasant, he was a real pleasure to have aboard.

It always appeared to me that Hannaford was the engineer who kept the Reagan train on track. This was quite a balancing act, considering the turf battles which eventually developed among such independent personalities as Sears, Lake, Charlie Black, Nofziger, Bill Casey, Richard Allen, Ed Meese, and Dick Wirthlin. The country would have benefited had he chosen to serve in the White House along with the other campaign survivors.

Deaver had enjoyed a longer association with Reagan than Pete. Mike was director of administration on the governor's staff when he hired Hannaford in 1973 to assist in an issue project. As a confidential aide to the candidate he served as a general "utility" man with responsibility for the overall direction of Reagan's activity. Ostensibly Deaver enjoyed a closer, personal relationship with the Reagans. Nancy, in particular, evidenced great confidence in his advice.

It was not until after the New Hampshire campaign that I realized Mike was a closet hardball player. He had sent me an article written flatteringly on "Remembering Reagan." I reminded him that some of our recollections were not quite that flattering.

He had programmed Reagan into believing, largely because Governor Thomson had predicted it, there would be a victory margin of over 50%. Yet from the beginning it had been our realistic objective to achieve a figure of around 40%, which was agreed as acceptable by the Reagan forces when I signed on as chairman. We far exceeded our expectations, but Reagan perceived we had failed.

Furthermore, after Reagan picked Senator Richard Schweiker as his running mate, Thomson was the first to abandon ship. In defense of the choice it was my unpleasant task to condemn Thomson's intemperance as "hapless." Still, thereafter Thomson was paid expenses to attend the Republican National Convention and receive amenities there, whereas none of the hard-working volunteers who had actually done the job here received any compensation or recognition whatsoever.

The final straw came after the convention when Reagan returned to New Hampshire for the sole purpose of raising money for Thomson's gubernatorial reelection effort. Not even a courtesy call advising of the visit was made to any of the loyal Reaganites until the deal was made, the date confirmed and announced to the press.

It was one of the shabbiest performances in my then-thirty-years of politics. Deaver had played a significant part in its manipulation. Our memory of Reagan was, indeed, not fully in sync with Deaver's.

———

My warm fellowship with George Bush and most members of his family for over ten years has made possible my acquaintance with many intriguing personalities. But the purpose of this chapter is to treat only those with whom I have had an association pertaining to our political relationship.

The most prominent of these would be James Baker. Possibly George's most dedicated and reliable friend, Baker served as Bush's 1980 national campaign chairman. After Reagan was elected Jim became chief of staff at the White House, serving with Deaver and Meese.

To this day his concurrent affiliation at that time with Reagan and Bush conjures for me an enigma I've never been able to resolve. Clearly Baker is the epitome of the accomplished, pragmatic politician.

Though Baker worked out of the Houston headquarters, he was in constant telephone contact with Bush. I began exchanging memos with him early in 1979. An attorney, Jim was quick, definite, and to the point. Whenever we needed anything, from scheduling dates to promotional materials, the service was prompt. While much of the credit probably belongs to his very talented assistant, Margaret Tutwiler, operations were handled in an efficient, businesslike manner.

A confident, composed, competent administrator, he directed George's first campaign with a fraction of the personnel and layers of staff which became a hallmark of the 1988 Bush effort. He was domineering and could be tough, but understanding.

Interviewed on the subject of the infamous Nashua debate I was once loosely quoted as saying of Jim Baker, " . . . but he'll stomp on anyone in his way, even a friend. Probe a bit, and you'll find that he doesn't really have much compassion for people."

I have since had a hard time convincing his friends that these remarks were intended as a compliment. In retrospect, I admit that I got carried away by hyperbole, spurred by unhappy recollection of that event.

In apologizing to him I expressed my esteem and the sincere view that the country is, indeed, fortunate to have a man of his caliber willing to accept major positions of leadership, including secretary of Treasury and State.

Standing right beside Jim Baker as possibly the Bush family's most faithful and dependable companion was a man little known to the public, Don Rhodes. Don has served as a longtime ex-officio aide, without portfolio, for George. Always there, he was forever cheerful and beloved by all the Bushes.

In thinking of him I'm reminded of the postal service's slogan, "Neither snow, nor rain, nor heat, nor darkness keeps him from accomplishing his appointed course with all speed." Whenever I wanted to put a confidential memo directly in George's hands, it got prompt delivery if sent to Don. He would reciprocate by contacting us if his friend (George) needed to identify correspondents from New Hampshire or embellish his Christmas card list.

Without meaning to snub other members of the Bush clan, it would be ungracious not to mention Don's kinship with a very special member, late lamented, C. Fred Bush. C. Fred wrote a book once, slightly edited by Barbara Bush, and said, "I love Don more than anyone else in the world." The author went on to explain that he was a "people" dog. Indeed, he was, having hobnobbed with such celebrities as Happy Rockefeller, Margaret Thatcher, King Hussein, and Charlton Heston.

The stress of running for president is staggering. A candidate needs to relax now and then, which requires the consoling backup of such professionals as Don and C. Fred. George is lucky to have had them.

Nor could you face a New Hampshire Primary without a full-time traveling assistant, like Dave Bates. Perennially unperturbed, always affable, he was a great houseguest, except on those mornings when he would oversleep and still be putting on his pants as George and I would be stepping into the car. Notwithstanding, Dave never missed a beat on the job, with an infinite capacity for remembering names, recognizing people, and refreshing Bush's memory on important contacts and even unimportant ones.

Of course, Cay will never forgive him for the night when he and Bruce Rounds had been swigging a few en route from a North Country Bush rally. She was in the front seat, Dave driving, as they were stopped for speeding by a state trooper. "I smell alcohol in this vehicle," said the trooper. "You're right," replied uncharacteristically loquacious Dave, "Mrs. Gregg has had a couple of beers."

After Bush became vice president, Bates' job was assumed by Tim McBride, who had previously worked with us on Advance. By then the position of power and prerogative of the White House made the task even more challenging, but Tim mirrored the multiple talents of Dave.

Frequently mistaken for a Secret Service agent, this tall, skillful aide gracefully steers Bush through a crowd with the mastery of a doctor plying a scalpel. The travel and responsibilities are now endless, as I noted on TV when Tim held an umbrella over George in Warsaw, Poland. Once more the president had found another good right hand, so necessary in carrying the load of his office.

Trailing along not far behind Tim is the smiling face of Dave Valdez, easily recognizable because he's always fitted out like an American tourist in Rome. Strapped around his middle and hanging from both shoulders are a conglomeration of cameras, lenses, and light meters. Dave's assignment is to take the candid shots as the candidate moves from person to person. For maintaining the presidential image he's the most vital craftsman of the lot.

The laborious follow-up is not the developing of his photos, rather it's to identify the subjects and, more importantly, where to send the picture. You should not consider running for president unless you first have the commitment of a tireless picture-taker. Further, you'd be hard pressed to find another Dave Valdez.

The press secretary may also function as a vigorous image maker. One of the best was Bush's Pete Teeley, bright, risible coiner of words who could have written the dictionary. Like Nofziger, he is respected by the press for his straightforwardness.

Pete had a great sense of humor, totally unassuming, and was always the thoughtful gentleman. He enjoyed a warm relationship with George, who had the utmost confidence in him, perpetually soliciting his counsel for the best approach to the problems of the day. Teeley exuded a sense of independence from other staffers who were often imbued with hustling their own images rather than that of the candidate. In fact, at one point Pete left George to write a book. It would have been a crime story about drugs but the Lorelei of politics quickly summoned him back to the White House and eventually to private lobbying. When asked why he didn't join Deaver, Stockman, Regan, and Speakes in publishing some type of tell-tale book, his answer was, "I'd have to disclose a lot of insider stuff and I wouldn't do that."

Two of Bush's most steadfast champions, Ron Kaufman and Andy Card, I dub the Gold Dust Twins (once the best-known commercial symbol in America. Gold Dust was a washing powder and the illustration was meant to show the product would not cause fading.). Ron married Andy's sister, and the twins' fidelity to Bush was eclipsed only by the fervency of their family effort on his behalf.

Kaufman is the wily one of the two. Blessed with a Machiavellian touch for chicanery, he's a habitual plotter of political strategems. At the same time, he retains an affable familiarity with the star players on everybody's campaign stage and can address most of the audience by their first names. I doubt there is one person whom Ron has even casually met who has not been granted a return call. He's an inveterate diplomatic operative.

Card, whom President Bush appointed as his deputy chief of staff, is more issue-oriented and approaches the fray with less concern for the personalities of the participants. Unflappable, modest in manner, he personifies the "nice guy" image. His penchant is to administer strategy while building esprit de corps. Andy is the kind of fellow who both answers and returns phone calls, an attribute uncommon among highly placed staffers.

This pair is perfectly counterbalanced and represents the kind of cornerstone essential to erecting a campaign structure, as recurrent contact with the candidate's loyalists is its lifeblood. Practitioners like these two are the mucilage that keep the whole operation intact.

Seldom did I have occasion to link up with the vice president's three top professional advisors of the 1988 campaign: Roger Ailes, Robert Teeter, and Lee Atwater.

Ailes, the media advisor and producer, appeared as a gruff, hands-on doer who set the scenarios and molded the harsh radio and TV ads in his own image. He appeared to enjoy unlimited authority in creating television commercials.

Teeter was a more unassuming senior strategist. It was among his responsibilities to determine the issues on which the candidate would concentrate. Yet, as the pollster, he surprised me when quoted in the *Wall Street Journal:* "People don't really vote on issues; they vote on people."

Since subsequently receiving so much notoriety as Republican national chairman, Atwater, Bush's 1988 campaign manager, is firmly portrayed in the minds of many. He's a pragmatic, grassroots combatant motivated by a furious ambition, with winning as his sole objective. He is the epitome of the politician's politician, blessed with superior administrative ability and boundless energy. Nor could any man have proved greater personal courage than Lee in fighting his life-threatening illness.

This triumvirate arrived as a unit for the first time in New Hampshire after the Iowa defeat, and assumed command. The media projected defeat. They were wrong again. It turned into a major victory. Success came from our ignoring the rigid Washington-ordered schedules. At last the vice president was allowed to move freely in unrehearsed situations.

Ironically this was precisely the approach for which we had been pleading from the beginning. But it was not until the tacticians were desperate and on the scene that they recognized we were right.

While Gallup, Roper, Harris, Caddell, the Opinion Research Corporation, and others have a long history of taking political soundings, their research did not necessarily play any part in determining the major platform planks of campaigns in the 1950s and 1960s. Rather, the candidates associated themselves with philosophical positions developed from their own personal experiences and sincere beliefs.

In those earlier days, such as in 1948, the pollsters were primarily concerned with the voters' preference of nominees. The last Gallup survey completed on October 25 of that year showed Dewey ahead by five percentage points, yet on November 2 Truman won by nearly the same margin for approximately a ten percent polling error. Even then, polls were not reliable.

Rockefeller's theme on the stump was derived from his Harvard lectures on "The Future of Federalism," wherein he expressed personal pride that New York had "been a pacesetter in effective legislation for individual opportunity and human rights." Goldwater wrestled with broad conservative opinions which, though inspiring to him, were not reflective of majority public sentiment at that time.

Beginning in the 1970s the pollsters have had an increasingly important role in identifying the issues of current public interest. The viable candidates weighed much more carefully the findings of the most renowned pollsters, and of those newspapers and radio stations which conduct regional polls. Most aspirants began hiring their own professionals who served on staff, as Dick Wirthlin did for Reagan and Teeter did for Bush.

But even in the 1976 campaign, Reagan pretty much modeled the issues which had been set during his terms as governor of California, and implemented his personal concept of how the federal bureaucracy should be run. His pollster appeared to be more involved in gauging how Reagan was coming across with the voters than with identifying the important issues.

Once into the eighties, professional pollsters sprang onto everyone's in-house staff. In addition to tracking the candidate's place in the race it has now become an equally important function to assess the voters' concerns. Built upon the results of phone calls or interviews, the pollsters put together a composite of ideas with national appeal, from which the contestant can form a viable election plan.

There is no such thing as accurate polling. It's speculative at best. Most professional pollsters adopt a random selection of potential voters using a myriad of classifications such as age, sex, income, occupation, and geographic, religious, and ethnic backgrounds. They are usually conducted by telephone surveys or brief interviews. Because the interviewer is not personally acquainted with the interviewee, the sincerity and motivation for the answers given may be suspect.

If the questions pertain to issues, often the person interviewed gives a spontaneous answer on subject matter to which he or she had never given any serious thought. Or, the voter doesn't understand the question yet wants to sound knowledgeable. If it's a straight "yes" or "no" question on voting for a particular candidate, the reply is often based on name familiarity rather than potential support. Or, a voter preference on the day of the interview can be changed that night by the evening news.

Candidates also use the results of their own in-house polling, when it's favorable, as a promotional tool to validate their popularity. Obviously the media are skeptical of such affirmations, regardless of how well respected the pollster may be. Again, it should be a warning to the public that polls are not worth much.

Many pollsters argue that polls do not influence elections. They claim their profession is only concerned with recording statistical facts. What rubbish! Certainly they are familiar with the human nature factor: "Everyone wants to be with a winner." Not only does a candidate who is way ahead in the polls capture additional converts, more importantly, many others will feel their vote is unessential. Besides, if polls did not manipulate elections, why are contestants always anxious to release favorable predictions?

The worst thing about polls is that, more often than not, they are treated by the media as critical news. Results get front page headlines in leading newspapers, prime-time TV coverage, and priority with columnists. Such emphasis adds to the pollsters' presumed authority in predetermining voting results.

It's unfortunate that the public fails to recognize that polls, like chameleons, can quickly change color when adjusting to new environments. Even the political community seems mesmerized. It disturbs me that the Republican National Committee proposed in its 1990 budget to spend $1,600,000 on polling during what was not even a presidential election year.

Presidential speechwriter Peggy Noonan touched on the subject in her book, *What I Saw at the Revolution: A Political Life in the Reagan Era.* In it she expressed her distaste for the White House's obsession with polls and the focus groups upon which some of them are based: "I felt that polls are now driving more than politics, they are driving history."

The professionals also claim a favorable track record in foretelling national presidential results. Considering the pollsters know the results of the fifty primaries or caucuses, are familiar with the emotions generated at both national party conventions, and have observed the nominees crisscrossing the country a half-dozen times, I presume the law of averages would lead to the same conclusions.

Polls have misled forecasters of other election outcomes as well. Remember how the ABC/*Washington Post* and other polls predicted an overwhelming victory for Daniel Ortega on February 26, 1990, over Violeta Chamorro when, after counting, she beat him by fifteen percentage points?

Still, the increased reliance on samplings of public opinion has spurred remarkable growth in the polling industry. Curiously enough, even with all the techniques of the computer age it still has not reached any scientific accuracy in predicting the outcome of New Hampshire primaries. In fact, they've had a dismal track record, as often off as on the mark.

In major cases lawyers also have developed their own breed of pollsters, known as litigation consultants. For this new science a simulated jury is hired which reflects the backgrounds of the real jurors. The ersatz jury sits in on the actual trial and predicts the human behavior of the appointed panel. Fortunately, I don't think one could ever corral a large enough sample of voters to apply this principle to predict their votes.

An entirely new craftsman has emerged almost simultaneously with the pollster: the professional strategist. The apprenticeship for this trade requires only having served well on the staff of a victorious presidential candidate, and being at the right place at the right time.

It used to be that a man running for president formed his own inner circle of advisors, most of whom were volunteers and friends. Those paid staff members who were also members of the group were individuals experienced in the folkways of national politics. They were not, however, proprietors of independent consulting businesses which did little else than run campaigns or lobby in Washington.

Now we have high-priced firms concentrating on political matters established along the lines of the modern advertising agency. But quite unlike most such agencies this new generation of consultants senses no ethical problem in representing two or more clients running against each other for the same presidential nomination. Nor do they have any compunctions about lobbying clients whom they have helped to elect after they are in office. Some apparently satisfy their consciences for such shams by forming two associations, yet both are staffed by the same account executives.

Similar to an advertising agency selling a commodity, these managers are hired to market their candidates to the electorate. It is their expertise which drafts the blueprint of the tactical plan, outlining everything from image to organization. It's their job to manipulate the press without damaging the candidate's credibility. And all the while they keep tabs on the opposition's strategy, which may be managed from the same office!

Running campaigns has developed for them intimate relationships with presidents, would-be presidents, and other influential people on the national scene. As a result these consultants have now become powerful influence-peddlers who command substantial retainers for their access to the White House and Congress.

Charles Black, one such successful entrepreneur who has taken political soundings for the president's chief of staff, has said, "The worst you can say about us is that it's a bad system and that we participated in it."

His firm, for example, was used by Puerto Rico to pressure the Federal Emergency Management Agency (FEMA) for faster service after the devastation caused by Hurricane Hugo in the fall of 1989. FEMA is one of the few federal agencies that are directly responsible to the president, not reporting through any cabinet secretary.

Though Charlie and his associate, Roger Stone, had been employed by Kemp in the 1988 Primary, they later signed on with Bush for the fall campaign. Previously even Atwater had been in partnership with them.

It seems to me there is something unsavory about this system if professional "insiders" are necessary to curry favor after a natural disaster from a federal agency which is charged with responding to the needs of our citizens in such a catastrophe.

Roger Ailes and Roger Stone have worked together in Republican campaigns and directly or indirectly helped Democrats in others. Nonetheless, both pledge their high-minded interest in the Republican cause. To some of us they may appear more like members of the oldest profession rather than of this new one.

The professional pollster and strategist work informally in a pseudopartnership. The latter relies on the former for the defining of the issues to be used. Then, once under way, it's the pollster who keeps the strategist informed as to the acceptance of their presentation. When the polls are not favorable, it's time to change direction. Thus, communication with the voters is increasingly regulated by professionals—not by the candidates themselves. The more professionals there are between the candidate or president and the people, the thicker is the Teflon coating.

In contrast, the physical distancing which has developed is countered by the effects of television, which stimulate unusual and perhaps undesirable familiarity. In the "old days," the Office of the Presidency was truly awesome. Even senators like Robert Taft and Hubert Humphrey inspired some reverence. Television has changed all that. The White House is now a familiar scene, used frequently as just an overnight stop by our increasingly well-traveled chief executives. "Have red phone, will travel" should be their new dictum.

This has resulted in more distancing of the authentic candidate from the populace. As one of George Bush's own sons has noted, "Consultants tend to treat their candidates as red meat." Many of these political advisors have achieved their success while self-serving at the expense of their employer. Others, once established in positions of power, play the field and bad-mouth a prior client if it serves their current purpose.

Dave Keene, a true Republican professional who was later fired by Dole, has been around the track a few times. According to authors Goldman and Mathews, Keene describes the ideal candidate as one "who understands that he is a necessary pain in the ass and does as he is told."

235

In contrast, it was amusing to read in *Insight* magazine that Frank Greer, popular Democratic professional strategist, proclaimed: "I may be able to help them [candidates] amplify or communicate their message, but a lot of it comes from the candidate and the political environment. I wish someone would write that a consultant said that, because I don't think consultants and pollsters win campaigns. Good candidates win campaigns."

Recent campaigns have proven unequivocally that this rising class of hired specialists has largely replaced the volunteer political leaders whose counsel formerly steered the candidacy. Local chairmen have become figureheads whose contribution has been reduced to that of merely lending credibility to the cause.

When we reach the 1992 New Hampshire Primary, it's doubtful they will have any part other than to give their endorsement and organize locally. No longer will their input on strategy be solicited or receive credence. Whatever deference the locals get from the professionals will likely be window dressing.

From the candidates' outlook, I suppose one cannot condemn this shifting of attribution of responsibility away from themselves as long as it wins elections.

For the country's welfare I believe we are losing something very precious in our democratic process. There will be a gradual erosion of interest by many who now actively participate in its functions. There will not be much excitement to spur the "political animal" of days past. It will result in considerably less involvement by the individual worker. Elections will become rote.

————

Political patronage persists, integral to the system, though it has taken strange new twists. Today elected presidents and vice presidents tend to reward their hired campaign hands with staff positions in the White House or VIP assignments elsewhere in the federal bureaucracy, with job descriptions totally unrelated to their special talents. It is a device for keeping them on ice until the next campaign, as was the case when Ron Kaufman was assigned to the Department of Health and Human Services.

When an incumbent president or vice president seeks reelection, he maintains two separate and distinct staffs, one for the campaign and the other as part of his administration. Yet, when elected, the first one is disbanded and technically he must rely on the national committee for political activity during the off-years.

But, as presently practiced, the intermingling of political and official duties and objectives at the White House gets out of balance.

Perhaps it would be better if the president or vice president openly retained his campaign organization during his term, at a much-reduced performing level, until it was needed again. It would offer an alternative to saving jobs for some of those persons whom he might otherwise have appointed to important offices for which they were not qualified.

To adopt this suggestion, because financing would be involved, would probably require amending of Federal Election Commission legislation. Still, it should be noted that in the Bush administration, his loyalists in the state of Washington already have instituted such an ongoing campaign organization on a volunteer basis, without White House support.

Also, of course, the incumbent has the further alternatives of directing some of his former campaign workers to serve on the staff of the national committee, or they could be loaned out to private industry by arranging such temporary assignments with appropriate business supporters.

No matter how it is accomplished, a cleaner division of political and official tasks initiating from the White House would improve the public's attitude toward government in general and could still preserve the patronage system. Further, it might serve for many, between quadrennials, as a continuing opportunity to spark their concern for good government.

Campaigns are designed to elect, not to govern. The two objectives are not the same. Still, they are becoming increasingly fused to each other. Political photo ops have become more important than the message and everything the president does is choreographed for political advantage.

ADVANCE: A critical correlative professional ingredient.

It is vital to a candidate's success that the site of his every appearance be scrupulously scouted in advance of his arrival, both for reasons of security and staging. "Advancing" requires considerable physical stamina and diversity of skills, but it is unquestionably the most challenging and fun of all traditional campaign assignments. Other jobs can become pretty monotonous because, as they say about dogsleds, if you're not the lead dog, the scenery never changes.

Here, too, professionals predominate. The core are career people in federal government service. If the aspirant is not an incumbent running for reelection, the Secret Service (USSS) and specialists on the campaign staff assigned to Advance make up the advance team. If he is an incumbent, the White House Office of Communications (WHCA) is added.

Unless the candidate is already a president or vice president, he or she will not necessarily be granted the protection of the Secret Service. Even if protection is granted, it is not normally assigned until several weeks prior to our Primary date. The decision of which candidates will receive Secret Service protection is left to a joint legislative committee, headed by the secretary of the treasury (for whom the Secret Service works), and leaders of the House and Senate.

There was no precedent for the degree of security required in the 1987-88 campaign. Never before had a president or vice president visited the state as often. When security had been involved, we did not have the population or traffic density we have now. In 1979-80, most of the candidates, including George Bush, did not ask for the Secret Service. In 1983-84, President Reagan came only twice, and Vice President Mondale infrequently.

There are at least four components of their work that the Secret Service will not discuss: number of personnel on any particular assignment, equipment used, security methods, and the cost of it all. Their dark glasses are worn to prevent others from observing their line of sight. They are not permitted to converse with curious onlookers while on duty.

Protection is provided on a 24-hour basis in four shifts on a multiday rotation cycle. The government pays the agents' salaries and expenses as they remain under the exclusive control of the Treasury Department.

In order to have enough personnel, especially when there are several presidential candidates needing protection, the Service augments its own ranks with reserves from other Treasury agencies such as Customs, Narcotics, and the IRS, or from the military. For example, prior to the vice president's Winnipesaukee cruise on July 4, 1985, Navy frogmen inspected the ship from bow to stern.

A lead agent is in charge of each protection detail which has its own or a combined command post in the state. Other supervisors also have specific assignments. A site agent is responsible for each stop. Travel routes and motorcades are directed by another individual. Dissidents in the area are checked by an intelligence agent. If the vice president spends the night, it's yet another job to secure the facility and the food.

Government vehicles are used to guide and guard the candidate as he travels. Also, assistance is rendered by the resident agents who have a local office and serve year-round on the many other activities of the agency.

The resident Secret Service staff is invaluable for the efficient handling of a candidate's welfare while he is campaigning here. With their intimate knowledge of the state, these men are better able to relate our local concerns to those agents who are transiently assigned to the area. More importantly, they are personally known and respected by all other in-state law enforcement agencies, with whom everyone has to work in setting up a candidate's visit. Frequently they provide information which makes the campaign staff's job much easier.

In the 1988 campaign we were blessed with the good fortune of having two exceptional resident agents: Fred Kratz and Jim

Fitton. Also, I would mention the willing assistance always received from Special Agent Tom Clark of Kennebunkport, with whom we were in constant contact, particularly when the vice president landed at Pease.

Except in the case of an incumbent, where protection is mandatory, one of the most important decisions a candidate makes in entering the New Hampshire Primary is whether it is advantageous to employ the Secret Service. There are contrasting views on its effects. Some weigh the trappings of the entourage as image-enhancing, whereas others consider the restraints as detrimental. The candidate must request the security; it is not required unless he is an incumbent.

For the contestant who does not have a large or experienced staff, the Service offers many advantages. It lends its expertise to the seven- to ten-day initial inspection of potential locations as a part of the Advance. It also assists in smoothing out the rough edges during the walk-throughs preceding the visit. In prerunning the motorcade tours the agents not only lay out the best routes, they compute accurate time segments which are so essential to scheduling. While in no way intended as a service to the candidate, still their internal communications system is frequently a major asset for the traveling party.

The disadvantages vary greatly with the personality of the lead agent. If all agents operated strictly by the book, then the candidate would find it very vexing to close in on the New Hampshire voter. Fortunately most of them recognize reasonable latitude should be allowed. Still there are many limitations which become real irritants, such as having to walk within confined ropelines, regulating street strolls (if allowed at all), entering side or rear doors of buildings, riding in freight elevators, restricting the numbers comprising greeting groups, or forbidding spontaneous stops along a motorcade route.

When the Secret Service is not involved, the candidate has considerably more flexibility. It made a substantial difference in conducting the Rockefeller effort of 1964 and Bush's in 1980, when there was no such restriction (although Bush accepted Secret Service protection after our Primary), and that of Reagan in 1976 when he did use it.

Rockefeller's one bodyguard, Ed Galvin, a plainclothes New York State police officer, doubled as an aide. Had he been a Secret Service agent he would not have been allowed to take photographs, introduce supporters, exchange on-site notes with the crowd, or undertake any similar promotional activities.

Except for the last few weeks in 1980, Bush opted to have no security whatsoever. If he had done so, he could not have shaken hands with thousands, nor would it have been practical to use my home as a cost-saver and convenience center. Near the end when we were joined by Bob Gambino, former director of security for the CIA who had worked under George, even he served more as a friend and all-around assistant than as a security escort.

With Reagan in 1976 the situation was quite different, as the Secret Service was with us from early January. They even changed our choice of airport for his first arrival. They set up a command post directly across the hall from his suite at the Highway Hotel and studiously monitored our access to him. If we wanted to move the caravan or make changes in the itinerary, we had to get their compliance. Whenever Reagan was allowed out of the bus for a street walk, which was not often, he was so surrounded by agents and photographers that the friendly voter had to be pretty agile to shake his hand. He'd lose his hand if he tried to snatch a button from Ron's coat, differing markedly from 1964 when Rocky's buttons were occasionally snatched by a souvenir hunter.

Of course the 1988 campaign with the incumbent vice president as our candidate was the ultimate exercise in personal security. Resulting from the attempted assassination of Reagan in 1981, security measures had been materially tightened. Even magnatometer machines and sniffing dogs were not in evidence twelve years earlier. Bush now rode in a bullet-proof limousine with heavily armed escorts, front and rear, accompanied by a helicopter overhead and an ambulance trailing along behind.

All personnel surrounding the vice president who wear a wire plugged to their ears are not necessarily Secret Service agents. The Bush Advance is also so equipped, though on a different wavelength, and are frequently mistaken as agents. When Bush is in a crowd and needs a personal service such as a pen, a note taken, or an autograph card, it is provided by the accompanying staff aide and not by a Secret Service agent.

We've come a long way from the old days when President Truman exercised regularly by walking the streets of Washington, sometimes even stopping to give an autograph to a tourist. But any cost or care is insignificant compared to the loss by a single rifle shot of a potential president and wiping out the whole process of electing our leader in this open society.

Ease of instant communication is essential to the president and vice president whether they are inside the White House or on the road. Thus, when they travel anywhere they are preceded by some exceptionally talented people under the jurisdiction of the Office of Communications. The mission of these technicians, many of whom are in the military service, is to establish instantly available worldwide electronic and telephonic facilities for every moment covered by the president's or vice president's itinerary. This responsibility even includes movements of travel, and the WHCA vehicle is always an integral part of the motorcade.

New Hampshire has been a singular challenge for the advance communications team because we did not have the convenience of cellular phone service (we do now), and because of the hazard of our mountainous North Country where electronic signals are deflected by land mass. The technicians have often had to carry heavy equipment through rugged terrain to set relay disks on lonely summits. In other situations, like in the secluded town of Salisbury, they mounted an antenna on the belfry of Old Church. The command post was set up in the Hearse House adjacent to a horse-drawn hearse built in New Hampshire in 1885 by the

Abbott and Downing Company, which made the famous Concord Stagecoach widely used to open the "wild West."

At every scheduled stop, holding rooms are predesignated for both the incumbent candidate and his staff. Days ahead, arrangements are made with the phone company for the team to install a secured line for his possible use, and separate lines for other officials. On a busy campaign day there can be as many as a dozen such installations in different locations. Fax machines and office support equipment are carried in the convoy.

The core of the Advance team is, of course, those members from the candidate's organization. These can usually be further categorized as the so-called professionals from the national staff and local volunteers. As indicated earlier, the two groups often do not work harmoniously, as the outsiders tend to be turf-conscious, less loyal, restrained from delegating authority, and disparaging of the natives. This condition is most prevalent when paid staffers are rotated with each trip into the state.

Good advance work likely goes unnoticed, whereas bad advance work is obvious immediately and the candidate suffers from a poor portrayal over which he has no direct control. Preparations vary widely depending on the type of event, from parades to political forums, service clubs, a chamber of commerce speech, factory tour, social mix and mingle, or a street walk.

Whatever the nature of the event, meticulous planning does not overlook the smallest detail. The format must be run and rerun with all the participating parties, including the sponsors (and the USSS and WHCA when involved).

The procedures of Advance had not been practiced in New Hampshire gubernatorial or congressional campaigns, thus it was new to us when Rockefeller ran. For his largest rally at the Manchester Armory, massive velvet drapes were flown in from New York to be used as backdrops. Today, the routine is refined to the point where a phone call to Bob Molloy of Manchester, an audio-visual exhibits expert, produces all the pipe, drape, and sophisticated sound equipment required.

Though trained Advance staffs were used extensively in New York, none were sent to pave the way for Rocky's tours here. In fact, we did not give detailed daily schedules to the traveling party until it was physically in the state. Additionally, we were short of personnel at our headquarters, so Advance was a casual, unsophisticated operation.

Reagan, on the other hand, with his years of experience as governor of California, brought a seasoned advance team to supplement his effort here. Paul Russo, who later became a key Dole advisor, headed up the operation. Because he was unassuming and gregarious, Paul related easily to Granite Staters. He set his own pace in working with us and was not under the strict discipline of the Reagan high command.

The Russo approach contrasted sharply with the advance as practiced by the professionals after Bush became vice president, and particularly in the 1988 campaign. Many of the transient operatives sent here to assist in Advance were new to the game. Some were volunteers who had signed on with the national effort for expenses and the political experience. They lacked knowledge of the state. At times undiplomatic and tactless, they often stirred bad relations with site sponsors.

Among their number were those who hoped to do so well in the hustings they would eventually end up in some government position. In advance of arrival it was customary to place upon the beds of senior staff a memorandum detailing information about the accommodations, the community, and services available. We were both shocked and amused when the out-of-state author of one of those memos included the sentence, "Hats off to _ _ _ [his name was included here] who has done a great job and has not taken one detail for granite here in New Hampshire."

Rigid rules had been determined by the Washington managers on all aspects of preparing for a Bush visit. To deviate from the norm for the amendment of itineraries, adding one-on-one interviews or seizing opportunities for unscheduled photo ops required approval from supervisors who were not on the scene.

At the site location, the placing of pipe and drape, the press platform, ropelines, and the use of the multbox and sound systems were all done according to a standard operating procedure which did not allow for deviation to fit unique circumstances. More often than not this pseudomilitary severity caused bad feelings and prevented the candidate from maximizing his appearance.

While this insistence on repetitious standards for the presentation of the candidate may play well for the national media, it is sometimes counterproductive to our New Hampshire plan. Our foremost objective is to solicit the votes of those in attendance, not an overriding concern for the photo ops on the evening news. There were numerous instances, for example, when the rearrangement of living rooms to accommodate television cameras at a private home reception caused bad relations with the hosts.

In concluding this chapter, it is clear that professionals are becoming increasingly dominant in the electoral process. Pollsters, strategists, or Advance people now vie with the media as perhaps the most potent element of the mix which elects presidents.

Do these differences and new approaches to the "professional" running of national campaigns represent irreversible change? Are they symptomatic of an unavoidable and progressively impersonal electoral process?

These days, those imperious, tenacious technocrats who survive the longest are best rewarded. Are they not, in fact, the ones who can best fit, sort out, squeeze, distill, dispel, extort, and expel the local people? How sad it is that the traditional, ardent, dedicated grass-roots volunteer is being so casually dismissed.

Chronicling the 1988 election, *Newsweek* reporters in the foreword of *Quest for the Presidency* have written, "It is the collective memoir of a presidential election, perhaps the first, in which the handlers so completely upstaged the candidates as to become the principal players."

More ominously, the candidates are delegating their burdens and responsibilities to these professionals who, in turn, fabricate their own image of the candidate. The *Wall Street Journal* stated clearly that " . . . the words, policies and soundbites pouring out of their mouths were poured into their heads by someone else."

CHAPTER 11

Media Magic

The media seek the political candidate and the politician needs the media to promote the message.

The message may not amount to much and the candidate may amount to nothing at all. But here in New Hampshire politics is the opportunity to be known, to amount to something, to see one's name in print and to read one's words quoted with those of mighty power.

The message of the candidate requires cooperation of the media and the media feed on the message and how it is presented. The press, radio, and television all feed on the events and non-events of a political campaign or argument to sell the product.

The rewards for political involvement do not require victory. Harold Stassen, former governor of Minnesota, has run in nearly every preference primary since the date of enactment of the statute, and he was seeking to build a base in New Hampshire more than forty years ago. His early success after World War II gradually eroded, but still he ran and was much admired therefor. His message perhaps became confused but the media still looked to him for quotes and color.

The evolution of media communication, especially television, has had a dramatic impact on the fundamentals of political campaigning everywhere.

Since the Eisenhower-Taft contest of 1952, the national press has enjoyed coming to New Hampshire. There's something very picturesque about our snow-covered hills and sometimes bitter winter days, which stir the adrenalin and provide a rigorous

247

respite from ordinary press assignments. They used to view us as a rural nowhere, inhabited with feisty characters who live in colorful Christmas-card settings.

When Walter Cronkite turned from war correspondent to television reporter in 1950, the TV industry was in its infancy. At the 1952 Republican and Democratic national conventions, Betty Furness received more attention and air time selling Westinghouse refrigerators and ranges than did the candidates. Television did not become a major factor in New Hampshire politics until the 1970s.

During Rockefeller's 1964 campaign, the press traveled with us by bus. It was always a happy group. Most of the reporters were columnists, or represented the major newspapers, radio stations, and wire services. Occasionally NBC, ABC, or CBS had a filming crew aboard. It was a small club of only fifty to seventy-five people who knew each other well. There wasn't much change in personnel from trip to trip. Competition did not cause discord. At the end of a long day, the reporters would come off the buses and get together before dinner. They were much more informal than they are today—a jovial bunch, swapping stories at the bar. Sometimes Rocky would sit in on their bull sessions.

Few newsmen traveled independent of the bus, thus all were exposed to the same information. Stories were developed from interviews with the candidate or from Rocky's activities on the street. Press releases were also a major part of the briefing diet. It would be fair to say that the reporters were somewhat herded—still a problem today—making it difficult for them to be innovative in preparing their material, since everyone heard and saw the same things.

There were midmorning and late-afternoon deadlines by which their daily stories had to be transmitted to the editors. Still, the only time our campaign staff assumed responsibility for insuring that sufficient telephones were made available to accommodate these filings was in late afternoon or evening. Most of the routine accounts did not get published until the following morning.

If Rockefeller planned to say something of particular substance during the day, the press releases were prepared and everyone was alerted well in advance. It was not customary for him to plan a major speech as the highlight of the day. There was no such service as instant, on-site television broadcasting.

Except for Manchester's *Union Leader*, the local print media did not have enough personnel, nor could they afford to track every movement of the candidate. Reports were generally limited to those from the statewide news service or from a newsman riding the bus while it was in his territory. Whenever a newspaper office was conveniently on the route of a street walk, Rocky would enter informally and have a preappointed talk with the owner or publisher.

The programming of a candidate as protection from the media was not yet a priority, although the lessons learned during this campaign, particularly by Senator Goldwater, led to a new wariness. It is largely believed that his campaign underestimated the effect of his spontaneous, startling pronouncements, triggering shock and concern from his most ardent supporters. Even the strident support of Bill Loeb's *Union Leader* could not protect Goldwater from himself, although the paper's pounding diatribes against Rockefeller's marital situation did him irrefutable damage.

It's interesting, too, that although television coverage of that campaign was relatively sparse, both candidates were not playing to the camera when they could have, much to their disadvantage. Senator Goldwater disliked the glaring lights and often insisted on dismissing the crew. His inability or unwillingness to adapt to the use of the medium may well have been intuitive, since eventually it was the famous daisy TV ad sponsored by the Johnson campaign in 1964 which contributed to his final demise in the national contest.

Even the experienced public relations advisors for Rockefeller were so naive as to use Massachusetts settings for ads to be broadcast in New Hampshire! This was an early faux pas—another lesson learned. Never again will savvy media consultants bypass the Old Man of the Mountain in favor of old Cape Cod.

By the mid-1970s and the Reagan versus Ford campaign, things had begun to change. The press was becoming more aggressive and TV news programming was beginning to shape the candidate's schedule. The retail politics of hand-shaking street walks were becoming more structured and one or two major events were planned for every day.

Also, Congress had authorized Secret Service protection for selected presidential candidates in the final weeks of the New Hampshire Primary. The agents sometimes made it more difficult for the media to have the same free access to the candidate which they had enjoyed in the Rockefeller days.

Still, a relatively small number of the national and international press traveled in the bus, stopping at towns like Millsfield with its seven voters. These expeditions made great news, and some reporters joked that Reagan's New Hampshire campaign should have been given the award for the "Best Media Event of 1976."

The reporters were becoming increasingly sophisticated in political judgments. A few were White House correspondents whose questions were considerably more scrutinizing. There seemed to be a certain sameness to their backgrounds and training, often reflected in their observations, as if they were all patterned from the same cookie cutter. There was also a discernible liberal trend.

Reagan, the conservative, avoided some direct confrontation with the media by the creation of his Citizens' Press Conferences. Still, recognizing the need for constant coverage, events were planned around at least one major pronouncement each day. These were filmed for later broadcast. Even then, film had to be flown for processing to New York, or elsewhere, before it could be shown on TV. There were no anchormen or correspondents on site, questioning each statement as it was made.

By the time Bush appeared on the scene in the late 1970s, television had begun to emerge as the major influence on the political conscience for millions of viewers. It had assumed a primary role in delivering news of the candidates' daily activities and was beginning to focus on in-depth commentaries. Though the technology of live TV filming had still not been perfected, camera crews from the major networks became an established part of the media assemblage which accompanied the candidates.

What a physical impact these changes made on the campaigns—requiring more personnel, added transportation, special facilities, directional signs, platforms, blue pipe and drape backdrops, multboxes, and special sound equipment. The traveling corps was no longer called "the press"; now, it was referred to as "the media." The nomenclature changed altogether, as visuals became predominant.

If the candidate is a front-runner, there are now usually two buses instead of one, but these are only a small part of the procession. Private vehicles, especially satellite trucks and portable broadcast booths, add drama to the parade. Emmett Buell, Jr., professor of political science at Denison University, has accurately depicted New Hampshire as the mouse that gets "the lion's share of coverage."

Prior to the 1988 Bush versus Dole contest, orbiting satellites were introduced, offering the new facility of instant replay.

C-Span and CNN joined the media corps, meticulously transmitting every minute detail of campaign action. Even independent television stations or local affiliates of the national networks began participating on a regular basis. Meanwhile, new, lesser-known radio stations and newspapers from all over the world sent their representatives.

The fraternity which used to exist among transient journalists in the entourage seems to have disappeared. Many are strangers to each other, more concerned with simultaneous feedback to their points of origin. Preoccupied with their technological apparatus, there seems no time for camaraderie.

Competition has sharpened; it has become a dangerous game. The medium that gets the news to the public the fastest meets the objective, and to that end television has the clear advantage.

Meanwhile, soaring costs have begun to cap the resources of the major networks. Commercial television is primarily an entertainment medium and must sell advertising for its support. In television's infancy, the networks intended to inform and educate. Today their survival primarily depends on making money. The three major networks compete with the public broadcasting service, cable news services, and pay television. A major change in demographics, the raised sophistication of baby boomers, and the popularity of VCRs have provided us the luxury of selecting our own programming.

Already the TV networks cannot afford to send camera crews on full-time assignments with every candidate. They are being forced to make greater use of tape from local affiliates or share with them the expense of satellite up-link trucks.

Even the perceived "leading" candidates are no longer assured of the free coverage they request when in New Hampshire, such as when CBS refused to accompany George Bush on his initial announcement swing in 1988.

For the dark-horse candidates here, television has become a critical factor, forcing a change in strategy. Without television exposure they must struggle much harder to gain visibility and credibility, even though they may offer the most provocative ideas.

Such restrictions have resulted in limiting the most favorable times of day when a candidate can generate news. For maximum national coverage, a newsworthy event must fall within the framework of television's planned programming. As one example, staging the thirty-second sound bite for early-evening viewing has taken precedence on everyone's schedule.

Much of this trend peaked in the 1988 contest, when issues took a tertiary place to flattering camera angles and backdrops. Al Hunt of the *Wall Street Journal* says that television's unquestioning use of pretty pictures is cheapening the campaign process: "TV producers are like nymphomaniacs when it comes to visuals."

Ken Bode wrote in *TV Guide*, "Conventions are now scripted and directed by Hollywood experts—speeches, demonstrations, balloon drops all timed to the second. And the networks have begun to withdraw from an event that is all pageant . . . " If television coverage were minimized, conventions would be reduced to what they used to be, a big bash for the pols. Of course, this is a catch-22 because as long as television cameras cover any segment of any political happening, no politician would ever deny himself or herself a shot at national exposure. As long as there is any TV coverage of conventions there will be plenty of available stars. What's most significant about Bode's article is that it appeared in *TV Guide*. It's encouraging to see this vital, serious subject published in a magazine that is likely to be read by a broad constituency.

Bode quotes John Chancellor as saying, "We ought to treat campaign stories as if we worked for the FDA—apply a 'truth in packaging' standard." Hooray for Bode and Chancellor. They're right on target.

News anchors used to preside at their desks when delivering the news. Now they stand and walk while performing—actually stepping back and forth into time itself. Everyone enjoys these antics; it's kinda fun to watch and would make an extra ring for Barnum and Bailey.

Though candidates depend on building their public image during these prime-time news segments, even the best-choreographed sound bite is subject to the whims of the programmer. Reporters create their own focus by picking and choosing the quickie quote they feel best fits their interpretation.

The proliferation of political talk shows, such as "The McLaughlin Group," "Washington Week in Review," and "Crossfire," is a real phenomenon. White House reporters like Tom Petit, Britt Hume, and Cokie Roberts have become household names and are accepted as reliable friends. Thus, their analyses can do more to identify the candidate than he or she can do personally.

How easily Bob Novak, George Will, or Jack Germond can ridicule the candidates and their positions on every issue. How effectively they can reinforce their own views, since the most popular shows often repeat analyses of the same events.

It is to their credit, though, that both sides are usually well represented, and it behooves the viewer to learn and discriminate between the liberal and conservative pundits' interpretations.

Then there's the increasing competition for glitz, drama, excitement. "Crossfire" is a perfect example of a talk show where Pat Buchanan and Michael Kinsley incite controversy with quick, sharp repartee. The louder the argument, the better the show. They deliberately create riot, animosity. Kinsley's neck becomes visibly tighter, with pulsating veins belying his otherwise youthful mien.

"The best of the shows put a premium on essentially superficial reactions. Insight and any depth of analysis, any nuance, is completely gone . . . " The Washington-based TV talk shows are "the most insidious, the most destructive (force) to independent thinking," says Hodding Carter III, former assistant secretary of state for public affairs.

Journalists themselves question the influence of "pack journalism" and media consensus, the development of "conventional wisdom." The factors which particularly affect this undesirable scarcity of daring and individualism have been frequently cited, such as the practice of herding or the use of pools of reporters where a certain few are selected to represent them all, usually for logistical reasons. This is a practical problem which obviously limits access to the candidates and many of their activities.

Another problem is that most newspeople tend to use the same reliable sources on whom they can depend for quotable remarks, though the danger here is clear. Those anonymous sources are likely to be the same spinmasters who are well prepared to articulate views which benefit either their candidate or themselves. Once a "policy" has been established, it is likely to be repeated over and over again, whether the inquirer is Fred Barnes or Morton Kondracke.

254

Further, there is safety in consensus and much less risk of going out on a limb. Since all reporters have access to the same basic television news services, which monopolize and docket the major stories of the day, the time-consuming task of seeking out the unusual story, or perhaps the less dramatic, less intriguing issue, is sacrificed to haste and expedience.

Getting the scoop, especially for newspapers, is much more harrying today than in yesteryear. Now TV can upstage even the most Herculean effort by the print press.

What's remarkable is that all of the networks so frequently replay substantially the same film clips. It's almost as though they all employed the same news editor. We used to have two major news services: AP and UPI. The latter has lost nearly all its New Hampshire clients, thereby eliminating considerable competition in the speed, accuracy and identification of news.

Offsetting this loss are a number of special feature services such as the *Washington Post, New York Times,* and *Los Angeles Times* which give us a lot of attention during presidential primaries.

We all recognize that television projects what the camera wants to see, presenting favorable or unfavorable images, excerpting and clipping as it editorializes, providing the "look" of a candidate and perhaps not capturing what was really said or done or intended. In many instances, it has reduced political rhetoric to slogans or generalities.

Sometimes the Madison Avenue approach goes too far in deceiving the public with its pseudoevents. In the last few days of Roger Ailes' stampeding effort to save what he considered a sinking ship, he staged a phony "Ask George Bush" evening meeting in the Hollis town hall. The purpose was to develop a thirty-minute television ad showing a composed candidate fielding questions in a typical New Hampshire town meeting.

All the specially selected participants were told to face the cameras, be quiet on the set, and to frame their questions succinctly. (Obviously Roger had never attended a real Hollis Town meeting.)

At 2:30 A.M., after the session, one of our workers, Shirley Cohen, was awakened by a call from Ron Kaufman to determine if there would be any objection if a particular question-and-answer sequence initiated by one of the more colorful participants was eliminated from the tape.

The request got a few people out of bed but the offending material was scratched so that the show could be aired. Oh, if only Doctor Jim Squires, the Hollis town moderator, could do that!

There is also the alarming new trend by some of the networks where they artificially reproduce incidents to create a retrospective documentary of past events. If this approach were applied to political situations which the media wanted to remake with more detail than old TV footage on hand, it could be devastating to a candidate, not to mention history. Can you conceive of a bunch of character actors replaying the Nashua debate, structuring a scene around Bush's "voodoo economics" statement or his "kick a little ass" incident after jousting with Geraldine Ferraro?

Television news looks more and more as if it were produced in Hollywood. Joan Konner, dean of the Columbia University Graduate School of Journalism, put it right when she said, "Once you add dramatizations, it's no longer news, it's drama, and that has no place on a network news broadcast."

It's too bad there is no limitation on poetic license when reproducing history for an alleged documentary of political events, particularly when it is being made for commercial profit. Producers and actors recreate for effect situations where they were not present and, perhaps sometimes inadvertently, without a correct representation of fact. Such distortions can be very prejudicial to a politician's reputation.

The net result of such exploitation is that the viewer is likely to be swayed more from the visual artistry than from the substance of the subject matter. The voter finds it more difficult to differentiate the bona fide candidate from the image. Or, as the *Wall Street Journal* stated editorially, "Republicans have to learn the difference between a political position and a clay pigeon."

Even they are physically there, on-site (not doing reenactments), TV commentators are susceptible to flashing ad-lib remarks which may be totally untrue or may emphasize situations which should be insignificant.

The danger remains that most voters tend to accept what they see on television as factual reporting and what they hear as reliable information. Its sphere of influence has magnified to the point where Arthur Schlesinger, Jr., and other professionals now believe television has replaced the political party! More than ten years ago, even Democratic writer R. M. Koster had arrived at the same conclusion.

While I think those observations are far-fetched, admittedly TV has substantially encroached on the party's prerogative to set its own agenda. It has the power to create conflicts within the party establishment, cause disruption of its policies, and originate issues which otherwise would, and should, have been ignored.

The print press, on the other hand, has the opportunity to dig more extensively into political postures. It is less likely to make mistakes of judgment. Columnists have plenty of time to write indepth on particular issues.

The distinctive personalization of each candidate as generated by both the electronic and print media tends to separate them from the party they represent. The Primary victories of presidential contenders normally have no coattail advantage for seekers of lesser offices.

In New Hampshire, where presidential contestants are the only names on the ballot in our early Primary, they are competing exclusively with each other and may take positions not reflective of their party. Thus they are seldom helpful in electing other Republicans or Democrats, at least until one becomes the party nominee after the national convention.

In this sense the media does contribute to the weakening of the parties. For it is the function of the Primary elective process to select a president, not his supportive congressmen, governors, or even local officials. The real damage to the political system comes not only from TV but rather from the media, as a composite of press, radio, and television.

————————

Although the number of media representatives covering the 1988 Bush-Dole campaign far exceeded the rather exclusive, tight group which followed Rockefeller in 1964, there is a similarity in the reporting of the key media correspondents from the sixties to the eighties.

The well-established political writers of this age, along with the prime-time anchors and commentators of television, still tend to consolidate their perspectives into consensus conclusions, much the same as was done by the closely knit press fraternity of the 1960s.

A disturbing change from the past is the saturation effect this small clique of kingpins has on the electorate, because their views are now instantly disseminated to trusting, sometimes gullible, television audiences worldwide.

It has been repeatedly demonstrated in New Hampshire that when the media muddles voter percentages, they can make winners out of losers and losers out of winners, without regard to the actual number of votes a candidate actually received.

If victory had been determined by the recorded tallies, then President Johnson would have won in 1968. Instead, the media decided to declare McCarthy the winner, because it decreed the president's margin of only 7% over the senator should have been greater, allowing for the president's status as the perceived front-runner. The same situation occurred in the Democratic presidential primary of 1972 when Muskie tallied only 9% more than McGovern and less than 50% of the total vote cast. Or, in 1976, perhaps a reverse situation, when Reagan lost to incumbent President Ford by only two percentage points!

The business of media projections borders on being no more than a treacherous pastime. It has reached a point where the press has less interest in the number of votes a contestant racks up than its prediction on how he or she should fare, even before the balloting takes place. In 1988 Dole was the media favorite to carry New Hampshire, after his win in the Iowa caucus. But Dole came in second here, so the media declared him a loser, and his campaign was never able to regain momentum thereafter.

A more sympathetic understanding of the newsman's situation would be to acknowledge that he is not, and probably never has been, a campaign manager. Those of us responsible for the planning of schedules and strategy approach the political perception we attempt to create quite differently from the reporter who is interpreting it. Moreover, our presentations are part of a long-range plan, not for the facade of the moment.

Dave Broder expressed it well in writing, "I wish that I just once worked inside a candidate's headquarters, felt the pressures, and learned how people operate when the press is not around." As he further observed, the press must caricature people from conflicting signals.

Fortunately for us in New Hampshire, the potential of media misdirection is not as extensive as it can be in other states. Candidates make news wherever they are, but they have to be here physically for extended periods of time.

Retail politics remains the basic thrust of our Primary. The contestants are live, they come into our homes, tour our factories, walk our streets, and we gain a close acquaintance with them. It's the see, hear, touch and smell syndrome, not privileged elsewhere, except maybe in Iowa. And that's what makes our Primary essential to a realistic appraisal of the candidates.

Professor David Moore of our state university has advanced a theory that extensive face-to-face campaigning is no longer necessary; rather, New Hampshire has become another "media" state. I disagree. Except for unique situations, such as Eisenhower's or Lodge's, a candidate must be physically present to build a grass-roots image, which can only be accomplished by "retail" politics. Perhaps the candidate's presence triggers mass media attention—perhaps not. "Wholesale" politics, standing alone, has not won. Our judgments are not as susceptible to the media.

Rather, they are formed by lengthy observation and scrutinization of the candidates, which would not be possible in a larger state. As Bill Gardner, our secretary of state, has said, "Those living in other states may not be actually participating, but they are nevertheless vicariously participating."

To the extent TV conveys our intuition to others, our style of one-on-one politics is of inestimable value to the entire election process. According to Theodore White in *The Making of the President 1964*, "New Hampshire Republicans are as good a cross section of the old-fashioned Republican faith as the nation offers anywhere. Hampshiremen are earnest about their politics; they vote seriously. . . ."

The vision of a pastoral, bucolic New Hampshire has long given way to the reality of its success. A thriving, eclectic ambiance has broadened the scope of its citizens, complementing what many have been seen as a unique microcosm, from which has emerged a learned consensus.

———————

In recent years the media have initiated the practice of exit polling. Voters are interviewed as they leave the polling place to determine how their ballots were cast. Most people give honest answers, so that the polling results show reasonably accurate trends, even before the votes are counted. In the fall general election, polls close earlier in the East than in the West because of time zones. If the media declare a national winner based on eastern exit polls, people in the West may feel their votes won't count.

Sometimes competing networks would arrive at different conclusions from their independent polls. Fortunately, to save money, the major TV networks including Cable News are now financing a consortium through the 1992 elections to be known as Voter Research and Surveys. It will conduct the random exit polls used by all of them on which the projection of winners will be based.

It's just one more case of how the media, television in particular, have affected the electoral process. Certainly the industry cannot be faulted for creating the initiative. It is probably up to Congress to find a solution, by establishing uniform hours for voting during federal elections—an almost impossible assignment if it considers voter convenience.

Media statisticians have also studied the historical trends of specific precincts in New Hampshire. From such research they predict by computer the outcome of the presidential primary for the entire state, based on the early returns from these specially selected communities.

Exit polls are also used as part of this technique, and they possibly affect a miniscule number of voters. But such media predictions usually come after all the polls have closed in New Hampshire, or after we've compiled our own figures, so there's no prejudicial effect. Besides, we know they are frequently wrong.

Another trend which has escalated because of the free promotion provided by television is that of picketing protestors, with their signs, their placards, and ardent, articulate spokesmen. Perhaps we have the Iranians to thank for popularizing the art of dramatic public protests, but whoever's to blame really started something! Whatever the issue, from abortion to protecting the environment, mass demonstrations are almost assured of coverage.

Fortunately, only once in all the presidential campaigns in which we've been engaged was there such a demonstration in New Hampshire—a small group showed up in Manchester to harrass Vice President Bush on his stand regarding nuclear energy and the Seabrook plant.

Since the 1988 campaigns the abortion issue has created polarization, with outpourings of both prolife and prochoice groups appearing everywhere. Picketing has become an accepted method of demonstration, particularly where there is a political assemblage. This new ingredient of unfriendly people, showing up at a campaign appearance with signs and sarcasm to ridicule the candidate, will affect presidential styles and appearances throughout the 1990s.

Television's treatment of such activities may well present new problems for the candidates in New Hampshire. Too often these outbursts are carefully organized by out-of-staters as part of an overall national media strategy. Participants are sent into the state to lead the charge and attack the candidate, somewhat in the same fashion as the "People's Bicentennial Commission" followed Reagan in the 1976 campaign. Their message is usually one the candidate would prefer to ignore. The demonstrators are usually so emotional, there is no right way to address them anyway.

Debates have become popular, perhaps more with the public than with the aspirants. Because of their importance and the guaranteed media assemblage, the candidates concentrate on avoiding mistakes rather than scoring knockout blows. Still, their briefings are designed to trigger replies to some questions with answers totally unrelated to the subject of the inquiry. This is often the only way that positive positions on some issues can be articulated in such a forum. Even though the media thoroughly understand this stratagem, the campaign has to balance the chance of a bad press rap for doing it, as against the favorable effect of getting its thesis on the record.

It's a political postulate that no matter what happens in a debate the candidate must claim victory. It is in support of this axiom that the relatively new use of "spin doctors" has emerged. These well-rehearsed handlers promptly follow up the debate session by meeting with the media to eulogize their candidate and berate the opposition. The best negotiators usually win the day with the press. Curiously enough, the public, even though it saw the debate itself, will still anxiously await the media's verdict and be influenced by it.

It is generally conceded that Nixon lost the famous debate with John Kennedy not so much for substance, but rather for his dark, furled eyebrows. If television cameras had been there, maybe Lincoln wouldn't have looked so good against Douglas.

Presidential handlers are now wary of all aspects of their candidate's appearance, and makeup artists are engaged to correct facial flaws and sallow complexions, voice coaches teach oratorical skills, and fashion consultants do color screening.

Everyone is aware that from control of the microphone, as in Nashua, to the positioning on stage, as at Dartmouth, any slip in looks or demeanor can result in undesirable camera shots of enormous consequence. Image can make or break the candidate, regardless of his rhetorical or intellectual skill.

It is conceded that direct mail is the most cost-effective method of communication limited to a targeted audience, but perhaps the day is not far off when TV will rival it, now that over 50% of American households enjoy the diverse choices of cable television. Today it is possible by this medium to address specifically all types of special interest groups, such as sports fans, art lovers, health addicts, and the elderly.

––––––––––

In politics, truth is what people believe. Thus, when free publicity has ignored or misrepresented what a candidate believes, then he must rely on paid advertising to present his opinions. Television is, of course, the most successful means of projecting image, although it strains the budget. Radio and newspaper advertising have the advantage of being less expensive.

Although approximately fifty percent of the campaign budget is allotted to advertising, gratuitous promotion has a much greater impact. The candidate sometimes does better in a state where he spends less money in advertising, such as when Bush won Iowa after being outspent by Reagan. Or, to prove the theory, when Bush outspent both Reagan and Anderson in Illinois, he came in a poor third.

Still, "media buys" are considered vital in the life-or-death primary effort. Their principal objective is to provide name identification or to counter specific attacks by the opposition.

It may be wise to stipulate that in order for a candidate to receive federal funds there are limitations in each state as to the total amount that a candidate may spend on the campaign, thereby limiting to some degree the share that can be allocated to paid media. Otherwise, even more money might be wasted.

The impact of paid media strengthens the benefits of free media, and vice versa. Sometimes the candidate stirs excitement with a provocative statement during a speech or at a press conference. It is picked up as newsworthy by the media, then later repeated through paid advertising. Conversely, paid media might come first. A prime example of the counteraction of these two approaches occurred in the 1988 Bush-Dukakis skirmish, when the GOP took off against the Democrats on family values, the environment, defense, and patriotism. For weeks the TV sets blared commercials and news broadcasts on the sins of Willie Horton and pollution in Boston Harbor. The ingenious use of television campaigning is just beginning. During the 1988 campaign, Senator Dole, sitting in a Washington studio, answered questions from newsmen located at stations in Iowa and Massachusetts (which reach New Hampshire), all linked by satellite. The half-hour satellite feed cost the campaign less than a thirty-second ad would have cost, if it followed a Boston evening newscast.

Congressman Gephardt hired his own camera crew to track him around our state. From this filming, short videotapes were cut, then sent by satellite to stations nationwide as an integral part of his publicity plan.

With the availability of candidate-purchased video filming and satellite transmission, campaigns now have a relatively untapped field with which to enhance their capacities for image building. Unsophisticated programmers frequently weave into local newscasts self-serving political material furnished to them. When a candidate is interviewed by the press on paid TV time, there's always the question of who is in control of the action. Is the candidate buying news coverage? It may be a case of the campaign manipulating the media, rather than the other way around.

Some stations welcome unsolicited clips from a candidate, as it enriches their programming; whereas others are suspicious that it's only a subterfuge to obtain free advertising. When Bush talked with Gorbachev during the 1988 campaign, his promoters bought studio and satellite services to publicize the meeting all over the country. One station solved the problem by reimbursing the campaign for its share of the cost.

————

The tone of a campaign also affects media coverage. The decent, honest, high-principled approach never gets as much ink as does the scurrilous attack. Of course, this has always been true in American politics, even before the days of Lincoln Steffens' muckrakers. Sensationalism sells newspapers.

In the presidential campaign of 1852 our own Franklin Pierce, a veteran of the Mexican War, was portrayed as the "Fainting General" with a drinking problem and "a hero of many a well-fought bottle."

The flagrant use of what we now call negative advertising, which I thought reached its peak in the general election of 1988, became that election's most incendiary issue. Its effectiveness against Dukakis was probably what assured Bush's success; albeit Bush was later quoted by Tom Raum of the Associated Press as saying, "What some consider negative, others consider factual."

Apparently it had not reached its peak because, in reporting about the New York City municipal election and the gubernatorial elections of New Jersey and Virginia in November of 1989, James M. Perry of the *Wall Street Journal* said, "This is the year of the negative ad." He quoted Douglas Bailey, a political consultant: "Unlike a few years ago, you don't even have to worry whether the ad is truthful."

Then there are others, like Woody West writing in *Insight* magazine, who claim that low voter turnout results from boredom with electioneering. His solution: "Let's have more negative campaigning, more verve and fire and, yes, wickedness."

The acceleration of hardball politics is largely fueled by television, an industry which requires action and speed to keep it competitive. In political races, confrontation is vital. The public has come to expect some vitriole to spice up the program. If the 1988 experience was a real sample of what's happening, the 1992 Primary may reach the pinnacle of acrimony, even within the political party. Campaign strategists will count on such divisiveness as a lure for media attention.

New Hampshire Senator Warren Rudman introduced a bill in the Senate which would have required the candidate or his identified representative to appear in person on any TV ad of less than ten minutes. It would have eliminated anonymity in content and presentation of political advertising. The idea took cognizance of the mudslinging problem and perhaps might not have violated the First Amendment.

Maybe we'd be better off to leave the matter to the viewer's standard of decency. President Bush himself said, "I put confidence in the American people—their ability to sort through what is fair and what is unfair, what is ugly and what is un-ugly, and be as positive as possible."

President Lyndon Johnson's campaign in 1964 ran the shocking ad, aforementioned, where a child was picking petals from a daisy, followed by a mushroom cloud, giving rise to a not-so-subtle suggestion that his opponent, Senator Goldwater, might start a nuclear war. Neither Goldwater nor the campaign was mentioned. Its producer, Tony Schwartz, explained, "It was not what the ad said, but what the people thought it said that made it so effective." There was such an anguished howl from viewers that the ad was immediately withdrawn.

Ken Bode examines in his *TV Guide* article the ethical lapses of politicians, approaching the trend from another direction: "One reason the political beat is changing is that when ethics and scandal are not at the center of the news, politics is considered dull stuff."

Meanwhile, the "hit-and-run" factor of the evening newscast continues its insatiable consumption of the new and different. When the day's excitement is sparse and the news is scant, the newsdesk scrapes for good copy. This is particularly true during a lengthy political campaign. The ongoing, in-depth review of the

New Hampshire Primary, night after night, can become monotonous. Thus, the search for conflict is inevitable, often leading to fabrication or emphasis on controversy, which otherwise would be considered insignificant.

A side effect of these TV symptoms is that they infect the viewers' judgment. The public is now conditioned to expecting rapidly changing images, and psychologists say our mental capacity to sustain is limited. Voters who are TV addicts are said to come to quicker decisions and hold them for shorter periods of time. While this is an annoyance to the TV scheduler, it's a momentous problem for the campaign. The political strategist must be constantly aware that a quick vote earned on TV today can be lost just as quickly on TV tomorrow.

As James M. Perry wrote in the *Wall Street Journal,* "The TV clutter means that the shelf life of ideas is reduced and people are less durable. People make up their minds faster, then change them readily."

As we move into the 1990s television will continue to innoculate more and more voters before they go to the polls. The negative aspects of its influence threaten the traditional grass-roots and retail politics we've practiced here since 1952.

Should this occur it would be a serious consequence for the rest of the country, as New Hampshire would no longer serve as the nation's guide in choosing its president.

CHAPTER 12

New Hampshire: "Always First, Always Right"

From colonial days New Hampshire citizens, pressed by the long, cold winters and unyielding soil, turned to politics to enrich daily living. They created easy access to the ballot and the largest state legislatures, encouraging everyone to participate in government.

Today our practice of politics has progressed to offer anyone the opportunity of beginning here to seek the presidency. It costs little to file and requires nothing in the way of qualifications —just endurance—though height may be a factor. Four-foot, eleven-inch Senator Barbara Ann Mikulski of Maryland said she couldn't run here because, "I can't figure out how to be seen above the snowdrifts."

Sometimes the media and the candidate are one in providing the message and expanding the themes of a campaign.

Nor have times changed much in this candidate-media relationship. Witness the close ties to the press enjoyed by the late, long-gone George Sibley of Manchester, who would count on the local press and radio to promote his several crusades while he served in the legislature.

He sought legislation to stop carnage on the highways by instituting a compulsory eight-hour sleep bill. The press loved it and dwelt at length on the inspectors and time pieces that would be required to enforce the law.

Sibley's fame grew and his views were carried as far as Maine, Vermont, and Massachusetts. He introduced a bill that would require at least one seven-foot bed in every hotel to accommodate tall tourists. Another reform would have imposed a fine on any member of a household who refused to open the front door to do business with a salesman or political canvasser.

Still, as Ted White wrote years ago, nothing could be more wrong than "the myth holds that New Hampshire is full of twangy, skinflint Uncle Ephs or Uncle Calebs who make their living by whittling antiques, milking cows and fleecing tourists."

Although in today's technological age greater emphasis is placed on the electronic media by candidates to communicate their message, the voters of New Hampshire have consistently ignored this method by requiring all presidential aspirants to meet them, one-on-one.

Our process affords a unique opportunity for the entire nation to observe ordinary citizens, instead of network commentators, asking the tough questions. Views are expounded in person, not distilled by television editors. Positions are analyzed by each of us, not by hired pollsters.

Decisions are made on what candidates say and how we perceive their leadership, not on how they come across on the tube. Television is one-way communication. It speaks to you; you can't speak to it.

To those who say the state is too small to be representative of the electorate at large, I say that its smallness testifies to the openness of the system. It allows for the testing of new ideas while spotting the shams. Wary people ask sharp questions. It's pretty hard for a candidate to fake it when talking face to face. Since 1952, through ten primaries, the fanfare hasn't fooled us. Neither money nor media can dictate what is a truly democratic approach.

Ron Brown, Democratic national chairman, thinks our primary is "grossly overestimated." Not surprisingly he was further quoted in the Manchester *Union Leader* as saying that the national leaders of his party "wring their hands" about the impact of the role our tiny state plays in selecting presidents. Considering that in the ten times our Primary has been tested it has triggered the election of seven Republican presidents, his concern is easily understood. Lyndon Johnson (and perhaps even Jimmy Carter after he ran the second time) would probably have agreed with him.

In 1976 Representative Morris Udall got taken here by a relatively unknown Jimmy Carter. Predictably, in 1984, the usually good-natured Udall took revenge by introducing legislation which would shorten our Primary season. It bothered him that we've had more to say about choosing our president than the people of New York or California.

So what? We've culled a lot of losers, including the good congressman. Pollster Pat Caddell discovered that Granite Staters are better informed and generally more discerning about candidates and issues than are voters in other primary states. In national campaigns we rarely get hung up on local issues.

It may be absurd to say that New Hampshire people were chosen to elect our chief executive, but it sounds like envy and sour grapes from those who lament that our influence is too great.

In 1988, for example, even the Democrats tried to forewarn the country about Dukakis' slim chance for success. A next-door neighbor we knew very well, he received only 36% of the Democratic vote. Over 60% of New Hampshire's Democrats did not vote for him. Weren't they trying to say something?

If and when California decides to move its primary up from next-to-last, immediately following ours, we would have to worry. Some of their legislators have felt their primary was almost meaningless because they did not have the benefit of looking at all the candidates. According to Fresno assemblyman Jim Costa "We haven't had an impact on the Democratic primary since 1972 and the Republican primary since 1964."

We think the voters of the Golden State should be happy because we saved the country from their Mayor Yorty and

Governor Brown. Besides, California may be typical, but typical of what?

California has six times as many convention delegates as we do and, to make matters worse, as applied to Republicans, has a "winner take all" law. Obviously the candidates would spend less time here and our Primary would become less important.

The importance of the New Hampshire Primary to the would-be nominees for the presidency comes from the national attention which they receive by participating in it. But it is not our Primary, the national party conventions, nor even the fall general election which nominates the president. It's the Electoral College which makes that final decision.

Thus, once the Granite State Primary is over, New Hampshire becomes totally unimportant in the overall strategy for the surviving candidates. They concentrate on the larger twenty-five states which hold the balance of the Electoral College votes. The public is either not aware or tends to forget that a nominee can win the fall general election and still not win the presidency. Our state with its mere four Electoral College votes is insignificant in this context. Once the Presidential Primary returns are counted, the political sun sets in New Hampshire, not to rise again until four years later.

From the viewpoint of convention delegates, there are those who argue that because the Super Tuesday of 1988 did not diffuse the New Hampshire Primary, an early California primary would likewise not lessen the impact of our event. This logic is skewed, since California represents a single state and obviously would be easier to manage than another dozen or more in a subsequent Super Tuesday.

Due to its geographic size and because more than ten percent of our national population lives there, the inordinate expense of campaigning in California would virtually eliminate the opportunity for self-starters. As Lou Cannon has written, "Californians are so numerous that candidates can reach them effectively only through television, which means it costs millions of dollars to wage even a rudimentary campaign."

The level playing field which New Hampshire has provided for unknowns would become a thing of the past. Which might be okay as long as they are Democrats, but suppose they were Republicans?

A Nashua *Telegraph* editorial stated it very well: "Candidates are not likely to withstand the expenses of California campaigning without a hefty war chest. This, in turn, heightens the pernicious influence of special interests. Candidates of modest means will be deprived of the opportunity to present their causes." It went on to point out that California's treasure trove of delegates should appropriately not be mined until later in the schedule, because "after all, the National Football League does not stage the Super Bowl during the middle of the regular season."

Or, it was put another way by a *Concord Monitor* editorial: "Any change that forces candidates to raise more money to communicate with voters through admen and image-builders will be detrimental to a system that with each election turns off more and more voters."

I believe it is an impractical and illogical view expressed by the *New York Times* that "By winning Iowa and New Hampshire, such a candidate might attract enough free media attention to offset a big paid advertising campaign."

For openers, how many unknown candidates have carried both Iowa and New Hampshire? If one ever did, how would he put together in one week or two a campaign in California which could compete with the money and resources that would already have been spent in that state over the previous months or years to elect a nationally recognized contestant? While we relish our long primary season, we have no quarrel with Iowa, which precedes us. It represents a different economic environment. In 1988, for example, Iowa was struggling with agricultural contraction while we were dealing with high-tech expansion. Theirs is a caucus, which is not a free expression of broad public sentiment. Consequently, the choices made there have to be corrected here anyway.

In fact, it's probably healthy for us that Iowa is out there providing a media appetizer. It leaves them salivating in anticipation of the main entree here. By the time they get to dessert elsewhere, they've been pretty well stuffed from New Hampshire, especially those who have enjoyed our comfortable accommodations and low-priced liquor.

Then there are those like Democratic Senator Alan Dixon, who would mandate that we join a regional primary for the alleged lofty purpose of compelling candidates to discuss broader issues of national interest than those of a single state. The truth is they want to demagnetize our first-in-the-nation position.

Quite apart from the foolishness of tinkering with a system that has worked so well, there is the constitutional question of states' rights. We resent the concept of Democrats in Congress regulating how we'd conduct a Republican primary.

Ironically it is a Democrat, Senator John Glenn, after campaigning unsuccessfully here in 1984, who put a regional primary in its proper perspective: "A New England regional primary would prevent the less well-known, less well-financed candidates in our party from having an opportunity to campaign in a primary where person-to-person, grassroots democratic politics is still more effective than the impersonal media campaign."

The senator expressed the further opinion that New Hampshire should be allowed to continue holding its primary earlier than all other state primaries and that beauty contest primaries, such as Vermont's, should be discouraged.

The downside of regionals was patently demonstrated when a group of states, in the so-called southern regional primary, all counted their ballots on Super Tuesday, March 8, 1988. More than a dozen states voted that day, making it physically impossible for the candidates to visit most of them for more than abbreviated in-and-out hellos.

Maybe more hands were shaken at airport short stops than were shaken in all New Hampshire, but in the time frames allowed it's a cinch that more of us had the opportunity to size up the candidates from close personal contact than the combined population of all those other states. Their impressions were primarily fixed from intensive media coverage and advertising.

It's oddball Yankee humor that one of our voters was asked if she'd vote for George Bush. Her answer: "Don't know, only met him three times."

Nonetheless, the moth-eaten anecdote illustrates the value we place on perseverance. Were it not for the opportunity of allowing unknowns to establish themselves in our Primary, the perceived front-runners would have little competition. The creative ideas of a Pete DuPont, an Al Haig, or a Howard Baker might otherwise not be articulated . . . yes, not even a Harold Stassen.

New Hampshire offers the only viable proving ground for the popular axiom that any American citizen, not just the political moguls, can aspire to the presidency. Here a candidate has the one and only opportunity to be recognized by the national media and dissected by a heterogeneous though compact population.

Simultaneously, we perform a service by providing gravestones in our vast political cemetery for fallen candidates. As Senator Eugene McCarthy recalled on a 1989 visit to Dartmouth, "I think more people die in New Hampshire than win." If an ambitious candidate cannot "outsnow" our rigorous winter analysis, why should the rest of the country be made to suffer his shortcomings?

Should an incumbent be running, even a vice president, without our Primary as a preliminary test, the odds would be insurmountable against his being effectively challenged elsewhere. It's a perk of the Office that the incumbent gets prime time at almost any hour requested and full coverage for the rest of the day.

But on three occasions our Primary has delivered a clear message of "no confidence" to the occupants of the White House: Truman in 1952, Johnson in 1968, and perhaps Mondale in 1984, though he was not in there then and had only been a vice president. Of course, they were all Democrats.

As long as both parties endorse open primaries to give any citizen the chance to run for president, the New Hampshire Primary is the practical place for contestants to start.

I must admit that the New Hampshire Primary tends to nurture more interest in the candidates themselves, as individuals, than for the party they represent. Since we have more Independents than Democrats, many of them will take a Republican ballot in the Presidential Primary (they can regain their Independent status thereafter by meeting certain requirements), just because they like a particular Republican who has campaigned effectively here, but certainly not because they consider themselves to be of Republican persuasion.

Obviously neither the Republican nor Democratic machines will operate in an open primary. The Primary contestants attempt to define themselves as dissimilar from their opponents within their respective parties and frequently with themes which are not necessarily those yet endorsed by their party.

Following a strenuous nationwide campaign, by the time the party nominee is selected at the party's late-summer convention that candidate has, in a sense, become more identifiable in the public mind than the party. For the same reason that some Independents will vote Republican in our Primary, others in the subsequent nationwide general election will vote for the individual—not the party.

In my view the average voter, unless he or she happens to be a one-issue zealot, is not solemnly concerned with the text or substance of a presidential campaign. The best evidence of this is that hardly anyone seems to care about what is written in either the Republican or Democratic platforms. Except for the few days of hearings to determine what goes into them, nobody ever hears any more about them. Nor are they often cited thereafter by the parties, the Congress, or elected officials. Until questioned by a reporter or pollster on a particular issue, the voter probably had not given it any serious thought.

Of course if he or she is hung up on a single issue like abortion, nuclear energy, drugs, or women's rights, then the issue

276

takes priority over either the party or the candidate. These individuals are the exception and are sometimes so ardent as to be dangerous to our system. As long as a potential nominee will vote "right" on their pet cause, they will vote for that candidate regardless of his or her other qualifications or lack thereof. The candidate could be an idiot or a Communist; it would not make the slightest difference.

All the foregoing leads to the conclusion that parties are playing a lesser role because the candidates are hyping themselves with the ever-increasing influence of television, to a considerably greater extent than ever before. I agree with pollster Bob Teeter that "People don't really vote on issues, they vote on people." In more and more cases it's not the party line which determines the choice, rather it comes down to a gut feeling about the candidate.

Then, too, there are those of us who pride ourselves on being good Republicans yet do not always support the party. Seldom have I voted a straight Republican ticket. Nor was it surprising when Frank Fahrenkopf, Jr., former Republican national chairman, told me he had not always voted for Republicans either, shielding his admission by adding, "I wouldn't have said that when I was the party's chairman."

It's anyone's guess as to why the percentage of voters participating in the national election between Dukakis and Bush in 1988 was one of the lowest in history. Any number of things could have turned off the voters—over-saturation from television to the blandness of the candidates.

But considering the mix, I would wager that the diminution of party influence had a lot to do with it. Actually it reflects the continuation of the trend that there's a substantially smaller percentage of voter turnout in the twentieth century than there was in the nineteenth. I believe this condition will worsen in the 1990s, as voter turnout continues its decrease in nearly all states.

Dr. Raymond Wolfinger, a professor of political science at the University of California, points out that the legalities and difficulties of reregistering for the estimated seventeen to twenty percent of voting-age Americans who move each year are a substantial cause of our low voter turnout. He estimates that voter turnout could be increased by nine percent if our mobile population could be easily registered.

His solution has been incorporated in congressional bills (National Voter Registration Act of 1989) which would establish national voter registration procedures for federal elections by utilizing Postal Service change-of-address cards and motor vehicle drivers' license applications. Unfortunately, this answer may violate the principle of states' rights and lead to ineffective checklist verification, or perhaps easier voter fraud.

As an aside, I also agree with Dayton Duncan, former press secretary to Governor Dukakis, that "character in the broad sense is the most important criterion in assessing who should lead our nation." The president can give leadership by formulating policy, but his job is to execute what our legislative leaders direct.

The chief executive does not make laws; the Congress does. Besides, what appears to be fact from outside the Oval Office may be quite different from within. Conditions change and unprecedented situations arise in our rapidly changing world which a president could not have anticipated when running for office.

Some describe New Hampshire as atypical, usually because we have such a miniscule percentage of ethnic minorities. But is any state typical? As our secretary of state, Bill Gardner, pointed out, Florida has an abundance of elderly, Alaska an oversupply of young people, and every state has something that sets it apart. As he says, "If you look at all the criteria . . . percentage of population over 65, under 18, college-educated, as well as median income, family income, median age, and the like, then we are typical."

Having suffered a few skirmishes with other states which have attempted to share our limelight, in 1977 we believed we had insured our first-in-the-nation status by amending our Primary law. It now reads that the election will be held on "the second Tuesday in March or on the Tuesday immediately preceding the date on which any other state shall hold a similar election, whichever is earlier, of each year when a President of the United States is to be elected."

We had felt quite secure in our preemptive date until we received word from a group of eager American self-starters from Guam. They noted that America's day begins in Guam, so why shouldn't the primary season begin there also? It was a threat to undertake a presidential primary on the same date as ours. Because their island empire is on the west side of the international date line, the results of their tabulation would hit the newswires one full hour before the polls would open here.

In further torment we were reminded we could not change the situation unless we could make the earth spin the other way. Assuming that under their tropical sun they'd gotten into too much papaya juice, we've chosen to ignore them.

Our status became more tenuous when columnist Mike Royko of the *Chicago Sun* suggested New Hampshire should get a choice of either moving our Primary back "into the pack where it will receive the attention it deserves—which is none—or be thrown out of the United States." Obviously he had either been frostbitten or lost his snowshoes here in 1979. We ignored him, too.

––––––––

Ten years ago Robert W. Merry wrote in *Quill* that Hugh Gregg's "views on the growing political significance of the news media reflected a perception shared by more and more analysts of American politics." By now it has become universally apparent that columnists, reporters, and commentators, all aided by the pervasive potency of TV, are doing a lot more than just informing the public.

Now, after enjoying ten more years of self-perpetuating psephology (the science of interpreting elections), what could foster more frivolous frolic than taking on the giant pundits? Jousting with the media greats could become a provocative political sideline.

We in the political community have a high regard for Jack

Germond, coauthor with Jules Witcover of their latest caper, *Whose Broad Stripes and Bright Stars.*

Before the 1976 primary Germond had all but dismissed the chances of the incumbent, Gerry Ford, for winning the Republican Primary in New Hampshire, practically conceding the primary and nomination to the rising star of Ronald Reagan. This was an unfortunate prognostication because, added to Governor Mel Thomson's last-minute braggadocio in predicting a 55% win, Germond and the rest of the pack resoundingly proclaimed the 49% Reagan vote a solid defeat!

In response to an interview with Merry, I had commented on another Germond pronouncement that George Bush's campaign had already peaked when he announced his candidacy for president in May of 1979. "That prediction and the later interpretation of the result (echoed in other journalistic reports) still rankle former New Hampshire Gov. Gregg," wrote Merry.

My remarks to Merry had been succinct: "The press has too much power. . . . It's a great example of how the national media make or break a candidate."

Jules Witcover reacted on behalf of his partner: "To say we make or break Presidents is preposterous.... It's our job to report what candidates and people say, and in 1976 they were saying that Reagan's 49% was a defeat, which it was."

And so came down the toothsome twosome's defensive declarations. They couldn't have been more wrong.

One of the real perks of being a campaign chairman is the opportunity to interface with such media stalwarts as Jack Germond, Hedrick Smith, Al Hunt, and Theodore White. Of course now that it's over I fall into the category to which Jack relegates faded governors in his book: "Because the state's governors serve only two-year terms and seem to be a hardy lot, any candidate with any pretensions of seriousness could find a former governor to be chairman of his committee."

That's okay with me, Jack, because we're still one up on the eminent political journalists of this world. As Dave Broder expressed in *Behind the Front Page*, none of you has yet sat and worked inside a candidate's headquarters for months on end, experiencing the pressures and realities of a vigorous political operation when the press is not around.

The daily maintenance of a spirited stallion, not to mention keeping the stable stainless, is stirring serendipity, indeed, but newspaper reporters don't stay long at the fair. They come to watch the race and kibitz with the jockeys. "We are voyeurs, not participants," asserts Broder.

As Merry put it, " . . . a related, and perhaps more serious criticism concerns Mr. Germond's addiction, frequently shared by Mr. Witcover, to political handicapping—the effort, often called 'horse-race reporting,' to divine who's up, who's down and who's going to win. The criticism takes on added importance in light of those new perceptions about the news media's growing role in the political process."

Says Germond, "I don't apologize for the horse-race school of journalism; I'm an advocate of it."

An equally serious Dave Broder counterpunches in his own book: "Horse-race journalism does everything the critics say. It short-circuits the system."

This fundamental disagreement between two extremely successful political reporters adds fodder to the frenzy, since not only do Broder and Germond acknowledge the chasm in their styles, but apparently Germond is not too compatible with George Will, either. Referring to Will's describing George Bush as a "lapdog" for his courtship of the ultraconservative wing of the Republican party, he declares Will's imagery "a somewhat ironic label coming from one of the right's prime bootlickers."

The fact that Fred Barnes, now a popular political writer and talk-show guest in his own right, worked under Germond for several years and wanted to "emulate Jack's way of reporting," and that Mark Shields (the Bob Hope of the columnists) also attests to Germond's considerable influence, confirms that Germond is still regarded as a guru of sorts, though now a self-admitted victim of dismay, perhaps too often "kept at bay."

Journalists resent any button-up quality in a political operation, and lament the trends which keep them at bay, whether because of security precautions either necessitated by recurring violence against our presidents, or created by the mediaphobia of fear- or tear-ful candidates.

There are few other instances in which Germond and I disagree, particularly in the way he credits polls for the direction of the New Hampshire 1988 campaign. In a chapter entitled "New Hampshire: the Resurrection of George Bush," he uses the word "polls" fifteen times and "surveys" five times. Admittedly, Bob Teeter, Bush's pollster, was a conspicuous and highly valued member of the inside team. But the sophisticated New Hampshire electorate is so traditionally independent it is nonsensical to believe they all jumped on the Bush bandwagon because of what the polls dictated. Quite the opposite. It was the enthusiasm of an aggressive organization, well-nursed for a very long time, which created the surge of momentum, plus an innate sense of knowing where the action was.

Again, so many of our citizens already knew George Bush personally. He'd only been working the terrain for ten years! Even his son, Neil, was better known than any of the contenders who competed with his father, including a well-recognized but less popular Bob Dole.

As for the straddle ad, to which is attributed much of the Bush-Dole campaign's ultimate success, it did define the differences at exactly the right time. But to suggest that any television advertising can deliver the coup de grace is almost insulting to a discerning viewing audience who detest blatant manipulation.

The ad may have reinforced the convictions of those who needed it, and may have lured a few, but the hunch that there may have been a hint of truth, or even potential truth, in the contrast between Dole and Bush was already there.

Bob Dole's previous performances on the campaign trail, his

record in Washington, and his general political philosophy were not a secret. It seems far more logical to conclude that New Hampshire people did make their choice based on what they knew about the two men, not on what they saw or didn't see on television.

At least Germond attributes some weight to the "staged media events" which he says were perhaps effective in reaching the average viewer. Bush's driving the forklift truck and Dukakis' riding in an army tank, for instance, did make a lasting impression, though in retrospect it was all very amusing—and perhaps that's why the spots were memorable. A few entertaining events, though contrived, amidst an otherwise disturbing exhibition.

Other than a passing reference to the superior organization of 1988 under the control of Andy Card, Atwater, and Sununu, the book gives little consideration to the part that Bush's ten-year buildup, before the threesome was even on the scene, might have had on the final result.

The very fact that his popularity endured for that long in New Hampshire, that the people here continued to believe in him, and that the organization survived for a decade should prove unequivocally that George Bush had the "right stuff" all along.

It seems unfair to continually discount so completely the efforts of those stalwart Bush supporters who carried the Bush banner, working and proselytizing on-site and behind the scenes for a solid decade. This is another one of those cases where self-appointed analysts cannot possibly know what's going on in New Hampshire when they're sitting down in Washington.

As Germond and Witcover said so well in their previous publication, *Blue Smoke and Mirrors*, "Exactly why one candidate wins and another loses a presidential election is always difficult to say with any precision. The voters make their decisions on the basis of a whole complex of factors: national and parochial issues, the personality and character of the candidates, voters' own personal situations, peer pressures, information and misinformation from the news media and advertising, sometimes simple impulse.

Not even the most sophisticated opinion poll can sift out all of these elements and assign them relative weights, although that task is among those the new technocrats of politics always strive to accomplish.

It was a refreshing respite romping through Germond's and Witcover's latest energetic exercise. By contrast, it elevated in my own esteem the perspicacious Dave Broder, whose *Behind the Front Page* frankly discusses an honest writer's woes. He uses descriptive chapter titles such as "Missing the Story" (by taking statements out of context or caricaturing the candidate), "Plots That Failed" (which touches on all sorts of journalistic pitfalls), and "Bias—and Other Sins."

Broder admits, "Whether we acknowledge it or not, we are constantly devising the scripts we think appropriate for the events we are covering." And, that " . . . those who are seeking to 'make news' . . . must, ideally, do something unusual, unexpected, or unprecedented. But they must do it in a time, place, and manner that fit the unvarying routine of the news organizations."

Hence the sound bites and vital importance of making the evening news.

———————

In spite of the "insider" practicing politician's view of the foreboding changes in the election process versus the "outsider" traveling journalists' converging conclusions, a number of interesting parallels can be developed.

A widespread alarm is being sounded, which somehow must resound beyond the political community to a much too preoccupied, apathetic electorate.

Interestingly, the span of time that Germond and Witcover covered in their latest publication is almost the same, 1964-present, as I've attempted to cover. Clearly it has been such a disappointing evolution that we are now pleading for enlightenment, declaring a war on contrivance and negativism, and almost unanimously begging to be heard.

All of which reemphasizes the need for continuing primaries

in small states where the effects of media can be offset, at least minimally, by personal interaction.

Quite apart from all the reasons that foreign forces allege for doing away with our "first status," there is very sober reasoning for its retention. We are the last remaining vestige of hope to preserve the spirit of democracy as it was conceived and practiced by our forefathers.

Our ancestors suffered no massive distillage of election information beamed in living color to every household. Professional pollsters did not mine for issues, professional strategists did not turn the news into political imagery, and nationwide television networks did not feed their self-proclaimed conclusions into every hearth.

New Hampshire still offers the opportunity for all its citizens to make their own independent and undeluded judgments after seeing, hearing, and touching the candidate himself. If voters did not talk to the candidate, it's because they did not want to.

At the same time it is conceded that our state, like the world, is vastly different in the Bush age than it was in the Rockefeller age. The *Keene Sentinel* summed it up succinctly: "We could leave our cars wherever we liked, stick our trash in a hole in the ground and put our boats where we darn pleased . . . now we have restrictions on parking, we are instituting mandatory recycling, and we have a new boat mooring law."

Along with everything else, the art of campaigning is also changing. As Nancy Reagan noted in her book, old-fashioned door-to-door campaigns are the kind of politics which is quickly dying out in the age of television.

Still, the idea that Washington, or wherever national presidential campaigns may be directed, knows more about how to do things here is absurd. Just because electronic technology has changed the focus of information for most voters, the personal approach remains vital to success in the Granite State. It's the traditional way of political self-expression basic to our democratic system—one we can ill afford to lose. Reliance on polls, professionals, and packaged publicity allows too much latitude for pitching phony perceptions to the people.

———————

What's more, with the advances being made in high-tech communications and the direction which political contrivance is taking us, let's muse upon a possible horrifying scenario for the national general election in the year 2000, or maybe even as early as 1996.

Envision yourself in front of your TV screen, watching an election week documentary series on that year's presidential candidate. Each party's contenders are uniformly videotaped, using a biography, positions on issues, fragments from the candidate's most significant speeches, and his or her own "pitch" or commentary.

The Public Broadcasting Service has already produced a similar program. They won the George Peabody Award for "The Choice," a "Frontline" *Time* special aired during the 1988 campaign. The piece presented candid, balanced studies of the two major presidential candidates.

The climax to this fantasy comes on Election Day, prime time. With a preregistered electronic voting device cupped securely in your hand, wired to an enormous worldwide satellite system controlled by the Federal Election Commission, you are now expected to cast your vote for the next president of the United States.

Within an authorized four-hour span, secluded from the influence of exit polls, time-zone sequences, and network forecasts, even the nation's shut-ins and Americans all over the globe will have cast their ballot.

The technology is already in place.

"Call Interactive," a joint venture of American Express and American Telephone and Telegraph Company, might allow such service by the voter dialing a 900 telephone number. The *Wall Street Journal* says that ABC Sports' marketing director reports that "tens of thousands" of fans already call its 900 number each week to vote on game action during the football season.

The Nielsen rating system established long ago a means of identifying those who regularly participate in its system of monitoring the popularity of certain TV shows. Voter checklists could be generated and updated from a central data bank by similar procedures.

Let's examine the advantages of this idea:

1) It would no longer be necessary to go to a polling place to cast your ballot.

2) The elimination of voter precincts would obviate the cost of maintenance, staffing, paperwork, voting machines, and all other related expenses. The money saved would perhaps more than offset the support costs of the TV network.

3) Weather would no longer be a factor.

4) There would be greater convenience in being able to vote in nearly any location. Public TV facilities would be provided for those who did not own one.

5) Absentee ballots, if not eliminated, would be required only for extreme circumstances.

6) The ease of voting would substantially increase participation.

7) The opportunity for fraud at the local level would be greatly reduced.

8) Everyone, everywhere, would vote within the same time frame.

9) The media could no longer manipulate election results from early returns or exit polls.

Do I hear my friends saying, "Gregg, you're reaching"? Well, maybe, but consider that forty years ago political campaigns were, in fact, grass-roots efforts. Today the designation is no more than a term of endearment.

Our constituencies here previously framed the issues from local appearances or personal contacts with the candidates. But no longer is the Granite Stater allowed to be quite as much a part of the framing procedures, unless he is tallied in the miniscule sampling used by national pollsters. It's a far cry from the days when

Joe Citizen's views were expressed and actually adopted at a local candidate's forum.

Political strategists from inside the Washington beltway, abetted by pollsters, are framing the issues. A new profession of self-styled "consultants," earning exorbitant salaries, is calling the shots. Enlightened from their computers, manuals, demographic and psychographic documentation, a unidirectional modus operandi is established for each candidate's campaign. Variations create turmoil. Personalization at the local level is anathema to the prescribed agenda.

Even those long-term, well-experienced, and dedicated volunteers who regularly participate in campaigns are directed by outsiders whose playbills are inflexibly fixed by out-of-state tacticians.

Polls and surveys "tend to take on a life of their own," says Leo Bogart, executive vice president of the Newspaper Advertising Bureau. "A poll is a snapshot, not a guide to action," wrote a noted columnist.

It is assumed that all fifty states reflect similar priorities of interest and concerns. Campaign decisions are made without reference to neighborhood precincts. For example, abortion and illegal drugs are national issues, but matters of major concern to New England voters, such as acid rain or the Seabrook nuclear power plant, are not issues west of the Rockies. Nor are we in the Northeast worrying about immigration along the Rio Grande or the problems of the timber industry in the Northwest.

Once issues are determined by these ersatz methods, the national media, particularly television, hype the public and set the course for political debate. The sheer power and intensity of ABC, NBC, CBS, CNN, C-Span, and other cable networks compel the voter to accept political agendas set by a few.

How much longer will there be a "bellwether state"? Soon all the bells will be pealing the same tone. We'll no longer need to go to the polls to vote on Election Day, because the results will have been predetermined for us by computerized consensus.

So, perhaps my scenario isn't so far out after all. Besides, it would solve Congress' problem of finding a way to standardize nationwide poll closing hours!

But then, if you still think my projection is hallucinatory, I offer another solution which would retain and yet expedite our traditional values.

New Hampshire may be a small state geographically, but presidential primaries have time and again demonstrated that the judgment of its citizens is an accurate reflection of our country's political posture.

As stated so many times before, since the process began in 1952, no candidate has ever been elected president of the United States without first having won the New Hampshire Primary.

Which suggests an interesting possibility: Rather than perpetuating the expense and effort of primaries or caucuses in all the states and possessions, why not hold only the New Hampshire Primary?

The other states would be spared the costs of their elections; it would be an inexpensive way of eliminating those candidates who couldn't make it to the presidency anyway; it would cut down on the use of political TV, leaving more prime time for coverage of other sporting events; and, finally, it would confine the selection procedure to a much shorter span of time.

Moreover, after the system had been tested for two or three elections, it might even work out that the Republican and Democratic parties would discover their conventions were unnecessary.

Trouble is, this suggestion could never catch on. No self-respecting politician would give up his or her quadrennial five-day escapade with fellow carousers, skittish lest it might interfere with their exercise of good government!

All of which brings me back to square one, our Presidential Primary slogan, "New Hampshire—Always First, Always Right."

Luckily there are still enough of us here who are either political activists or involved citizens and have conscientiously worked the process since its inception in 1952. New volunteers appear for every campaign, lured by the excitement of friendship with a potential president or for sincere patriotic reasons.

They are all bucking the trend, proud of their contributions, spurred by altruistic vision. Thanks to their strength and tenacity, the unique State of New Hampshire continues to offer some hope for traditional democracy.

As we approach the 1992 elections there will be continued resistance to our partaking of such a pivotal chunk in the electoral process. There was similar pressure prior to the last four presidentials. Auspiciously, none of them resulted in our last hurrah, nor do we intend to surrender our status in the future.

It was back in 1976 when Al Hunt wrote in the *Wall Street Journal*, "As long as the nation is saddled with the present system, New Hampshire, with its imperfections, really isn't a bad place to start." Since that time the system has not changed and for four more times we served it well.

"Boy, there is no place like New Hampshire," the journalists proclaimed, according to Broder, the night of the Bush-Reagan debate of 1980 in Nashua.

"The New Hampshire ritual is not an easy one for politicians or those who write about them. Uncertainties abound. Minor lapses can damage a man's prospects. And journalists who happen to be looking the other way may miss the meanings. Yet, the New Hampshire primary transcends all that. It has proven itself a good place to start great political adventures and to end unpromising ones. New Hampshire answers a lot of questions," says Hugh Sidey in his foreword to *First Step to the White House*.

Paced by the overwhelming influence of television, polling, and the professionals, presidential elections have glamorized politics. The glitz and gloss by which we've become mesmerized have distracted us from the serious objective of politics, which is to establish a responsible and responsive government of qualified leaders.

Thus, when the country votes for its chief executive in 1992, it is more imperative than ever that New Hampshire should again have the first opportunity of preserving the electoral system which has been the very foundation of our democracy for over two hundred years.

Index

ABC-TV, 48, 233, 248, 286, 288

Abbott, William, 105, 112, 120, 127

Adams, John Quincy, 2

Adams, Sherman, 217

Ailes, Roger, 159, 162, 229, 235, 255

Allen, Richard, 224

Anderson, John, 69, 72, 84, 98, 222, 263

Anderson, Marty, 52, 223, 224

Annenbergs, The, 114

Annis, Genevieve, 80

Apple, R. W., Jr., 166

Arel, Maurice, 106

Atwater, Lee, 127, 131, 159, 180, 181, 229, 230, 234, 283

Bailey, Douglas, 265

Baker, Howard, 69, 72, 73, 75, 87, 194, 222, 275

Baker, James, 74, 75, 96, 97
    as Secretary of State, 177, 225, 226

Balsams, 33, 50, 54

The Baltimore Sun, 217

Banks, David, 114

Barnes, Fred, 254, 281

Barnicle, Mike, 5

Barry, James, 89

Bartlett, Lee, 143

Bartlett, William, 122, 143, 156

Bates, David, 75, 76, 77, 78, 176, 195, 227

Beauvais, Henry, 108

Behind the Front Page (Broder), 281, 284

Bennett, Edward, 114

Biden, Joseph, 196

Black, Charles, 43, 224, 234

Blue Smoke and Mirrors (Germond, Witcover), 283

Bode, Ken, 252-253, 266

Bogart, Leo, 288

The Boston Globe, 5, 72, 110, 134, 140

Boutin, Bernard, 217

Boyles, Peg, 140

Breen, Jon, 97

Brereton, Charles, 1

Bridges, Styles, 13, 14

Broder, David, 31, 41, 176, 259, 280, 281, 284

Brokaw, Tom, 162

Brown, Edmund (Jerry), Jr., 272

Brown, Phyllis, 38, 39
Brown, Ron, 270
Buchanan, Patrick, 122, 254
Buell, Emmett, Jr., 251
Burbank, Jon, 130
Burke, Merle, 147
Burton, Raymond, 45
Bush, Barbara Pierce, 65, 173, 174, 226
  1980 primary campaign, 76, 89-90, 95,
  1988 primary campaign, 128, 137-139, 141, 143, 150, 163-164, 166, 175
  as wife of vice president, 82, 105-106, 108, 114-116, 118, 121, 122, 123, 124
Bush, C. Fred (dog), 108, 123, 226, 227
Bush, Dorothy (daughter), 90
Bush, Fred, 111
Bush, George, 7, 15, 65, 66, 285
  1980 primary campaign, 69, 71, 73-100, 222
  1988 primary campaign, 127-167, 277, 282, 283
  as vice president, 100-126
  author's review, 170-181
  media image, 58, 183-198, 250-252, 256, 258, 261, 263-265, 280
  organization, 200, 201, 206, 208, 210, 212, 214, 275
  and Secret Service, 238, 240-242
  staff, 225-231, 234, 244
Bush, Jamie (nephew), 90
Bush, John (nephew), 90, 162, 163, 164, 196, 213
Bush, Margaret (daughter-in-law), 163
Bush, Marvin (son), 90, 163

Bush, Neil (son), 76, 80, 81, 90, 173, 282
Bush, Prescott (brother), 103

Caddell, Pat, 230, 271
Cahill, William, 120
California primary, 271-273
Calloway, Bo, 39, 40, 46, 47, 63
Cannon, Lou, 107, 111, 177, 272
Card, Andy, 128, 129, 228, 229, 283
Carmen, Gerald, 89, 96, 217
Carney, David, 127, 180, 217
Carter, Jimmy, 54, 61, 64, 86, 271
Carter, Hodding III, 91, 254
Casey, William, 224
CBS-TV, 88, 248, 252, 288
Chamberlin, James, 75, 77
Chamorro, Violeta, 233
Chancellor, John, 253
Chandler, John P. H., 139
Charbonneau, Rhona, 132
The Chicago Sun, 279
Citizens for Reagan, 37
Citizens' Press Conference, 44, 48, 49, 52, 55, 57, 196, 250
Claneil Foundation, 114
Clark, Thomas, 240
Clarion Somerset Hotel, 158, 159, 160, 164, 175, 180
Clegg, Billy Joe, 54
Cleveland, Hilary, 75, 141, 217
Cleveland, James, 30, 38, 39, 40, 64, 71, 73, 75, 103, 141
CNN (Cable News Network), 158, 251, 260, 288
Cohen, Shirley, 256
Colebrook News & Sentinel, 54, 83, 93
Common Cause, 49

Conable, Barber, 96
Concord Monitor, 273
Conger, Clem, 115
Connally, John, 42, 69, 70, 72, 103, 188, 207
Coos County Democrat, 23, 81
Costa, Jim, 271
Cotton, Norris, 5, 34, 38, 39, 40, 41, 58, 60, 64, 77, 117, 118, 187
Crane, Philip, 69, 70, 75, 95, 222
Cronkite, Walter, 98, 248
Crossfire, 254
Croteau, John, Jr., 110
C-Span, 108, 251, 288
Cudhea, Lucille, 140-141
Cummings, Catherine, 181
Currier, David, 181

D'Agostino, Michael, 87, 106
Damm, William, 54
Daniell, Gene, 5
Daniell, Jere, 4
Dartmouth College, 15, 17, 19, 27, 60, 80, 117, 118, 153, 221, 263, 275
Davidson, Donald, 136
Davidson, Jean, 194
Deaver, Michael, 52, 223, 224, 225, 228
DeNobile, Vincent, 135-136
Dewey, Thomas, 194, 230
Dixon, Alan, 274
Dixville Notch, 33, 53, 54
Dole, Elizabeth, 113, 195
Dole, Robert, 69, 107, 113, 196, 214, 235, 244
  1980 primary campaign, 70, 75
  1988 primary campaign, 114, 127, 132, 155, 157, 159, 162, 164, 175, 176, 197, 222

media image, 190, 251, 258, 259, 264, 282
Doonesbury, 162, 172
Dukakis, Michael, 157, 191, 192, 264, 265, 271, 277, 278, 283
Duncan, Dayton, 278
DuPont, Pierre, 112, 127, 148, 154, 160, 275
Durkin, Daniel, 80
Durkin, Patrick, 80
Dwinell, Lane, 102, 103, 106, 111, 152

Edwards, Steve, 130, 149, 181
Eisenhower, Dwight, 1, 34, 184, 186, 214, 247, 259
Ellis, Nancy Bush, 110, 172

Fahrenkopf, Frank, Jr., 277
Federal Election Commission (FEC), 96, 127, 151, 158, 206-207, 237, 286
Ferraro, Geraldine, 256
1590 Broadcaster, 58
Finnegan, James, 91
First Step to the White House (Brereton), 1, 290
Fisher, Parkie, 80
Fitton, James, 239-240
Fitzgerald, Jennifer, 78, 176
Fitzwater, Marlin, 121
Flanders, Ann, 47
Ford, Betty, 58
Ford, Gerald, 27, 30, 70, 75, 101, 102, 108, 186, 187, 210
  1976 primary campaign, 38-41, 43, 45-46, 49, 51, 53, 58-62, 64, 185, 198, 201, 204, 208, 250, 258, 280

Fortune, 2
Fort Worth Star, 84
Foster, Robert, 96
Foster's Daily Democrat, 96, 98
Fuller, Craig, 121, 131, 153, 176
Fund for America's Future, 111, 112, 120, 121, 122, 124, 127
Furness, Betty, 248

Gallen, Hugh, 73
Galvin, Eddie, 18, 241
Gambino, Robert, 90, 173, 241
Gardner, William, 57, 260, 278
Gephardt, Richard, 264
Gergen, David, 96
Germond, Jack, 45, 87, 253, 279-284
Gifford, W.H., 123
Glenn, John, 274
Godwin, Roger, 124
Golding, William, 130
Goldman, Peter, 165, 235
Goldwater, Barry, 52, 191, 230, 249, 266
    1964 primary campaign, 13, 23, 24-27, 30-31, 33-34, 36, 41, 184, 186, 199, 210, 211
    support for Bush, 160, 164, 198, 212
Goodman, Robert, 87, 88, 153
Gorbachev, Mikhail S., 155, 174, 265
Graham, Billy, 114
Greer, Frank, 236
Gregg, Catherine (Cay), 11, 13, 16, 17, 21, 30, 32, 36, 40, 65, 69, 77, 95, 109, 114, 150, 164, 166, 227
Gregg, Cyrus, 145, 146
Gregg, David III, 181

Gregg, Kathleen, 145
Gregg, Judd, 75, 77, 88, 103, 105, 112, 116, 118, 123, 124, 145, 166, 180, 181, 217
Griffin, Ruth, 181
Gun Owners, 113, 157

Haig, Alexander, 114, 155, 275
Hannaford, Peter, 99, 222, 223, 224
Harrigan, Frederick, 33, 54, 83
Harrigan, John, 81, 82, 83, 190
Harris, Fred, 64
Hart, Gary, 121, 214
Hawke, Prime Minister of Australia, 114
Heckler, Margaret, 111
Heston, Charlton, 227
Hinman, Barbara, 11
Hinman, George, 11, 12, 13, 221
Hippauf, Georgi, 57, 75, 76, 79, 129, 130, 181
Hope, Bob, 21
Horton, Willie, 264
Hugel, Max (Project '88) 113, 121, 122
Hume, Britt, 253
Humphrey, Gordon, 70, 104, 108
Humphrey, Hubert, 235
Hunt, Al, 252, 280, 290
Hussein, King, 227
Hynes, Thomas, 66, 77

Indian Stream Republic, 3
Insight, 236, 265

Jackman, J. Richard, 31
Jaskiel, Faustyn, 59
Johnson, Carl, 22

Johnson, Lyndon Baines, 185, 208, 249, 258, 266, 271, 275
Jordan, Ed, 164

Kaufman, Ronald C., 111, 112, 118, 119, 120, 127, 129, 132, 228, 229, 236, 256
Kaye, Peter, 2
Keene, David, 176, 219, 235
The Keene Sentinel, 34, 79, 121, 285
Kefauver, Estes, 1, 25, 53, 208, 213, 214
Kelleher, Robert, 55
Keller, John, 131
Kemp, Jack, 1, 113, 127, 139, 160, 213, 234
Kennedy, John F., 24, 217, 262
Kilgallen, Dorothy, 29
King, Martin Luther, 4
Kirkland, Lane, 114
Kinsley, Michael, 254
Kirkpatrick, Jeane, 109, 113
Kirsch, Jonathan, 73
Koblinski, Mitchell, 59
Kondracke, Morton, 90, 254
Konner, Joan, 256
Koster, R. M., 257
Kratz, Fred, 239

Lake, James, 37, 38, 39, 40, 52, 60, 66, 89, 107, 222
Lamb, Brian, 108
Lamprey, Stewart, 45
Lankler, Alex (Sandy), 16, 25
LaRouche, Lyndon, 6
Laxalt, Paul, 93
Lehrman, Lew, 112
Lodge, George, 30, 31

Lodge, Henry Cabot, 30-36, 58, 184, 186, 198, 199, 214, 218, 259
Loeb, Nackey, 105, 106, 108, 112, 122, 145, 157, 160, 165
Loeb, William, 157
  1964 primary (opposes Rockefeller), 26-27, 30(1974), 36
  1976 primary (supports Reagan), 42, 58, 60
  1980 primary (opposes Bush), 70, 72, 73, 86, 89-92, 98, 188
  post-primary, 103-104, 109, 118, 121-122, 145
Looking Forward (Bush, Gold), 98
Los Angeles Times, 41, 74, 84, 194, 255
Lyons, Elaine, 89

McBride, Tim, 195, 227
McCarthy, Eugene, 2, 49, 185, 208, 258, 275
McCloskey, Paul, 91
McGovern, George, 185, 258
McGrory, Mary, 43, 58, 64, 110
The McLaughlin Group, 253
MacMillin, Guy, 34
McQuaid, Joseph W., 91, 109
The Making of the President 1964, (White), 36, 260
Makinson, Larry, 208
Maiola, Joel, 81, 105, 145
Mally, James, 4
Manchester Union Leader, 23, 26-27, 42, 70, 86, 88, 91, 102, 105, 122, 125, 145, 156, 157, 165, 177, 188, 249, 270
The Manchester Union Leader in New Hampshire Elections (Veblen), 26

Mangini, Victor, 21
Marshall, George, 152
Mathews, Tom, 165, 235
Mauro, Robert, 91
Meese, Ed, 82, 224, 225
Meet the Press, 62
Merry, Robert W., 279-281
Merton, Andy, 61
Meserve, John, 130
Mikulski, Barbara Anne, 269
Molloy, Robert, 243
Mondale, Walter, 214, 238, 275
Monier, Robert, 89, 106, 107, 111, 112
Monroe, James, 2
Moore, David W., 96, 259
Morrell, Robert, 50
Morrow, Hugh, 25
Morse, Walter, 154
Morton, Matthew, 18, 43
Morton, Richard, 18
Morton, Rogers, 58, 198
Mosbacher, Robert, 160
Muller, Lucy, 75, 79
Muskie, Edmund, 258
My Turn (Reagan), 65

NBC-TV, 23, 48, 62, 248, 288
Nash, Gerald Q., 158
Nashua Debate, 95, 104, 106, 158, 184, 185, 210, 222, 226, 256, 263, 290
Nashua High School, 95, 106
Nashua Telegraph, 15, 96, 97, 133, 157, 158, 273
National Conservative Political Conference, 42
Nessen, Ron, 164
New Hampshire Federation of Republican Women, 108, 113, 212
New Hampshire Highway Hotel, 18, 32, 43, 57, 63, 79, 107, 204-205, 241
New Hampshire State Constitution, 3
New Hampshire Sunday News, 86
New Hampshire Times, 27, 52
New West, 73
The New York Times, 79, 87, 90, 102, 121, 166, 189, 218, 255, 273
Newman, Bonnie, 217
Newsweek, 98, 146, 165, 245
Nixon, Richard, 5, 25, 26, 33, 34, 35, 41, 55, 58, 63, 210, 262
Noelte, Mildred, 140
Nofziger, Lyn, 50, 52, 56, 61, 71, 194, 222-223, 224, 228
Nolan, Lloyd, 59, 198
Noonan, Peggy, 159, 232
Novak, Robert, 82, 253

Olinger, David, 72
O'Neill, Thomas P., Jr. ("Tip"), 2
Oreskes, Michael, 218
Ortega, Daniel, 233
Osgood, Jonathan, 130

Packard, Vance, 82
Packwood, Lee, 54
Palmer, Rita, 181
Paquin, Paul, 111
Parker, Bertie, 33
Paul, Rod, 27
Pease Air Force Base, 106, 120, 142, 143, 165, 193, 207
Pease, Warren, 91

People's Bicentennial Commission (PBC), (or Bicentennial Common Sense), 48, 55, 58, 262
Perry, James M., 92, 265, 267
Peterson, Walter, 72
Petit, Tom, 62, 253
Pierce, Franklin, 5, 265
Pierce, Kent, 90
Pierce, Scott, 89
Plumer, William, 2
Porter, Geraldine, 72, 73
The Portsmouth Herald, 41, 47, 64
Portsmouth Navy Yard, 121, 154, 207
Pouliot, Herman, 157
Powell, Wesley, 26, 91
Project '88, 113, 121, 122
Public Broadcasting Service (PBS), 286

Quest for the Presidency (Newsweek), 165, 245
Quill, 279

Rath, Thomas, 113
Raum, Tom, 265
Reagan, Nancy, 43-45, 47, 51, 52, 56, 61, 64, 65, 71, 96, 190, 224, 285
Reagan, Ronald, 157, 158, 164, 165, 172, 173, 175, 199-200, 204, 205, 208, 210
  1976 primary campaign, 37-66, 250, 258, 262, 263, 280
  1980 primary campaign, 69-71, 73, 75, 79, 81-82, 84, 89-93, 95-99, 101-113

media image, 183-198
staff, 222-225, 231, 241, 244
The Reagans, 99
Regan, Donald, 228
Republican National Committee (RNC), 109, 111, 172, 212, 232, 237
Republican National Convention, 202, 248, 257
  1964, 33
  1976, 42, 60, 66, 224
  1980, 99, 101, 109
Reston, James, 121
Rhodes, Donald, 226, 227
Richardson, Elliott, 58, 198
Rifkin, Jeremy, 49
Roberts, Cokie, 253
Robertson, Pat, 112, 159, 160, 195, 213
Rockefeller, David, 86, 98
Rockefeller, Happy, 11, 12, 17, 19, 22, 27, 29, 30, 36, 64, 186, 227
Rockefeller, Michael, 19
Rockefeller, Nelson, 7, 52, 64, 74, 79, 157, 183, 186, 188, 197, 201, 202, 210, 221, 234, 285
  1964 primary, 11-36, 41, 184, 192, 195, 199, 204, 214, 240-241, 243-244, 248-250, 258
Rollinson, Keep Roll-in-son, 55
Rollinson, Magic Princess, 55
Rounds, Bruce, 47, 50, 53, 55, 58, 59, 73, 75, 77, 93, 105, 108-109, 115-116, 121, 122, 156, 173, 227
Roy, Aime, 139
Roy, Vesta, 105
Royko, Mike, 279
Rudman, Warren, 72, 113, 266

Rumsfeld, Donald, 39
Russo, Paul, 69, 244

San Francisco Examiner, 87
Schlesinger, Arthur, Jr., 257
Schwartz, Tony, 266
Schweiker, Richard, 60, 224
Scranton, Andrea, 110
Sears, John P., 37, 38, 39, 40, 43, 66, 73, 92, 187, 222, 224
Secret Service, 194, 197, 207, 238-243, 250
  1976 primary, 47, 50, 52, 56, 63, 65
  1980 primary, 75, 90
  with Bush as vice president, 82, 105, 124, 129, 131, 134, 136-138, 140-141, 143-144, 146, 150, 153, 158, 160, 162
Seib, Gerald, 174
Sewall, Alan, 130
Seymour, Thaddeus, 27
Sheraton Wayfarer, 44
Shields, Mark, 281
Sibley, George, 269, 270
Sidey, Hugh, 290
Simon, Paul, 194
Sixty Minutes, 5, 88
Smith, John, 2
Smith, Hedrick, 280
Smith, Margaret Chase, 26
Smith, Robert, 116
Smith, Sharon, 81
Spad, Karl, 25
Sparks, David, 176
Speakes, Larry, 228
Spencer, Stuart, 40, 63
Squires, James, 256
Stabile, John, 158
Stassen, Harold, 26, 29, 69, 92,

108, 247, 275
State News Service, 23
Steffens, Lincoln, 265
Steiner, Lee Ann, 139
Steiner, Robert, 138
Straus, Murray, 4
Stevenson, Tom, 25
Stockman, David, 228
Stone, Roger, 234, 235
Streeter, Bernard, 19
Stylianos, John, 15-16
Sullivan, Charles B., 77
Sununu, John, 122, 217
  fundraisers, 104-105, 107, 109, 113, 125
  supports George Bush, 118-119, 124, 127-128, 137, 140, 153, 155, 159, 162, 166, 171, 176-177, 180-181, 283
Sununu, Nancy, 105, 177
Sweatt, Etta, 95
Sylvester, Geraldine, 61

TV Guide, 252-253, 266
Taft, Robert, 34, 184, 214, 235, 247
Tamposi, Elizabeth, 217
Tamposi, Samuel, 58
Tandy, Roy, Jr., 111
Teague, Bert, 13-14, 15, 18, 19, 31, 32, 59
Teague, Joanne, 29
Teeley, Pete, 96, 153, 176, 228
Teeter, Robert, 159, 229, 231, 277, 282
Thatcher, Margaret, 227
Thayer, Steve, 89
Thimmesch, Nick, 41
Thomas, Lowell, 78
Thompson, Ben, 77, 116-118

Thomson, Meldrim, 38, 42-43, 44, 59-61, 62, 64, 73, 149, 185, 224, 225, 280
Thurston, Matthew 130
Tibbetts, Donn, 91
Time, 146, 175, 286
The "Today" Show, 48
Tracy, Paul, 91
Treat, Vivian, 11
Treat, William, 11, 12, 31, 107, 113
Trilateral Commission, 86, 98, 188
Trowbridge, Robert, 56
Trudeau, Garry, 172
Truman, Harry, 1, 208, 214, 230, 242, 275
Tucker, John, 105
Turner, Robert "Landslide", 129, 130
Tutwiler, Margaret, 225

Udall, Morris, 271
University of New Hampshire, 4, 13, 38, 96, 109, 134, 193
Untermeyer, Chase, 78, 176

Valdez, David, 227, 228
Vartanian, Elsie, 132
Veblen, Eric, 26

WMUR-TV, 25
Walker, James 152
Walker, Kelly, 129, 130, 131, 132
The Wall Street Journal, 4, 62, 91, 92, 174, 208, 229, 246, 252, 256, 265, 267, 286, 290
The Washington Post, 60, 233, 255
Washington Week in Review, 253
Watson, Harold, 43

Webster, Daniel, 2
Weinberger, Caspar, 188
West, Woody, 265
Whalen, Richard J., 189
What I Saw at the Revolution (Noonan), 232
White, Clint, 23
White House Communications (WHCA), 123, 124, 129, 155, 164, 238, 242-243
White, Theodore, 25, 36, 184, 260, 270, 280
Whitman, Ann, 25
Whose Broad Stripes and Bright Stars (Germond, Witcover) 280
Wieczorek, Raymond, 137
Will, George, 73, 84, 253, 281
Williams, Ted, 150, 198
Wing, Howard "Pete", 18
Winning of the White House 1988 (Time), 175
Winters, Richard, 153
Wirthlin, Richard, 224, 231
Witcover, Jules, 45, 280, 281, 284
Wolfinger, Raymond, 277
Woodman, Wendell, 86
Woods, Rosemary, 25
World Almanac, 51
Wyman, Louis, 38

Yankee Strummers, 147
Yeager, Chuck, 155, 198
Yorty, Sam, 271

Zachos, Kimon, 181
Zachos, Victoria, 71
Zekes, 80-81, 87, 105, 112, 202-203
Zeliff, William, 144
Zellner, Joe, 89

About the Author

Former governor Hugh Gregg of New Hampshire was the state's campaign chairman for Nelson Rockefeller in the 1964 Presidential Primary. He performed the same role for Ronald Reagan in 1976 and for George Bush in 1980. In 1984 he served as Reagan-Bush coordinator and in 1988 was chairman of Vice President Bush's New Hampshire Advance team. He is the Republican national committeeman from New Hampshire.

Born in New Hampshire, Hugh Gregg became its youngest governor in 1952, at the age of thirty-four. His swift ascent from alderman-at-large to mayor of his hometown, Nashua, marked the beginning of a lifelong political career. A graduate of Yale and Harvard Law School, he served as a special agent of the Counter Intelligence Corps in World War II and the Korean crisis. He is a well-known business and community leader. His son, Judd, currently serves as Governor of New Hampshire. Hugh Gregg writes from a broad background and a unique perspective of the New Hampshire ethos and its political temperament.